VINCENT D'INDY AND HIS WORLD

VINCENT D'INDY

AND HIS WORLD

Andrew Thomson

CLARENDON PRESS · OXFORD
1996

Oxford University Press, Great Clarendon Street, Oxford OX2 6DP

Oxford New York
Athens Auckland Bangkok Bogota Bombay
Buenos Aires Calcutta Cape Town Dar es Salaam
Delhi Florence Hong Kong Istanbul Karachi
Kuala Lumpur Madras Madrid Melbourne
Mexico City Nairobi Paris Singapore
Taipei Tokyo Toronto
and associated companies in
Berlin Ibadan

Oxford is a trade mark of Oxford University Press

Published in the United States
by Oxford University Press Inc., New York

British Library Cataloguing in Publication Data
Data available

Library of Congress Cataloging in Publication Data
Thomsom, Andrew, 1944–
Vincent D'Indy and his world / Andrew Thomson.
p.   cm.
"Catalogue of main works": p.
Includes bibliographical references (p.   ) and index.
1. Indy, Vincent d', 1851–1931. 2. Composers—France—Biography.
I. Title.
ML410.I7T56   1996   780'.92—dc20   [B]   96–9214
ISBN 0–19–816220–0

1 3 5 7 9 10 8 6 4 2

Typeset by Hope Services (Abingdon) Ltd.
Printed in Great Britain
on acid-free paper by
Biddles Ltd
Guildford and King's Lynn

In memoriam
Michael de Cossart
1944–1989

Preface and Acknowledgements

This admittedly brief book offers a new perspective on the life and work of the much maligned Vincent d'Indy; but I should first utter a word of caution to the reader. It cannot claim to be a definitive study, for to do full justice to the scope of its subject's manifold achievements, the author would have to be that modern impossibility, an expert in many fields, *inter alia* early music, Wagner, music theory, analysis, and aesthetics, Dante, symbolist art and poetry, political history, psychology, and even gender studies, and I am certainly not equipped to deal with all these subjects. Nevertheless, I have endeavoured to indicate the importance of ideas—musical, literary, philosophical, and political—in d'Indy's creative development.

Previous biographies, it must be said, have provided a restricted picture. Chief of these is the two-volume study by Léon Vallas (1946–50), which curiously begins to peter out when it reaches the 1880s, just when d'Indy's life was becoming increasingly interesting and intellectually complex. Above all, I would take issue with Vallas on his claustrophobic portrait of the man as essentially a cold rationalist, whose full personal development was stunted by the effects of his upbringing at the hands of a tyrannical grandmother. I am deeply obliged to Mme La Comtesse d'Indy for allowing me access to new information about his childhood found in his *Journal intime*. This was lodged in the Bibliothèque Nationale by his second wife, Caroline née Janson, just before her death in 1950; it was only to be seen by close members of his family, and even Vallas does not appear to have been privy to its contents.

From the journal, an altogether less inhibited picture of his youth emerges, which I find more plausible. Moreover, other source material—autograph letters and writings—reveal an emotionally intense character and a passionate intellectualism, his fabled self-discipline resulting from fear of the anarchic forces within him, which were liable to break out at times of acute tension. In fact, his complex psychological constitution invites much speculation, but I have tried to resist the temptation to provide an overdetermined view, with the accompanying danger of fitting facts to theories. Yet it cannot be denied that the Freudian idea of the father-figure and its projection loomed large in his imagination, and that his character contained both masculine and feminine elements, conceivable perhaps in terms of William James's 'tough and tender' mentalities, or Jung's *animus* and *anima* archetypes. His was an obsessive mind, prone to *idées fixes*, and with an immense capacity for symbolism, above all in the sanctification of his master, César Franck. But if, on the one hand, there was a highly conventional side to him, in his firmly held Catholic beliefs and values, as well as his intense patriotism, he was also capable of the utmost audaciousness and radicalism, which make him a vital part of the modern movement of his time.

I have made no attempt to play down or disguise his notorious right-wing views, utterly discredited after 1945. However, it should be remembered that such political ideologies were subscribed to by such leading twentieth-century modernists as Stravinsky, Pound, and Eliot, and that today, with the resurgence of nationalism within post-war Europe, the concerns of d'Indy and his associates may be seen in a rather less condemnatory light. The hard-fought aesthetic controversies in which he became embroiled will doubtless seem utterly remote from the present-day Anglo-Saxon mentality, but I consider some account of them to be essential for understanding d'Indy and his period. If, as a great teacher and theorist of symphonic composition, he possessed all the breadth of vision and wide culture of his counterparts across the Channel, Hubert Parry and Donald Tovey, his taste for fierce polemics brings to mind F. R. Leavis of the Cambridge English school! Indeed, this book may come across as excessively concerned with battles of one kind or another; but it does at least provide some corrective to the cultural cliché of *la belle époque*, in which French civilization is largely apprehended in terms of hedonism and immorality.

Preface and Acknowledgements

As a composer, d'Indy seems to me to excel in his orchestral works, his command of instrumentation being second to none. His three music dramas, alas long forgotten, are nevertheless fascinating in conception and full of interesting music; however, I would not like to speculate as to how well they could hold the stage today. So as not to overload the narrative with musical description and analysis, and so as to provide a balance of information, only passing reference is made to the chamber works, which I find less compelling. My hope is that, having put the underlying ideas and ideologies into historical perspective, his music will at last be listened to on its own, very considerable merits.

My research for this book was greatly facilitated by the kindness of the Comte and Comtesse Jacques d'Indy, who gave me access to the library and archives of Les Faugs, and submitted to my continuous barrage of questions cheerfully and with enormous fortitude. A number of friends and colleagues gave generously of their advice and encouragement: Professor Basil Deane, the late Dr Michael de Cossart (the dedicatee of the book), Felix Aprahamian, Dr Lynn Garafola, Daniel-Lesur, and Stéphan Giocanti. I am particularly obliged to Roger Nichols for reading the typescript, and, with exquisite tact, alerting me to numerous *faux pas*.

I would also like to acknowledge the great value to me in this enterprise of Bristol University's extra-mural classes on modern French philosophy, taught by Professor Ronald Grimsley and Edward Waring.

Thanks are also due to the staff of the Bibliothèque Nationale, the Bibliothèque Gustav Mahler, Paris, the British Library, Bristol University Library, and Bristol Central Library. My research visits to France have been made possible by grants from the Society of Authors and *Music and Letters*, for which I am most grateful.

Special mention must be made of my editor at OUP, Bruce Phillips, with his patient helpfulness and tolerance of my vagaries. Many thanks, too, to his assistant, Helen Foster, for nursing me through the maze of copy-editing and proofreading. And, above all, my wife Susan, my mother Sheila, and daughters Hannah and Clarissa should receive full credit for succouring this increasingly testy author with their customary fund of deflationary humour!

Plates 1–10, 14–15, kindly supplied by Madame La Comtesse d'Indy from the Archives des Faugs. Photographs 11–12 kindly supplied by Sotheby's; permission given by owner of the costume design, but purchaser of the décor design not yet located.

Music examples 1*a*, 1*b*, 4*a*, 4*b*, 5*a*, 5*b*, 6*a*, 6*b*, 7*a*, 7*b*, 7*c*, 8*a*, and 8*b* are reproduced by permission of Éditions Durand SA, Paris/United Music Publishers Ltd.; examples 2*a*, 2*b*, 3*a*, and 3*b* are reproduced by permission of Éditions Hamelle, Paris/United Music Publishers Ltd.; examples 9*a*, 9*b*, 10*a*, 10*b*, 11*a*, and 11*b* are reproduced by permission of Éditions Salabert, Paris/United Music Publishers Ltd. Passages from d'Indy's *Cours de composition musicale* are reproduced by permission of Éditions Durand SA, Paris/United Music Publishers Ltd.

ANDREW THOMSON

Clevedon, 1994

There is greatness only in fulfilment, in the fullness of awakening. Completion means the symphony. Sublimation means to condemn to immobility certain members of the body for the sake of the monstrous development of others. Like the abnormal sensitivity of the blind, the unusually keen hearing of the mute. It is monstrous. Psychologically, a great personality is a circle touching something at every point. A circle with a core. A process of nature, growth, not the ideal. The ideal is an error. Life is a full circle, widening until it joins the circle motions of the infinite.

Anaïs Nin, *Journal*

Contents

Plates

(between pages 112 and 113)

Abbreviations

AF	Archives des Faugs
BN	Bibliothèque Nationale
CCM	Vincent d'Indy, *Cours de composition musicale* (Paris, 1903–51)
CF	Vincent d'Indy, *César Franck* (Paris, 1906), trans. Rosa Newmarch (New York, 1910)
GR	Guy Ropartz
LV	Léon Vallas, *Vincent d'Indy* (Paris, 1946–50)
OM	Octave Maus
PB	Pierre de Bréville
RBM	*Revue belge de musicologie*, 14/1–4 (1960)
RM	*La Revue musicale*
TS	*Les Tablettes de la Schola Cantorum*
VI	Vincent d'Indy

1

Grandmother's Footsteps

Paul Marie Théodore Vincent d'Indy was born with the blood
of military and public service in his veins; the course of his
long and active musical life revealed how loyal he remained to
the patriotic, idealistic spirit of his ancestors. The family can
be traced as far back as 1388, when Enguerrand Indy was
Governor of the Dauphiné; the junior branch established itself
at Annonay in 1490. Little subsequently is remarkable until
the era of the Napoleonic wars, which gave Vincent's great-
grandfather and grandfather the opportunity to show their
mettle. Joseph d'Indy was Prefect of the Ardèche in 1814,
remaining faithful to Louis XVIII during the 'Hundred Days'
of Napoleon's return from Elba, but rewarded in 1819 with
dismissal from his post by Decazes, the King's minister.

A more apparently brilliant, if rather foolhardy, spirit was
Théodore Isaïe d'Indy, lieutenant of dragoons, then captain of
the mounted grenadier guards in Napoleon's army. During the
minor battle of Hanau against the Bavarians, and under
heavy fire, he is said to have fixed his sword to the pommel of
his saddle to rest his chin on and hold his head high—a somewhat misplaced act of bravado! Unable to give his support to
the July Monarchy of Louis-Philippe, he resigned his commission in 1830. Yet he retained the hereditary title of Comte,
granted by Charles X for military services.

His wife, née Thérèse de Chorier, and Vincent's formidable
grandmother, brought some particularly distinguished stock
to the d'Indy line. Of her forebears, Antoine-Joseph Pernety,
received the appointment of librarian to Frederick the Great,

King of Prussia, becoming a member of the Berlin Academy of Science. Another relative, General Joseph-Marie Pernety, Baron of the Empire, commanded the artillery of the First Corps of Napoleon's Grande Armée in 1812. Unlike Théodore d'Indy, his was a more accommodating nature. Having first accepted office as Councillor of State in 1817 under the restoration of the Bourbon monarchy, his career continued to advance throughout the various changes of regime; raised to a peerage by Louis-Philippe, he subsequently served as a senator under the Emperor Napoleon III. As for Vincent's great-grandmother, Madeleine de Chorier-Pernety, a certain mystique surrounded her, for she lived in Valence in the house of Amélie de Laurencin, one of Napoleon's lady friends, at the very time when the then unknown second lieutenant in the artillery found himself garrisoned in that town on the Rhône. Vincent's own mother, Matilde de Chabrol-Crousol, came from a hardly less notable background; her grandfather, having been made Prefect of Lyon, was made a peer of France in 1823, and served first as Minister of the Navy, then as Minister of Finance under Polignac.[1]

Thérèse de Chorier's own sons, Wilfrid and Antonin d'Indy, did not exactly live up to this intimidating pedigree. Rejecting the possibility of careers in public service under the Orléanist monarchy, they remained content to live on their very considerable inherited wealth and occupy themselves with charitable work and amateur music making.

Antonin's son, Vincent d'Indy, the subject of our study, came into the world on 27 March 1851 at 45 rue de Grenelle, Paris, but his mother tragically failed to survive the birth. Understandably, Matilde's death at the age of only 21, after only one year of marriage, left her husband Antonin in a state of acute shock and depression. The overriding need to get away from the scene of desolation and from his own state of misery took hold of him; leaving his newly born child in the care of his mother, Thérèse, he embarked upon a period of travel in Italy. On his return, evidently restored, he found a new wife, Catherine de Glos, whom he married in 1855, and

[1] A. Balsan, 'L'Hérédité Drômoise de Vincent d'Indy, notes généalogiques', *Revue Drômoise*, no. 421 (Oct. 1981), 373–7.

from this union three children were born: Marie, Pierre, and Agnès. Fortunately, Antonin did not neglect Vincent, although he acceded to Thérèse's request—very wisely, as things turned out—that she herself should take full charge of her grandson's upbringing and education in her own home at 97 rue du Bac.

A grossly distorted legend, fostered by Vallas and other previous biographers, has unfortunately been generally received, according to which Thérèse was a domineering, even sadistic ogress who subjected Vincent to a punishing, over-regimented regime of work and study. Certainly, from the start, she entertained the highest hopes and ambitions for him, loving him dearly and wishing to see him carry on the distinguished achievements of the Pernety family. Perhaps she was even secretly a little disappointed in her own sons Wilfrid and Antonin, both men of culture who made little mark in the world. Nevertheless, her insistence on a properly disciplined, organized upbringing, with all due emphasis on punctuality and meticulousness, was in reality rather closer to the approved methods of the twentieth-century Dr Spock than to the unnaturally forced education of the English utilitarian philosopher John Stuart Mill. If it is true that she once made him stand at the window during a fierce thunderstorm to cure him of timidity, this type of treatment of children was *de rigueur* in the nineteenth century; one remembers that Virginia Woolf was thrown naked into a pool by her father so that she would learn to swim!

If Vincent's timidity and reserve had originally been caused by the traumatic loss of his mother, Thérèse—familiarly known as Rézia—was able to bring about a marked change in his initially fragile state of health, and, thanks to her devoted care, he became physically stronger. And not only his body, but also his mental and moral faculties were a matter of her intense concern. Although he submitted cheerfully to her ministrations, she doubtless possessed sufficient human and psychological insight to detect—even at this early stage—a latent force of will and anarchic strength of passion potentially destructive if not bridled by the assiduous training of his reasoning powers. Yet her strict regime was not so repressive as to kill the very real affection he felt for her; indeed, the old lady in her turn would take in good part his good-humoured sense of mischief and the tricks and practical jokes he played at her expense. Above all, she wanted him to grow up to be his own man, independent in mind and fully in command of himself; a wish to break his spirit definitely had no place in her programme, let alone anything that today would be called abuse.

A private tutor was engaged to give Vincent his first lessons. Mademoiselle Saint-Pierre, a gentle soul who completely gained his confidence, encouraged him to love God's creation, nature and the birds. The fantastic imaginative world of Hans Christian Andersen also strongly appealed to him. At the same time, Rézia, a keen, well-informed amateur musician, singer, and lover of opera, began to teach him the piano, using studies by Czerny, Bertini, and Cramer; she would also play music by Haydn and Mozart to him, as well as some Beethoven sonatas, above all the 'Pathétique'. She felt especially proud when, at the age of 8, he played and sang at one of her musical parties, attended by such luminaries as the aged Rossini and Gounod. Vincent's greatest delight, however, was to play with his set of toy soldiers, the beginning of a lifelong obsession with all things military, and particularly the life of Napoleon Bonaparte; on the subject of Napoleon's battles the future composer was to become something of an expert.[2] This, indeed, was no mere hobby, answering rather to some deep-rooted craving on his own part for order and organization. Two present-day psychologists have argued that the painful breaking of the original bond between the intelligent male child and his mother—necessary if he is to launch out on his own—'leads him to create systems of ideas which can stand in the way of lost intimacy, and within which he can strive for coherence and harmony'. In Vincent's case, his mother's death in childbirth can only have exacerbated these tendencies.[3]

[2] VI, *Journal intime*, BN; LV i. chs 1–4 *passim*.
[3] L. Hudson and B. Jacot, *The Way Men Think, Intellect, Intimacy and the Erotic Imagination* (New Haven, 1991). Quote from *TLS* review, 13 Dec. 1991.

Meanwhile, under Rézia's consistent, methodical tuition, he made sound progress in his piano playing. When he reached the age of 11, however, she realized that his ability required a more professional approach than she could provide. Well-connected in the cultural world as she was, she sought advice from the distinguished pedagogue Antoine François Marmontel, who had pipped the great Charles Valentine Alkan to the post of Professor of Piano at the Paris Conservatoire. Marmontel helpfully recommended his excellent prize-winning pupil Louis Diémer, an arrangement which proved successful, for Vincent in due course developed into a most capable pianist, if not a virtuoso. According to Vallas, Marmontel monitored Vincent's progress under Diémer each week, and was not always pleased; as a result, Rézia supervised his practice armed with a ruler! Perhaps she really did use it; in later years Vincent certainly didn't like to give the impression that he had received a soft upbringing!

Did the wise old lady have any inkling that she was nurturing a potential musician of genius? Regardless, she was determined that he should at least be a highly competent amateur like Wilfrid. Lessons in harmony were arranged with a young 18-year-old student of Ambroise Thomas, Albert Lavignac, later to become Debussy's professor in the Conservatoire's *solfège* class. A pleasant character of some humility, Lavignac was not one to assert the authority of his position when faced with a pupil potentially more talented than himself. Just as he was to handle the difficult and argumentative teenager Debussy with tact and sympathy, so his friendly manner found an immediate response in Vincent, who regarded him like an elder brother. Moreover, despite his systematic methods of teaching, Lavignac was remarkably broad-minded in outlook, and would not have stifled discussion which strayed from the confines of the curriculum.

In 1863, Rézia moved house to 7 avenue de Villars, a location which must have excited Vincent with its clear view of the Invalides, Mansart's monument to the military glory of France, in which Napoleon's remains had been reinterred. He was thrilled with the large new apartment, too, and sent a highly detailed description and plan of it to Mlle

Saint-Pierre;[4] it was to become his home for the rest of his life. In very French fashion, Antonin proceeded to move into the house next door with his new family, joining up with Rézia and Vincent at mealtimes. Both Vincent and his stepmother must have accepted the tricky situation with a good grace, for there seem to have been surprisingly few tensions between the various family members, and he enjoyed to the full the predominantly adult company and their lengthy discussions. Frequently Wilfrid would appear with his wife Marguérite, the sister of Vincent's late mother, a clear indication of the exceptionally close-knit nature of the family.

Wilfrid and his nephew enjoyed a special rapport through their keen musical interests. The former, an amateur of no mean accomplishment, had composed, *inter alia*, an operetta *Les deux Princesses* (1859). As Vincent's own personal tastes began to develop, however, he began to dissent from those of his uncle, coming to detest his favourite opera composers, Auber, Boieldieu, and Flotow.

It would appear that Vincent never went to school, being taught instead by private tutors. Yet he was sensibly not denied contact with other boys of his own age, even if they all came from the same narrow social group. He became a member of the Société de Saint-Vincent-de-Paul, a charitable, albeit extremely paternalistic organization founded by Frédéric Ozanam in 1833, of which Antonin was a leading light. Its main purpose was to visit the poor and the sick, and to distribute alms; yet its increasing strength had alarmed Napoleon III sufficiently for him to dissolve its central council in 1861, seeing it in political terms as an arm of the legitimist revival. By the time Vincent joined, it was a shadow of its former self, but he greatly enjoyed the camaraderie with his fellows, whether or not their souls were saved by their actions, as the Society intended![5]

Paris at this time reflected the glittering though fragile apogee of the Second Empire of Napoleon III, and in another letter to Mlle Saint-Pierre in 1864, we learn that Vincent

[4] VI to Mlle Saint-Pierre, ?1863, AF.
[5] VI to Mlle Saint-Pierre, ?1863, AF. T. Zeldin, *France 1848–1945*, paperback edn. (Oxford, 1979–81), 252.

attended a military review at the Carrousel, inspected by the Emperor and the Empress Eugénie. The following Sunday, he watched the parade of the children's troup before the 9-year-old Prince Eugène—'a pretty sight'. As a special treat after reciting his catechism, Antonin took him on a tour of several churches—including Notre Dame de Victoire, Saint-Roch, and Saint-Thomas d'Aquine—sustaining his young son's interest with a series of meals. The subject of food was obviously an important one for this growing, energetic boy, since he provided his old teacher with a detailed account of the menu and price list of his family's Easter Day dinner in a restaurant. He also received an Easter gift of a map of France painted on a base of copper, with the mountains standing out in relief, a timely reminder of the importance of the regions of France and of his roots in Valence, in the Drôme.[6]

Valence, a historic town situated on the Rhône to the south of Lyon, and the birthplace of many of Vincent's ancestors, has its origins in the Roman Empire. Among its monuments are the Romanesque cathedral of Saint-Apollinaire, consecrated in 1095 by Pope Urban II; on the other side of the river, at the summit of a steep cliff, rise the ruins of the Château de Crussol, built in the twelfth century. During the Renaissance era, Valence entered into a period of brilliance with the founding of the university, notable for the study of law. In 1498, the county of the Valentinois was ceded to the notorious son of Pope Alexander VI, Cesare Borgia, returning to the French crown six years later. Unhappily, the Wars of Religion destroyed much of the town's growing prosperity, Protestantism having become strongly rooted in the area. With the restoration of order, a number of convents were founded at the beginning of the seventeenth century, among them an Ursuline community at the instigation of the celebrated mystic Marie Teissonier, whose visitors included Louis XIII, Anne of Austria, Marie de Medici, as well as those leading spirits of the Catholic Counter-Reformation, Pierre de Bérulle, François de Sales, Vincent de Paul, and Jean-Jacques Olier, *curé* of the church of Saint-Sulpice in Paris. In the

---

[6] VI to Mlle Saint-Pierre, ?1864, AF.

following century, a very considerable benefit accrued to Valence from the appointment as bishop of a more worldly and energetic figure, Alexandre Milon du Mesme—a doctor of the Sorbonne and chaplain to Louis XV—who left the cathedral embellished with a high altar in marble and an organ mounted on a Roman-style basilica. Napoleon studied artillery here in 1785–91. Less happily, after the invasion of the Papal States during the period of the Directory, Pope Pius VI was imprisoned in the Citadel, dying there in 1799.[7]

By the time Vincent came to know Valence, the forces of modern progress were firmly established; the railway had arrived in 1855, and the ramparts built by François I against the invasions of Charles V were demolished. In addition to its industries, the town also housed an army garrison in which many regiments were quartered. But although a distinctly Mediterranean atmosphere of light and air can be sensed here, even so far inland, a more remote, sombre scene awaits the traveller who takes the winding road towards Vernoux through the bleak mountainous, pine-covered terrain of the Ardèche. Near to the hillside village of Boffres, with its tiny ancient church, lies Chabret, once the home of the de Pampelonnes, Vincent's cousins.

It was to Chabret that Rézia packed Vincent off one summer when she felt the time had come for him, at the age of 13, to make the acquaintance of the de Pampelonnes. After the comparative rigours of his grandmother's regime, he must have found the slow rhythms of life in the depths of the countryside extraordinarily relaxing. Moreover, these relations did not represent the most energetic branch of the family, for Anton Victor de Pampelonne, an ex-officer in the navy, had preferred unduly lengthy periods of leave ashore to active service on the high seas. Bibiane, who had married him in 1848, was the daughter of Rézia's sister, Joséphin de Chorier, herself married to Jean Guillaume d'Indy, brother of Vincent's grandfather, Theodore; her mental horizons extended little beyond the cycle of births, marriages, and

---

[7] Much interesting historical information about the town is on display at the Musée de Valence. The cathedral contains a remarkably fine series of monuments and sculptured busts of its notable dignitaries.

deaths which she faithfully recorded in her *Mémoires d'une vie provinciale*.[8] If her nephew privately found these cousins intellectually rather dull and unstimulating by the standards of his Paris home, the warmth of their welcome was ample compensation.

In this beneficially peaceful environment, he could—without feelings of guilt—permit himself, year after year, to take a real holiday from the pressures of work and hard discussion with sophisticated adults; the understanding Rézia knew what she was doing. Of the seven de Pampelonne children, he found Isabelle particularly *simpatico*, and liked to play piano duets with her—an acceptable way of achieving some degree of intimacy! He joined them all in their outdoor games, walks in the forest, and rides over to Vernoux. During the latter, he was overwhelmed by the austere countryside, whose bleak aspects struck a chord in his own somewhat puritanical character. Above all, the wonderful dawns and sunsets, a particular feature of the area, deeply impressed him. His latent visual sense had been aroused; and indeed it was around this time that he took up water-colour painting, for which, like Mendelssohn, he possessed a marked talent. It revealed, too, the emergence of a more sensitive, feminine dimension in the boy, whose very masculine obsession with military matters was already leading him to contemplate a career in the army.

Already he had put down roots in the soil of his ancestors, and every summer he would return to Chabret, to his cousins' delight. Meanwhile, back in Paris his nose was kept to the grindstone, for under the tutelage of his private instructors Monsieur and Madame Pessonneaux, his academic studies embraced Latin, Greek, French literature, history, cosmography, geography, and mathematics, the last of which gave him a great deal of difficulty. As well as teaching him classics, M. Pessonneaux, a fellow student of Ozanam of the Society of Saint Vincent de Paul, also introduced him to the works of Dante, with even happier results. Yet his pupil still had some time left for leisure pursuits. Antonin presented him with a model yacht, which he sailed each Sunday, weather permitting,

---

[8] Balsan, 'L'Hérédité Drômoise', 373–7.

on the pond in the Tuileries, and racing matches took place with other boat-owners, both young and old. On these outings, he was accompanied by an older boy, the future poet Robert de Bonnières, a family friend deputed to look after him and protect him from the dangers and temptations of the wicked city.[9]

The years of adolescence were passing rapidly, and the state examination, the Baccalauréat, loomed. Vincent's intention, albeit opposed by Rézia, was to enter the military academy of St Cyr; but even so, music began to run the army a close second. A further stimulus in this area came from a new friendship with a student at the Jesuit Collège de Vaugirard, Henri Duparc, who took piano lessons from a faded former boy prodigy called César Franck, now a humble, peripatetic music teacher and church organist. Under Franck's guidance, Duparc changed from a bored pianist into an enthusiastic composer and student of scores by Bach, Gluck, and Beethoven. Vincent's acquaintance with him probably came about through a mutual friend, Ellen MacSwinney, a musical Scots girl who lived on the fifth floor of 7 avenue de Villars, and whom Duparc eventually married. It was Duparc who introduced Vincent to Wagner's works, with *Lohengrin*, *Rheingold* and *Die Walküre*. They were also devoted to *Bach's St Matthew Passion*, and even attempted to perform it with a small group of friends. Thus they anticipated Lamoureux's pioneering performance of 1874.[10]

The contrast between the two young men's ambitions could hardly have been more marked, however. Whereas Duparc sensibly contented himself with producing a small number of excellent songs and some piano pieces, Vincent attempted no less than a full-scale grand opera entitled *Burgraves*—an absurd proposition at this early stage in his career; perhaps a firmer hand from Lavignac was needed! Inevitably, Vincent did not get much further than writing the libretto, based on Victor Hugo, and composing the overture. His passion for

---

[9] VI to Alphonse de Pampelonne, 1866, AF. C. Photiadès, 'Vincent d'Indy', *La Revue de Paris*, 15 Jan. 1932, 459.

[10] S. Northcote, *The Songs of Henri Duparc* (London, 1959), 44–5. H. Imbert, *Profils des musiciens* (Paris, 1888), 41.

opera at this time centred mainly on Meyerbeer's *Robert le diable*, *Les Huguenots*, and *Le Prophète*, whose historically based drama, imposing massed effects and thrilling orchestration, thoroughly excited him. On the other hand, his dislikes were intense; above all, Italian *bel canto* opera earned his undying contempt. This prejudice may well have originated in Rézia's salon, where he perhaps found Rossini unbearably suave and complacent. But he did have more time for Verdi, especially for his Meyerbeer-influenced *Don Carlos*, premièred at the Paris Opéra in 1867.

Vincent succeeded in passing his Baccalauréat at the second attempt, in the autumn retakes of 1869, and wrote to his cousin Isabelle: 'I assure you that was a terrific weight off my chest.' In fact, he had managed to produce very satisfactory answers on the fables of La Fontaine and on the War of the Spanish Succession, but he was astonished to learn that he had actually shone in his worst subject—mathematics! Exhausted, he felt he had had enough of the Sorbonne and its dismal façade.

Rézia was delighted with his success, and sent him off on a trip to Italy as a reward. On the eve of his departure in November he told Isabelle how much he looked forward to visiting 'the monuments of Rome and the remains of the Empire—reading Dante in Florence—"seeing Naples and dying"—getting around Venice in a gondola and seeing the Bridge of Sighs'. He was also aware that the epoch-making First Vatican Council—which was to declare the doctrine of papal infallibity—was in session. From this grand tour, he brought back a forceful impression of the art and architecture of the High Renaissance—Michelangelo, Raphael, and Titian; yet this was not to be nearly so enduring as his growing love of Dante's *Divine Comedy*, which proved to be one of the fundamental influences in his artistic and intellectual formation. Indeed, it is not hard to understand why the great epic poem made such an appeal to this youth who took himself and the world so seriously. Repelled by the bourgeois pursuit of comfort and security encouraged by rapid advances in science and technology, he discovered in Dante an intellectually satisfying basis for the Catholic faith in which he had been nurtured.

Vincent was not alone among the conservative-minded to yearn for the certainties of the medieval age of faith, its theology guided by the light of both natural reason and divine grace—respectively personified in the *Divine Comedy* as the Roman poet Virgil and as Beatrice, a woman of supreme beauty, virtue, and power. If his own essentially commercial age appeared to lack a solid core of ethical and cultural values, Vincent, the future symphonist, found enormous sustenance in contemplating Dante's spiritual journey through the work's great structures and symmetries: the circles of Hell, the corniced mountain of Purgatory, and the Neoplatonic hierarchy of Heaven. Moreover, both the 'Purgatorio' and the 'Paradiso' are suffused with music, in the latter resounding throughout the heavens with the singing of angels and the souls of the blessed. There are frequent references to memories of earthly music in the former, as in Dante's important meeting with the singer Casella:

> 'Love which discourses with me in my mind,'
> He began to sing, and so sweetly
> That the sweetness still sounds within me now.

So overwhelmed was Vincent that he even contemplated writing a symphony based on the 'Purgatorio', another gigantic conception which inevitably came to nothing.[11]

Rézia's plan had triumphed. Her beloved grandson had returned from Italy full of his artistic experiences and totally confirmed in his natural vocation for music, as she may have foreseen. St Cyr was forgotten, but the growing power of a recently unified Germany, directed by the ambitions of the Prussian chancellor Bismarck, ensured that Vincent could not so easily escape the call to arms.

The outbreak of the Franco-Prussian War in July 1870 effectively brought Vincent's sheltered youth to an abrupt end. After the disastrous defeat and capitulation of the Emperor and his army at Sedan, the invading Prussians

---

[11] VI to Isabelle de Pampelonne, 27 Nov. 1869, AF. VI to H. Imbert, 15 June 1887, BN. C. Holmes, *Dante* (Oxford, 1980), 47, 75. Dante, *The Divine Comedy*, trans. C. H. Sisson (London, 1980), Purg. II, lines 112–14. E. Fubini, *A History of Music Aesthetics* (Basingstoke and London, 1991), 104–5.

pressed on to Paris itself. Defying Rézia's will for the first time, he cheerfully submitted to the call of his country, and enrolled in the National Guard, a militia normally formed from the 'reliable' bourgeois class. In this emergency, however, large numbers of 'proletarian' Red Republican sympathizers were taken on, to the dismay of the governor of Paris, General Louis Trochu, who soon came to view the National Guard as an unreliable armed rabble. Vincent's experience in the 105th battalion nevertheless proved to be something which he subsequently recalled with fierce pride. The initiation into army life certainly came as a shock, with daily roll-call, training, parades, and large-scale manœuvres, even if mitigated by an intense feeling of camaraderie. At this early stage, he remarked upon the total confidence in which the new Republican government was held by the National Guard and the whole of Paris, as well as the prevailing sense of discipline and respect for authority. But he also noted the inadequacy of the weapons—miserable, out-of-date *fusils à pistons*— issued to the battalion.

On 17 September the siege of Paris began; yet the city, surrounded by an *enceinte* wall, moat, and chain of sixteen powerful forts, seemed virtually impregnable. The Prussian forces found themselves fully stretched to invest a circumference of nearly fifty miles. The 105th was stationed in bastion 70 in the Vaugirard area, lodged in a cavity hollowed out under a ramp leading to the ramparts. During the long spells of sentry duty on the ramparts, absolutely alone in the darkness of the night, with only two or three cannons for company, Vincent kept up his spirits by recalling the happy times spent at Chabret; when dawn broke, he was reminded of the superb mountain panorama at Vernoux. Inevitably, his reveries would be interrupted by a rough shout of 'Who goes there?', or by a sudden flash followed by the dull roar of the guns. He couldn't deny that he was a rotten sentry, to which he attributed his promotion to the rank of Corporal!

Meanwhile, the Prussians' intention to starve the city into submission was beginning to have some effect; as normal foodstuffs ran out, the inhabitants resorted to the meat of horse, dog, and cat, and eventually even rat, not to mention the elephant in the Jardin des Plantes. As the situation worsened, Vincent's initial respect for authority evaporated, to be replaced by contempt and rage in the face of Trochu's inactivity and clichéd pronouncements, notoriously 'Le gouverneur de Paris ne capitulera pas'! The sufferings of the Parisians were further exacerbated by the bitter cold which arrived in December. On Christmas night, Vincent's battalion was quartered in the village of Issy, housed in an inadequate tent at a temperature of 15 degrees Fahrenheit, 'with a layer of ice for a mattress and a heap of snow for a pillow', as he described it later. In the ensuing skirmish at Val-Fleury, he experienced 'the inexpressible excitement which overtakes you during a bayonet charge, feverish, delirious, with the blood boiling in your head; a wonderful cure for the cold!' He found himself becoming hardened to violence and suffering, indifferent to the cries of the wounded. He realized that the age of Turenne had long departed, that bravery was irrelevant; modern warfare had little to do with fine uniforms, horses, and dreams of glory, being more like a terrible plague. In his published history of the battalion, he described how

Above all, everything in a war happens mathematically, by calculation . . . a battle is no more than an algebraic operation, a siege is a multiplication, a campaign is an entire nation hurling itself upon another nation, to the point of one annihilating the other.

Frustrated by the unexpected length of the siege, and in defiance of world opinion, the Prussians decided to bombard the city into submission, using Krupp's super-heavy guns dangerously elevated to the maximum angle of 30 degrees. Favourite targets were the areas around the Panthéon and the Invalides, with Vincent's own home receiving two shells. But the overall damage and casualties were comparatively light, while many of the enemy guns were starting to blow up under such excessive demands. The initial onslaught had been made on the southern forts, silencing the guns at Issy on 5 January; but only eighteen men were killed and eighty wounded out of a total of 1,900. Stationed on the ramparts, Vincent quickly learned to listen carefully to ascertain from which side a shell was coming, and take cover accordingly; the whistling noise

produced a particularly disagreeable sensation. Several times
he barely escaped death. He also witnessed some appalling
sights, above all one night when forty-eight shells fell within
two hours while he was commanding a detachment in
Grenelle.

It was entirely characteristic of him that throughout the
siege he carried his copy of Dante's *Divine Comedy* in a French
translation, and doubtless the 'Inferno' acquired an even more
intense significance in these grim conditions. Suffering from
the terrible freezing weather, he must have felt the irony that
the torments of the damned in the very lowest circles of Hell
consisted not of fire but of ice:

> Discoloured, up to where disgrace appears,
> So were the shadows tortured in the ice,
> And, with their chattering teeth, sounded like storks.

Vincent took part in the final disastrous sortie of the siege
on 18 January 1871, an attempted strike at Buzenal in the sec-
tor nearest to Versailles and strongly defended by the enemy.
After a chaotic start, a foothold was gained on the plateau of
Garches-La Bergerie; but, exposed to the Prussian guns, some
'proletarian' regiments went to pieces, refusing to go forward,
and even directing some fire on to their own side. Finally,
the French forces fled back to Paris in total disorder. Battle-
hardened as he was, Vincent could not but be appalled by the
carnage: 'men covered with blood, convoys of the wounded,
their cries masking the roars of the guns'. The news of 4,000
dead and wounded provoked a popular uprising in the city, a
clear sign to the government that an armistice with the
Prussians should be arranged without delay. Deeply embittered both by Trochu's pusillanimous conduct of the defence
of Paris and by his slurs on the honour of the National Guard
as a whole, Vincent resigned from his battalion.

Indeed, there was no longer any reason for him to remain
in Paris, in view of the election of a new conservative National
Assembly by the country as a whole, which was Catholic,
monarchist, and rural in its sympathies, and utterly opposed
to the advanced Republican ideas which found their hotbed in
the capital. He probably made his way down to Valence the

following month at the same time as the government transferred from Paris to Versailles. Thus he played no part in the
bloody events of the Commune, so ruthlessly crushed by
French troops on the orders of the Chief of Executive Powers,
Adolphe Thiers.

Vincent may have intended to recuperate in the country
after his wartime tribulations, but once securely installed at
Chabret, he launched himself into several schemes of work.
First, he had an overwhelming desire to justify the performance of the National Guard as a whole, which, it seemed,
Trochu had distrusted to the extent of committing only some
of his available forces to battle. Although it was true that the
'proletarian' battalions had earned their reputation for drunk-
enness and inefficiency, he stoutly maintained that the majority of the Guard showed excellent spirit and discipline; only
50,000 or 60,000 out of the total of about 350,000 men were
active communard sympathizers, out to shoot fellow
Frenchmen or flee from the Prussians. His case was presented
in a short book *Histoire du 105ᵉ bataillon* published the following year, which also provides a vivid and passionate
account of his experiences of the siege. Trochu's own defence
of his conduct, *Pour la verité et pour la justice*, appeared in
print in 1873.[12]

Having delivered his broadside against Trochu, d'Indy (as
I shall refer to him from now on) could at last settle down to
the main purpose of his existence. For a time he continued to
work on his opera *Burgraves*, only to abandon it when he
finally realized that the desired unity of form and treatment
eluded him. He had obviously bitten off more than he could
chew, and a thorough, systematic course in the basic subjects
of composition was now urgently required. He envisaged a
laborious musical apprenticeship, to include close study and
analysis of the symphonies of Haydn, Mozart, Beethoven,
Mendelssohn, and Berlioz, together with the operas of Gluck,
Mozart, Weber, Meyerbeer, Gounod, and Wagner. Orchestra-

[12] VI to Alphonse de Pampelonne, 8 Feb. 1871, AF. VI, *Histoire du 105ᵉ bataillon*
(Paris, 1872), *passim*. A. Horne, *The Fall of Paris, the Siege and the Commune,
1870–71* (London, 1965; rev. 1989), *passim*. Dante, Inf. XXXII, lines 34–9. *Catalogue
du bibliothèque de Vincent d'Indy* (Paris, 1933).

tion he regarded as a special challenge, with constant reference to Berlioz's *Grand Traité d'orchestration*. The road to mastery was to be long and arduous, but nothing less would have satisfied such a striving, self-critical nature.

2

Père Franck and the Abbé Liszt

On his return to Paris after the 'Bloody Week' of May 1871, during which the troops of the Versailles government had crushed the Paris Commune with merciless severity, d'Indy was confronted by a terrifying scene of damage and destruction. Raging fires had reduced many buildings like the Tuileries and the Hôtel de Ville to smouldering ruins. Doubtless the military man in him would have agreed with the grim verdict of the Goncourt brothers that 'The solution has restored its self-confidence to the Army, which has learned in the blood of the Communards that it was still capable of fighting'.[1] The national shame and humiliation of defeat at the hands of the Germans had indelibly marked the younger generation of Frenchmen—Joffre, Foch, and Pétain among them—for whom the experience was only to be expunged, and in the most terrible way, by ultimate victory in the Great War of 1914–18.

Meanwhile, normal life was beginning to re-establish itself. The Parisian bourgeoisie swarmed back to take possession of their city, and a stream of carriages brought back those who had taken refuge in the country. Soon omnibuses were operating and theatres had reopened. In fact, the national recovery proved to be nothing less than astounding, with an industrial renaissance which permitted the heavy burden of reparations to Germany to be paid off ahead of time. But d'Indy, sentimentally loyal to the Napoleonic ideal and its

[1] *Pages from the Goncourt Journals*, ed. R. Baldick (Oxford, 1962), 31 May 1871, 193–4.

legacy, however disastrous, could only view the bourgeois triumph of Thiers's Third Republic with utter distaste. Nevertheless, if his immediate intention was to turn his back on public life and retreat into an *exil intérieur* devoted to musical studies, his father had other ideas.

Antonin now stepped in to steer his son's hitherto unfocused, indeterminate way of life into the straight and narrow course of a regular career—maybe he had regrets about his own dilettante existence. For a youth of d'Indy's intelligence and social standing, the study of law seemed the obvious choice; no doubt Antonin envisaged him as a cultivated barrister with strong musical interests. To this end, he made him enrol in the Faculty of Law at the Sorbonne, where the arid grind of the *Code Napoléon* was hardly to his liking.[2] The pull of music remained too strong to be resisted, and, surreptitiously, he still attended concerts and the opera and associated with musicians. He even managed to continue his lessons with Lavignac, while working on a new, ambitious symphony in A minor. Some encouragement came with the publication of some songs and four *Romances sans paroles* for piano. At the same time, his life, seemingly so serious and purposeful, had its lighter side, for much fun and laughter was to be had at Saint-Saëns's soirées on Mondays, where the most progressive musicians gathered. There d'Indy met Bizet; Massenet; Charles-Marie Widor, the fashionable young organist of Saint-Sulpice; Bussine, a singing teacher at the Conservatoire; Alexis de Castillon, an ex-army officer; and—most significantly for the future—César Franck, a dowdy figure a little out of place in this sophisticated company.

Saint-Saëns's own compositions performed on these occasions won d'Indy's admiration: *Le Rouet d'Omphale*, arranged for two pianos, he considered 'a true jewel of grace and finesse'; while a programme of songs, including a *danse macabre*, had the added attraction of being performed by Franck's ravishing Irish pupil Augusta Holmès. Always highly susceptible to female charm, d'Indy found himself, like Franck, totally infatuated with her. On these occasions,

[2] VI, 'Impressions musicales d'enfance et de la jeunesse', *Annales*, 15 May 1930, 471.

amusing anecdotes circulated, such as the one about the Colonel who tackled a bandsman on parade for not playing his trombone. 'But, Colonel,' the unfortunate player replied, 'I'm counting rests.' The Colonel exploded: 'I've never seen that in all my life; I want everyone in my regiment working, and you are going to start blowing straight away and do fifteen days in the guardhouse!'

D'Indy became very friendly with Alexis de Castillon, who had resigned from the Imperial Guard to study with Franck. A highly promising composer of chamber music, he died only two years later at the early age of 35. D'Indy frequently visited him at his small apartment in the rue Bayard to talk about art and listen respectfully to his compositions. However, he thoroughly disapproved of Castillon's liaison with a certain woman of the world, an entirely sensual creature 'who exhausted him and certainly led him to his grave. . . . when she came to the rehearsals of Pasdeloup's concerts, veiled in her box, we couldn't resist saying to each other "Here comes the octopus".'[3]

Events took another turn with the death of Rézia on 21 February 1872. Grief there must have been at the passing of this formidable, though excellently intentioned old lady; at the same time, his inheritance of her fortune placed him in an independent position regarding Antonin, enabling him to withdraw from his legal studies and concentrate on music. In later years, he liked to play down the reality of himself as a man of means, and to foster the myth that he had been a typical poor student, cut off by a harsh, unsympathetic father, and forced to undertake the lowest grades of musical work—playing horn and drums at middle-class balls and copying band parts—in order to survive.[4] The truth was that at this stage of his career he regarded no task as beneath him in his quest for complete expertise and professionalism in his chosen field; to remain a wealthy dilettante he would have regarded as unworthy, even immoral. Anxious to be taken entirely on

---

[3] VI to Cécile d'Indy, 6 Nov. 1871 and 17 Oct. 1872, AF. VI to H. Imbert, 5 Oct. 1894, BN.

[4] VI, 'Impressions musicales', 471.

his own merits, he never relied on his aristocratic pedigree to secure himself any advantage. Another test of his powers of endurance was about to take place. During his regular summer vacations at Chabret, he had fallen passionately in love with his cousin Isabelle, and he now proposed marriage to her. To this, Antonin was firmly opposed, not merely because he hoped his son might marry a duchess! With good reason, he feared the genetic dangers of further intermarriage; for already the family history presented a veritable tangle of inbreeding in previous generations, as we have already seen. At the same time, Antonin respected his son's blind strength of feeling, and eventually he was prepared to compromise. With the agreement of both branches of the family, the decision to permit the pair to marry was postponed for two years, to test their resolution; Vincent was forbidden to visit Chabret or to write to Isabelle. Both faced the bleak prospect patiently, while Vincent sought consolation in playing Beethoven's sonatas op. 27, no. 2, and op. 90, which he sentimentally associated with love and married bliss.[5]

During this period of anxious waiting, he completed his symphony, considering it worthy of being shown to the conductor Pasdeloup, who used his Tuesday rehearsals to try out works by young composers. Plucking up courage, he took the Scherzo movement along to Pasdeloup's house in the avenue Bonne-Nouvelle; but overcome by a sudden attack of nerves on the doorstep, he fled. A second attempt proved no more successful: boarding a bus in pouring rain, he slipped on the step and dropped the packet of orchestral parts in the muddy gutter! Finally, he managed to deliver the music to Pasdeloup during a rehearsal. The story probably lost nothing in the telling at the end of his life, but after a wait of over two months, the Scherzo was duly played through, and the apparently satisfied conductor asked to see the rest of the symphony. Although it was eventually discarded, a good start had been made, and two years later Pasdeloup was to give a public performance of d'Indy's next work, the concert overture *Piccolomini*.[6]

[5] LV i. 120.   [6] VI, 'Impressions musicales', 471.

Yet there was little room for complacency. With Duparc's encouragement, d'Indy took a string quartet movement to Franck for his opinion. Expecting a favourable reaction, he was unpleasantly startled by Franck's brutal frankness:

'There are some good things in it; it shows spirit and a certain instinct for dialogue between the parts; the ideas would not be bad—but—that is not enough; the work is not finished—in fact, *you really know nothing whatever.*' Seeing that I was dreadfully mortified by this opinion, for which I was not at all prepared, he went on to explain his reasons, and wound up by saying: 'Come to see me, if you want us to work together. I could teach you composition.'

At first, d'Indy found this advice hard to accept. But on the following day, after having made himself calmly go through the pencilled comments on his manuscript, he realized that Franck was absolutely right. Thereupon he went back to him to ask for lessons. In addition to these lessons, in which the study of fugal writing played an integral part, Franck admitted him as an observer to the organ class at the Conservatoire.[7] This class came under the section 'Harmonie, orgue, et composition', as improvisation formed a particularly important aspect of the training of church organists in France, requiring a solid grounding in the principles of composition. The professor, therefore, had to be a composer as well as an organist.

In this, d'Indy took what proved to be the most momentous decision of his life, but it was not an immediately obvious step, but rather an act of faith. The previous year, Franck had surfaced, in rather mysterious circumstances, from the obscurity of private teaching and the organ loft of Sainte-Clotilde—not then the fashionable church it later became—to succeed his old teacher François Benoist as organ professor. There was minimal prestige in the appointment, for the organ world had fallen into the doldrums in the decades following the French Revolution, and a church organist post was generally regarded merely as a useful means of economic survival for struggling musicians, even for the most brilliant like Saint-Saëns. Reflecting this state of affairs, the ethos of the class

---

[7] CF 242–4.

under Benoist, who had held the post since 1819, was essentially workaday and uninspired.

With Franck in charge, the authorities assumed that this situation would continue as before. Indeed, in those years, his prolonged periods of artistic stagnation quite overshadowed the few outbursts of true creative energy, manifest in the precocious early piano trios (1842) and later in the *Six pièces* (1860–2), in which he showed himself the first to come to grips with the aesthetic potential of the new Cavaillé-Coll symphonic organ. Moreover, his modest demeanour and his appearance of a bourgeois music teacher, shabby but respectable, utterly belied the possibility that he might become a powerful force in his own right, even a threat to the *status quo*. In reality, however, the class provided him with an outlet for his pent-up creative powers, and d'Indy considered that none of the actual composition professors—Bazin, Reber, and Massé, whose horizons did not extend beyond the requirements of the Prix de Rome—could have provided him with such a thorough grounding: 'They did not properly understand either their *art* or their *craft*.'

It is an extraordinary fact that Franck had gained his profound knowledge and vision in the teeth of a continuous history of personal set-backs and frustrations, his general education sacrificed to his ruthless father's ambition to make him into a piano-playing prodigy. Little besides a valuable course in counterpoint at the Conservatoire under the excellent Anton Reicha, a friend of Beethoven, and Benoist's sound, if dull, organ pedagogy mitigated the relentless commercial pressures of a piano virtuoso's career playing popular show-pieces. A crisis point was reached in 1846, when he suddenly abandoned this life of false glamour for the organ loft. Fundamentally serious-minded, a natural student and autodidact, his confidence in the long-term development of his powers sustained him through years of near poverty and discouragement. He provided the ideal role model for d'Indy, whose contempt for easy success was as austere as it was profound.[8]

---

[8] L. Vallas, *César Franck* (New York, 1951).

At the time when d'Indy became his pupil, Franck was occupied with what can only be described as idealistic projects, the large-scale oratorios *La Rédemption* and *Les Béatitudes*, whose prospects hardly looked encouraging in the absence of a strong French choral tradition. In fact, it is arguable that the very distinctiveness of his teaching was the result of expertise painfully achieved in isolation, based on the continuous study of Bach and Beethoven, and unaffected by fashion. As d'Indy later explained in his book on Franck, the latter above all emphasized the need for architectural qualities in his students' work, for musical ideas to be distributed in a definite, logical order. Any faults in construction were immediately exposed, as also the failure to make a proper *selection* of ideas. Yet these timeless formal principles he applied with a sense of deep humanity and a respect for the individual student. An excellent psychologist, he gave each pupil the direction and subject-matter best suited to his or her temperament, encouraging initiative and rightly refusing to conform to the prevailing bureaucratic system which tended to reduce all intellects to one level. Rivalry he abhorred, preferring to foster an atmosphere of love and charity in accordance with his simple Christian faith based on the Gospels.[9]

The aura of Franck's personality extended beyond the classroom, drawing his students to the organ loft at Sainte-Clotilde. There, during Sunday masses, d'Indy heard the finest improviser of his age at the three-manual Cavaillé-Coll instrument, from which he derived much inspiration. But by comparison with Saint-Saëns at the Madeleine and the newly rising stars Charles-Marie Widor and Alexandre Guilmant at Saint-Sulpice and the Trinité, Franck was an organist of mediocre technical attainment. If, in class, his teaching of composition and improvisation was beyond praise, instruction in organ technique and management clearly bored him: all too often, he would himself change registrations while the student played on. To his credit, he did introduce some much needed new repertoire to the class, particularly the Preludes and

---

[9] CF 233–50.

Fugues of J. S. Bach—cheerfully assuming that the students already possessed sufficient technique to tackle them![10]

For d'Indy, the organ-playing side of the course was of less importance than the insights gained into the techniques of composition. He brought a sharpened critical faculty to the performance of Beethoven's Ninth Symphony under Deldevez in February 1873, commenting on the choral finale, 'It's so large! That immense phrase rising from the depths of the orchestra to the violas and cellos, then to the first violins, and at last to the whole orchestra, maintains a consistent interest, an equally great strength *without modulating a single time*.' He had absorbed a vital lesson from Franck that key changes should not take place unnecessarily, or in an arbitrary, haphazard manner, but rather with full awareness of their function in the overall structure. This may well come as a surprise to those who—like Debussy—regard the Franckian style as a sea of perpetual modulation! D'Indy's sensitivity to orchestral sonority was aroused by Beethoven's use of the contrabassoon—'like a 32' organ stop'.[11]

His admiration for Franck was immense, as if the older man answered to a deep-seated need in him. He fully involved himself in the preparations for the first performance of *La Rédemption* which took place during Holy Week in April 1873 under Colonne's direction. This provided him with a hard-won object lesson in tonal architecture. To underline the story of Christ's coming on earth to regenerate pagan humanity and, after its backsliding, the Archangel's proclamation of a new redemption, Franck had devised an ingenious tonal scheme, corresponding to the poem's contrasts of light and shade. In d'Indy's own description in his biography of Franck:

How admirably logical is the succession of sharp keys in this work! Starting with a neutral and colourless key, A minor, the first part is illuminated by degrees; as by a ladder, we seem to rise to the *greatest light* by means of E, the dominant, A major, and F sharp major.

The sections in the last-named key, deemed unplayable by the orchestra, became the breaking-point in a catastrophic

[10] R. Smith, *Towards an Authentic Interpretation of the Organ Works of César Franck* (New York, 1983), 41–3.
[11] LV i. 135.

series of rehearsals. The first had to be abandoned on account of excessive errors in the band parts; even the normally genial Franck could not hide his annoyance. D'Indy, who knew the score well, having accompanied the choir's practices on the piano, promptly came to the rescue. Together with Duparc and Benoît, he undertook the Herculean task of correcting the parts in the short space of one day and two nights, fortified by a good supply of brandy! Despite their efforts, nothing thereafter went right; rehearsals were curtailed, cuts made, and the performers took against the work. Not surprisingly, the concert was something of a fiasco, but any anger felt by the composer was as nothing by comparison with the violent reaction of his disciples. It seemed a matter of real urgency to persuade him to change the sections in the offending key of F sharp. According to d'Indy's own account in his biography of Franck:

I first undertook to broach the subject to him. I must own that I was not very well received on the first occasion, and, having sinned yet a second time, 'Father' Franck, throwing aside his usual amenity, forbade me, with some severity, to mention the subject again. But after several of his favourite pupils, led by Henri Duparc, had returned to the attack, he ended by resigning himself to the transposition of the Archangel's aria and the whole of the last number of the first part into E major. But the entire design of the work was changed, for although it is easier to play in E major, this key is far from giving that effulgency which we derive from F sharp, which is the dominant, not the subdominant, of the final tonality.

D'Indy lived to regret bitterly this advice which he had tendered so urgently to his master. Indeed, he subsequently made a full and contrite confession of his error, through which 'a perfect and wonderfully balanced structure was unfortunately modified in the second edition of the work—the only one now extant'.

Emotionally drained by this experience, he was badly in need of spiritual refreshment. He decided to treat himself that summer to a tour of Germany, his interest aroused by his enthusiasm for Brahms's German Requiem. This, however, was to be no mere holiday; in addition to sightseeing, concert going, and visiting galleries, his main object was to track

down Liszt and Brahms and, if possible, Wagner, the prime
movers in modern musical developments, whose work had, as
yet, hardly begun to make an impact in France. But he certainly hadn't the slightest intention of honouring Bismarck's
Prussia with his presence![12]

He went first to Cologne, where the cathedral absorbed all
his attention. 'What grandeur, what poetry, what true art
there is in this immense *petrifaction*, if I may call it that, of
the thought of the Middle Ages,' he wrote in a very long letter to Isabelle's brother, Roger de Pampelonne, describing the
entire tour. 'It's struck me as being at least as beautiful and
great as St Peter's in Rome; both uplift the soul, but
St Peter's inspires thoughts of vastness, of Michelangelo, and
great art, while at Cologne one is seized and transported,
dreaming of eternal truths and thinking of God.'

In Marburg, his eye for the picturesque took particular
delight in the traditional costumes worn by the inhabitants:
'the blue stockings, the green petticoats, and especially the
little embroidered bonnets of the Hessians which match the
countryside very well, not to mention the multicoloured uniforms of the German students and their own special songs'.
Moving on to Eisenach, he visited the thirteenth-century
Wartburg, the castle of the Margraves of Thuringia, full of
memories of Saint Elisabeth, Isabelle's patron saint. With
charming gallantry, he sent her via Roger a little red and
orange flower picked near the Roman fountain where the saint
came to pray. He also took vigorous walks in the forests and
mountains, during which he meditated in solitude.

The high point of the tour turned out to be Weimar, with
its shades of Herder, Wieland, Goethe, and Schiller, whose
works he had started to read. At this moment, by happy
chance, Liszt was in residence, still very much alive in his six-
ties, and surrounded by an adoring crowd of pupils. Bearing a
letter of introduction from Saint-Saëns, d'Indy approached
Liszt in his summer chalet in the middle of a wood. The first
glimpse was hardly auspicious; he recalled that

[12] CF 144–55. Imbert, *Profils des musiciens*, 43.

I was about to enter the study when I saw a long figure rise up before me in a state of total confusion with movements like the classical gestures of malediction. . . . after waiting some minutes, I saw the great artist reappear, mollified. He took me by the hand in a most courteous manner. Liszt had just received the Papal notification of his admission into a minor order of the Catholic Church, and he was bound not to receive anyone without being dressed in the long black cassock, the distinctive sign of his nomination.

D'Indy was immediately welcomed into the circle of Liszt's followers, who were mainly German, Russian, and American, finding them most congenial company. Much of each day was spent profitably discussing and making music, yet there was also time for amusement, with partying and dancing, all of which revolved around Liszt himself; his powerful charm enveloped everyone like a cloud, and the magic of his presence was irresistible.

To his pleasant surprise, d'Indy received invitations from Liszt to coffee in the mornings. These, indeed, were no mere social calls, for his conversation, in French, was most instructive. From him, the future reformer of French musical education claimed to have received the conception of a historically based pedagogy, provoking students to ascertain and relive, as it were, the successive developments of musical civilization in their own work. In addition, he took part in the piano master classes, and at the point when he arrived, the works of Schumann were being studied, among them the *Humoresque*, *Études symphoniques*, and *Waldscenen*. Occasionally, when an unfortunate student proved unequal to the task, Liszt would furiously push him aside and take over: then 'the piano appeared to us as a superior instrument, producing hitherto unknown sonorities'. As a special honour, d'Indy was asked to play duets with Liszt, and to score-read passages from his oratorio *Christus*. But he did not achieve all his hopes. He had come to Germany bearing some newly printed copies of Franck's *Rédemption*, and one of these he presented to Liszt. But, according to the American student Amy Fay, Liszt showed little interest in it. Sitting at the piano, 'he would skip whole pages and begin again here and there.'

After twelve days, Liszt left Weimar, and at once the student group broke up. The time had come for d'Indy to continue his journey, making his way to Nuremberg in the company of Amy Fay, who disappointingly made no mention of him in her book *Music Study in Germany*, published in 1881. Nuremberg, then still preserved in the Middle Ages, enchanted the romantic medievalist in him, particularly during his lengthy midnight wanderings:

The mysterious light of the moon lends this mysterious town a very special character; when the roofs stand out in black against the silvery sky, when the thrusting gables try to pierce the heavens like so many great spires, when you see no light, apart from the two lanterns lit upon the two towers of Saint-Laurent like two strange eyes; what a delight to wander completely alone in these Gothic alleys, to lose yourself in the Middle Ages without fear that a jarring frock coat or a Rabajas hat may come and destroy your illusion, to see when you raise your eyes a terrifying gargoyle looking as if it wanted to spit on your head, to stop at last on the bank of the river in which the sky is reflected, to look at the great black towers and the light of the moon which plays on the little panes of the Gothic windows, without hearing any sound but the river which roars like a torrent beneath the low arches of the Roman bridges; it is thus that you dream, that you feel yourself elated, thinking of poetry, great art, and those whom you love.

Such was the spell that the town cast upon him that he extended his stay there from two to five days, when the lure of Wagner at Bayreuth finally succeeded in drawing him away. Thanks to a letter of introduction from Liszt, Cosima Wagner received him graciously, but the master was not to be disturbed. Instead, she allowed him to look at her husband from a distance, moving about before a long, high desk, and nervously scattering sheets of lined paper in all corners of the room. These sheets were the final pages of the full orchestral score of *Götterdämmerung*.

After Bayreuth, Leipzig seemed like a fall from grace, for all its theatre could offer were some futile ballets and a Bellini opera. 'It's not worth coming to Germany just to hear that,' he remarked sourly. Dresden, by comparison, was a revelation. Adopted at once by the *artistes* of the opera, he was given a place in the orchestra so that he could attend every rehearsal and performance during his stay. It was an invaluable experience to see the workings of an opera-house at close quarters, as well as to make the acquaintance of the leading members of the company.

Fully engaged by the musical life of the town, he did not neglect the art gallery and its outstanding collection of pictures. It struck him forcefully how well hung these were in comparison with the museums of Italy. Certain pictures he knew and admired already from reproductions, and to see the originals was something worth waiting for. Of these, Raphael's famous *Sistine Madonna* floating in the clouds and Correggio's *Madeleine*, the embodiment of feminine charm, especially delighted him; at this stage in his life, these sensuous works of the Renaissance exerted an appeal far greater than the Italian 'primitives' of the trecento and quattrocento, whose austere spiritual qualities were to speak so clearly to him in the years of his maturity. He also made some new discoveries among the artists of northern Europe, finding Holbein's *Virgin* a revelation in its purity, truth, and grace, reminiscent of Lully's *Armide*. Rembrandt, too, impressed him greatly with his brush strokes 'à la Beethoven'.

After Dresden, Vienna came as an anticlimax: 'a not very picturesque city where you find Parisian boulevards, Parisian monuments, Parisian Englishmen, Parisian cafés, Parisian tarts. . . . at the Opera, they put on three or four times some filthy ballets for the benefit of the English.' His temper was not improved by failing to find Brahms at home. Continuing on his way down the Danube by boat, he arrived at Salzburg, where he visited the museum and even persuaded the curator to let him inspect one of Mozart's autograph scores. But more than the relics of Mozart, the salt mines on the outskirts of the town captured his imagination, and he graphically described his visit to one of them:

The mine is inside the mountain, and, in this mountain there are twenty-six salt lakes on which you navigate with miner's overalls on, a leather apron, large hat and lighted lamp; then you see grottos, rifts, precipices, and in the end, if you have any imagination left, you may conjure up Dante's *Inferno*, where the miners at the bottom of their pits seem like damned souls.

Faithful to his hardy outdoor philosophy, he explored the surrounding countryside on foot, setting off one morning at five o'clock to climb the mountain right up to the snowline, and returning at ten at night, tired out. The views had been magnificent, the experience enhanced by his contemptuous pity for the English Cook's tourists on the road below, roasting in their carriages in 30 degrees of heat! Proceeding to Munich, he was warmly welcomed by the members of the orchestra and students of the *Hochschule*. The cultural life of the city was hardly less stimulating than that of Dresden, with an unforgettable performance of *Fidelio*. At the *Alte Pinakothek* he was stunned by Holbein's painting of the Way of the Cross, 'of a colour which no painter has been able to equal'. But if he had hoped to catch Brahms in Munich, the bird had flown. At last, however, he found the composer of the German Requiem at Tützing, beside Lake Starnberg.

D'Indy might as well have spared himself the trouble. Like a surly bear surprised in its lair, Brahms received him on the doorstep of his chalet with scant courtesy, accepting the proffered copy of Franck's *Rédemption* with indifference. To d'Indy's request that he play one of his latest compositions, Brahms replied laconically that he did not play the piano. Then, with an abrupt 'Auf weidersehen', he showed him the door. Several months later, d'Indy learned from the pianist Madame Szarvady that Brahms was really a very kind, welcoming person, and that he played the piano exceptionally well! Under the circumstances, d'Indy took the snub most philosophically, reflecting that the older man had been put off by his youthful self-confidence and *candeur*; or perhaps he had even been the butt of a practical joke. But if the German tour ended on a rather sour note, the benefits in terms of widened cultural horizons were incalculable.[13]

[13] VI to Roger de Pampelonne, 27 July 1873, repr. in *Revue Hommes et mondes*, no. 39 (Oct. 1949), 234–9. VI, 'Impressions musicales', 471–2. A. Fay, *Music Study in Germany* (Chicago, 1881), 240.

3

Marriage and the Lure of Bayreuth

On his return to Paris, d'Indy immediately plunged back into his normal life of intensive activity and study. In January 1874, he re-entered Franck's organ class as a full student member, with the hope of gaining a first prize, an award which would justify his chosen path in the eyes of his family. In the same month, on 25 January, student in status as he was, he received the honour of a performance by Pasdeloup of his concert overture *Piccolomini*, laboriously composed under Franck's guidance. This work, the first part to be completed of an ambitious orchestral project, will be discussed later in this chapter.

There was progress, too, in his private affairs, for that spring his father agreed in principle to his marriage to Isabelle, but with the condition of a further year's delay. His end-of-year result at the Conservatoire proved to be rather less impressive than he had hoped, however. A *deuxième accessit*, a minor prize, gained in June nevertheless represented some measure of achievement, even if it fell far short of the much coveted first, or even second prize. Franck regarded him as 'an excellent hard-working pupil; he still lacks facility, but will gain it by work'. As a player, his natural ability lay more with the piano than the organ, and, significantly, he also lacked the necessary sense of freedom in improvisation. This last, indeed, is hardly surprising when one considers that he was in some ways an inhibited youth of uncertain aims, nurturing grandiose, over-ambitious plans; the act of creation he conceived in romantic, Beethovenian terms of a massive exertion of the will, rather than a spontaneous release. For a man of such a psychological constitution, progress could only be painful and slow. Doggedly, he enrolled in the class for another year's study.

If the organ was not really his true *métier*, he nevertheless took up the post of organist at the church of Saint-Leu-Taverny, near Ermont. This boasted a superb Cavaillé-Coll, presented by Napoleon III in memory of his mother, Queen Hortense; the association would have greatly appealed to d'Indy.[1] Avid for experience, he also took on the unpaid position of second timpanist in the newly founded orchestra of L'Association artistique des concerts du Châtelet directed by Edouard—originally Judas—Colonne. No better way of studying the craft of orchestration existed, d'Indy subsequently maintained. At the same time this young aristocrat lived by the principle of *noblesse oblige*. His own intense ambitions as a composer were for him inseparable from the wider aim of serving music itself and of assisting other composers in mounting performances of their works, frequently under the most unfavourable conditions; this he saw as a moral duty, part of a crusade for the higher values of civilization.

The bitter disappointments of a creative musician's life, which he had witnessed at close range in the case of Franck's *Rédemption*, again struck him forcefully during the rehearsals of Bizet's *Carmen* at the Opéra-Comique in October 1874; nothing but hostility was being shown to the composer by management, chorus, and orchestra alike. Attending the first night on 3 March 1875, having won a free ticket offered to the students of Franck's class, d'Indy observed Bizet in the interval sunk in total dejection, prophesying defeat, a definitive, hopeless flop. The next day, Bizet turned up at the organ class appealing for a volunteer to play the harmonium behind the scenes to support Don José's unaccompanied song in Act II, as the tenor, Lhérie, was incapable of sustaining the pitch. D'Indy immediately stepped into the breach, remaining at his post in the wings throughout the remaining performances,

---

[1] N. Dufourcq, *Autour de Coquard, César Franck et Vincent d'Indy* (Paris, 1952), 60–1. VI to Imbert, 8 June 1893.

sadly remarking on the gradually diminishing audiences. Within three months Bizet was dead, broken by despair.[2]

In these circumstances, d'Indy must surely have pondered seriously his own ambitions and hopes, without illusions as to the inordinate obstacles which lay before him. His idealism took a nasty jolt, moreover, in the course of a conversation with Massenet. Complimenting him on his recent opera *Marie-Magdeleine*, d'Indy asked, with reference to certain passages: 'How did you produce this music which seems at times to be divinely inspired?' Massenet's reply revealed a depth of artistic cynicism which utterly deflated the young enthusiast: 'Oh, so you think a lot of all these sanctimonious ditties, but I don't take them seriously. . . . but the public likes them, and we must always keep in step with the public.'

After this set-back, a strange meeting with the notorious recluse Charles Valentine Alkan brought him a welcome measure of reassurance. This already legendary figure—to whom Franck had dedicated his *Grande pièce symphonique*—d'Indy discovered by chance in a studio in the Maison Erard practising Bach's St Anne Prelude in E flat on a pedal piano, with great clarity and expression. A spark of rapport was struck between them, and, at Alkan's request, d'Indy played him Bach's Fugue in C major. Alkan, in his turn, gave his interpretation of Beethoven's Sonata in A flat major, op. 110, which roused d'Indy to the height of enthusiasm: 'This wasn't Liszt—perhaps technically less perfect—but it was more intimate, human, and touching.' Before he could utter a word of appreciation, Alkan pushed him towards the window violently and looked him straight in the eyes, pronouncing the momentous words: 'You will be an artist . . . a true one. . . . Farewell, for we shall never meet again!' At this, d'Indy protested strongly, fully intending to be present at his forthcoming series of *petits concerts*. Alas, the prophecy proved to be all too correct, for unavoidable engagements constantly prevented his attendance.[3]

The same year, he was presented with a great opportunity. Obviously impressed by his energy and efficiency, Colonne

[2] LV i. 201–2.   [3] VI, 'Impressions musicales', 473.

promoted him from second timpanist to salaried chorus master of the Concerts du Châtelet. Since rehearsals were held on Sunday afternoons, d'Indy was obliged to resign his organ post. The work of training a choir and teaching its members their parts suited him admirably, thorough and disciplined as he was. Moreover, the task constituted an education in itself, for it fell to him to prepare the choral parts of Beethoven's Ninth Symphony and of Berlioz's *L'Enfance du Christ*, *Roméo et Juliette*, and *La Damnation de Faust*. An unfortunate disagreement with Colonne, however, subsequently led to his resignation.

In July 1875, the great prizes of the Conservatoire once again eluded him. To Franck's intense bewilderment and general consternation, he gained a *premier accessit*—only a small advance on the previous year's result. On the other hand, it must be realized that very few first prizes were actually awarded during Franck's tenure of the professorship, therefore d'Indy's relative lack of achievement was small disgrace. But any sense of failure or disappointment utterly melted away before the imminent prospect of his marriage to Isabelle, to which both sets of parents were now reconciled. The wedding ceremony took place at Boffres on 11 August amid great festivities. During the service in the tiny church, a fellow student, Charles Langrand, played the harmonium; afterwards, d'Indy upbraided him for modulating to the subdominant in his improvisation during the *Offertoire*! The happy couple departed for their honeymoon in Spain, seemingly undeterred by the Carlist War then drawing to its close.[4]

D'Indy's marriage could certainly be counted a success. On his side, there may well have been a tendency to idealize Isabelle à la Dante's Beatrice; but she certainly represented for her husband the sense of his roots in the Drôme, or Ardèche region. Expending so much of his time and energy in Paris, he increasingly felt aware of the danger of deracination, the loss of contact with the soil of France. Indeed, this was becoming a major political and literary theme generally, expressed in Barrès' once celebrated symbolist novel *Le Jardin de Bérénice*

---

[4] LV i. 205–6. Imbert, *Profils des musiciens*, 45.

(1891), in which a young girl of Provence provides for her politician-lover the most complete image of the forces of nature: 'Sitting beside her, who represented to me the mysterious power and impulse of the world, I tasted in the light perfume of her young woman's body all the savour of passion and of death.' Similarly, it was as if Isabelle's own spirit, redolent of their ancestral heritage, infiltrated the surrounding countryside, bringing to d'Indy a much needed feeling of integration and renewal. And, as we shall see, the region was to become the source of inspiration of many of his finest compositions.

On the practical level, Isabelle proved to be an excellent wife in the conventional mode, giving him a son and two daughters; moreover, her superb talents for household management provided a peaceful atmosphere, so necessary for her husband's work. In every way, she acted as a firm support to him, above all bringing a sense of focus to his life, and encouraging the regular patterns of living first inculcated by Rézia. There is reason to believe that he in turn was an affectionate, considerate spouse, rather than the stereotype of the domestic tyrant. It has been hinted by Vallas that Isabelle assumed a position of dominance over d'Indy, on the slender grounds that she took every care to protect him from unnecessary intrusions and interruptions to his regular programme of work, as well as dealing with family and business matters. It seems more a case of a mutual partnership, however, remarkably progressive in an age which still regarded a wife as the legal property of her husband.[5]

Happily, and to Isabelle's great credit, the marriage did not have the effect of isolating d'Indy from his friends in a claustrophobic *ménage*. Perhaps she herself found the Parisian scene a stimulating change, for the tenement building at 7 avenue de Villars was transformed into a veritable artists' colony. Above the d'Indys on the second floor lived his old childhood friend, the poet Robert de Bonnières, on the fourth floor the well-known designer Willette, and at the top Duparc

---

[5] LV i. 206–7. M. Barrès, *Le Jardin de Bérénice* (Paris, 1891), Flammarion edn. (1988), 97. Jean d'Indy, 'Vincent d'Indy en famille', *Revue Internationale de musique*, 10 (1951), 326.

had moved in with Ellen MacSwinney, whom he married. On regular stated evenings, these friends held parties where unfamiliar music and poetry, old and new, could be heard in a heady atmosphere of youthful idealism. At Duparc's soirées, d'Indy was introduced to Gabriel Fauré, André Messager, Pierre de Bréville, and Emmanuel Chabrier, with all of whom he remained in close contact and active musical association.

De Bonnières, on the other hand, attracted a more literary following, among whom were Leconte de Lisle, Anatole France, and Jules Lemaître. To these were added a little later the cultivated barrister Paul Poujard, whose critical views made a powerful contribution to the intellectual development of that generation. Although only slightly older, de Bonnières adopted a rather superior, patronizing attitude to d'Indy, a hangover from the days when he used to chaperone him on Sundays. Having already gained some literary reputation, he offered free advice to the budding composer on the subject of general education, introducing him to the books of the historian Michelet, the philosopher Hegel, and the novelists Turgenev and Dickens. And not only on literary matters, but also on questions of dress and deportment; he would cast a quizzical eye on the absent-minded d'Indy and say: 'Vincent, take care of your appearance and your shoes!' Even in later years, he was wont to complain quite bitchily, 'Poor Vincent, when he's in evening dress, he does rather look like a village locksmith.'[6]

Stimulated by this milieu, d'Indy's compositions reflected his growing literary interests. That he had become a lover of Shakespeare is no surprise, for the Bard of Stratford had strongly influenced the French Romantic movement as a whole—not only Berlioz—in the earlier part of the century. D'Indy's favourite plays were *King Lear* and *The Tempest*,[7] whose wild, fantastic elements sounded a chord in his own character. But it was the lesser-known yet magnificent tragedy *Antony and Cleopatra* which he took as the subject of a concert overture of that name. This received a performance

---

[6] VI, 'Impressions musicales', 473. Photiadès, 'Vincent d'Indy', 459. *Debussy Letters*, ed. Lesure and Nichols (London, 1987), 52.

[7] VI to Imbert, 15 June, 1887, BN.

at the Société Nationale Musicale in March 1876 in an arrangement for two pianos played by Saint-Saëns and himself. A mediocre orchestral reading by Pasdeloup a year later probably persuaded him to withdraw the work.

Since its foundation in February 1871 by Saint-Saëns and Romain Bussine, with the support of Duparc and de Castillon, in order to 'give hearings to the works of living French composers exclusively', the Société Nationale had been providing an invaluable platform for native-grown music. Nevertheless, it laboured under certain disadvantages: namely, a lack of systematic organization and of a permanent venue. There was little money forthcoming to support the venture; performers gave their services without a fee, and the piano manufacturers Pleyel and Erard came to the rescue by allowing the use of their halls. Individuals with enough time at their disposal were urgently required to undertake the day-to-day running of the Society, and in 1876, d'Indy and Duparc found themselves elected as joint secretaries. D'Indy in particular made himself indispensable, keeping precise minutes and putting the files and records in order.

He also took an active part in the concerts as conductor and pianist, promoting the works of his colleagues no less than his own. In February and April that year, he and Fauré performed Duparc's *Suite de valses* for two pianos and in December a four-handed arrangement of his own *Piccolomini*. The same month, Saint-Saëns's *Suite pour orchestre* in an eight-handed version was tackled by its composer together with d'Indy, Eugène Gigout, and Jules Griset; and in February 1877, d'Indy and Fauré played Saint-Saëns's *Orient et Occident*.

Unfortunately, this almost idyllic state of mutual cooperation did not last for long. D'Indy's sheer competence in running the Society placed him in a strong position to influence policy making, and this he used to promote Franck. Moreover, his tour of Germany had convinced him that contemporary French music would be diminished by lack of contact with the dynamic developments in that country. To his proposal that the Society include foreign works, contrary to the intention of its founders, Saint-Saëns reacted with horror.

As his biographer James Harding has pointed out, he not unreasonably foresaw a return of the days when French composers were denied a proper hearing in their own country. But d'Indy's views prevailed, and in the following years music by Brahms, Borodin, and Glazunov *inter alia* were increasingly heard in the programmes. Understandably, Saint-Saëns felt alienated from both d'Indy and the Society, a situation which came to a head ten years later.[8]

Meanwhile, the triumph of Wagner was moving towards its apotheosis, with the first complete performance of *The Ring of the Nibelungs* in the specially built theatre at Bayreuth. With characteristic enterprise, d'Indy duly made his pilgrimage there in September 1876, together with a strong French contingent, in order to be present at the cultural sensation of the century. He wrote a long, detailed account of it to his father, whose ideas of opera, like Wilfrid's, remained conservative, wedded to the familiar Parisian scene. To one of such a highly emotional nature as d'Indy, the experience of the *Ring* proved utterly overwhelming, inducing 'a sensation of intoxication of which nothing else can give any idea', a reaction similar to that of the philosopher Friedrich Nietzsche. But d'Indy did not respond to the different parts of the tetralogy in the same way. *Das Rheingold* left a curious impression; although he was not bored for a moment, he had not '*vibrated*, with a frisson of the spine' as he did in certain French operas. The reason, he felt, was the lack of any human sentiment in a work which moved in an ideal sphere of logic and philosophy. Brilliant as he found the depiction of its supernatural world of gods and giants, his heart remained fundamentally untouched.

Die Walküre, on the other hand, struck him as an unequivocal masterpiece, rivalled only by Beethoven's symphonies. Never had he heard anything so beautiful and enchanting, overflowing with true human feeling. Nor had he ever seen such marvellous scenery. After this, *Siegfried* seemed a lesser achievement, despite the interest and amusement it provided

[8] J. Harding, *Saint-Saëns and his Circle* (London, 1965), 109–11, 154.

in the mime scenes, reminiscent of opéra comique, and in Act II's plethora of musical and scenic colours, not to mention the acrobatic virtuosity of the horn parts. Act III, however, left him cold; the great duet between Siegfried and Brünnhilde, which had seemed highly melodic when played on the piano, made a disappointing impression on stage. He could not be sure whether or not the singers were to blame for this. Finally, music drama of the highest calibre emerged in *Götterdämmerung* despite, in d'Indy's view, a weak, disagreeable second act, totally devoid of melodic interest. Above all, Act III attained sublimity, and at the death of Siegfried, he was overcome with grief, crying into his handkerchief, entirely oblivious of the rest of the audience. At the conclusion, he and his friends fled from the theatre to a nearby pine forest, where they could breathe and reflect in peace.

Although the *Ring* as a whole had shaken him to the depths of his being, the pragmatic side of his character resisted being fully submerged by the flood of intense feeling and emotion. Attentive to detail as ever, he described in his letter the unique design of the theatre, with its bare, unornamented appearance, the audience plunged into almost total darkness and silence, its attention entirely concentrated on the stage and the music. He remarked on the complete audibility of the singers' words, even when uttered *sotto voce*, and never masked by the orchestra, which was concealed from view. Cheekily, he thought that Verdi ought to take lessons in the accompaniment of voices at Bayreuth! Permitted to visit the orchestra pit, he observed the ingenious layout of the 107 players on different levels under Hans Richter's omniscient direction, the strings entirely separated from the wind and percussion.

He had been well received by Cosima Wagner and Liszt, yet he felt obliged to decline her farewell invitation to dinner, as he had not brought any evening clothes with him. In any case, he did not wish to linger any longer in this town where he was unable to relax. Perhaps he found the Wagner entourage impossibly self-absorbed. Pressing on to Munich, he was enchanted to hear Weber's *Der Freischütz*, but much less enamoured with Bellini's *Norma* the next day. Finally, he reached Geneva, his ultimate destination, where Isabelle awaited him. Together, they enjoyed a charming eight-day tour of Switzerland and the Dauphiné before returning home.[9] For his first major orchestral work of lasting quality, d'Indy turned to a favourite author from the Germanic tradition, Friedrich Schiller, whose dramatic trilogy *Wallenstein* (1779–91) presents a romantic episode within the grand historical panorama of the Thirty Years War, that cataclysmic conflict between Catholic and Protestant empires and nations which raged from 1618 to 1648. The enormously ambitious Wallenstein, General of the Imperial Habsburg forces, plans to bring his own huge army to the opposing side, in return for recognition as King of Bohemia. His treachery destroys the love affair between his own daughter Thècla and Max, the son of his lieutenant, Octavio Piccolomini, for the last named is involved in a counterplot to overthrow Wallenstein. As the General's troops melt away before Prague, Max sacrifices himself in a cavalry charge against the Swedish forces, and Wallenstein himself is murdered by mercenaries.

Such a military theme was certainly to the liking of the young veteran of the Siege of Paris. At the same time, it is possible to read his choice of subject as a rather self-dramatizing allegory of his own troubles, so painful and humiliating, in courting Isabelle. Just as Wallenstein's conduct destroyed the love of Max and Thècla, so did Antonin d'Indy attempt to frustrate the union of Vincent and Isabelle; in both cases, the father-figure emerges as a destructive, masculine force. The episode may have left a psychological scar which Vincent hoped to exorcize by means of his art, though it seems that he never adopted an overtly hostile attitude towards his father.

Surprisingly, perhaps, d'Indy did not conceive his own *Wallenstein* as a Lisztian symphonic poem, but rather as three thematically interlinked concert overtures, corresponding to the three parts of Schiller's trilogy. As we have seen, the second of these, *Piccolomini*—subsequently renamed *Max et Thècla*—was actually the first to be written, with Franck's sympathetic guidance; significantly, he had come to regard his

---

[9] VI to Antonin d'Indy, 15 Sept. 1876, repr. in *Revue Hommes et mondes*, 39 (Oct. 1949), 240–7.

beloved master as a veritable second father, one who embodied the more maternal qualities of love and creativity. But he
had set himself a tough task which brought him endless difficulties; the work in its entirety did not receive its première
until 1881. For all its high artistic aspiration, its shortcomings
are all too apparent. Much of the musical material is derivative; Wallenstein's theme is similar in character to the 'sword
motive' in Wagner's *Ring*, while those of Max and Thècla are
conventionally romantic in style, exuding the moral complacency of Mendelssohn's and Franck's commonplaces: d'Indy
indeed viewed his own union with Isabelle in terms of the
utmost respectability. And, despite the energy and will-power
which went into the work's construction, the musical flow is
constricted by an unfortunate stiffness of form. Inexperience
also resulted in passages of ineffective textures and orchestration, as he himself freely admitted in later years. Yet, for all
that, Wallenstein turned out to be one of his most popular and
widely accepted compositions throughout his life.

The first overture, *Le Camp de Wallenstein* portrays the
raw energies of the soldiers, their courage and devotion to
their General, as well as their violent desires for rape and
pillage. The opening theme, in G major, establishes the warlike character of the work by means of a rhythmic idea

♪ ♪ ♪ ♪ ♪ ♪ ♪ ♪ ♪   reminiscent of the 'forging

motive' in *Siegfried*; while the second theme, in waltz time,
depicts the gaiety of the soldiers arriving from many lands. In
a dramatic episode, a grotesque four-part fugato for bassoons
leads to the powerful, though derivative theme of the mighty
Wallenstein himself; the coda combines all these themes in a
stretto.

By contrast, *Max et Thècla* commences with a slow introduction, gradually exposing Max's 'heroic' theme, confidently
rising and expansive, yet menaced by drum taps evoking the
ominous presence of Wallenstein; Thècla's theme, with its gently drooping melodic contour, is merely hinted at. After a classical Allegro exposition full of rhythmic energy, the themes of
Max and Thècla are brought together and combined contrapuntally, and that of Wallenstein is recalled with a significant

sense of drama—an allusion to the sadness of Max on becoming convinced of his General's treason. After a shortened recapitulation, a poetic coda brings brief returns of the doomed young lovers' themes in the broken accents of grief, heightened by the fatalistic-sounding rhythms of the timpani (Ex. 1*a*).

Ex. 1a. *Max et Thècla*

The slow introduction of *La Mort de Wallenstein* is dominated by the most striking and original feature of the entire work: the alternation of the unrelated chords of B minor, D minor and F minor, played by divided strings to produce a mystical sonority evoking the forebodings of the stars which haunt Wallenstein's soul (Ex. 1*b*). In the ensuing Allegro, both themes are derived from that of Wallenstein, with the warlike

Ex. 1b. *La Mort de Wallenstein*

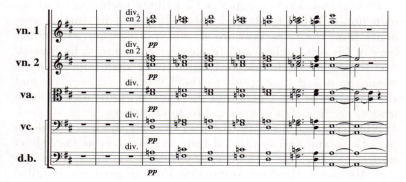

idea from *Le Camp de Wallenstein* reappearing to form the transition between them. An Andante tranquillo episode in the remote keys of E and E flat major brings a reminiscence of Thècla's melody to her father's mind, enveloped in a languid flute, clarinet, and harp texture, to which a solo horn adds fragments of Max's music. After the formal recapitulation, prepared by a violent orchestral crescendo of false entries, the astral harmonies return in a grandiose coda; as Wallenstein dies, so his theme is gradually extinguished.

Fully stretched as he was by a large range of activities and commitments, d'Indy never forgot César Franck, even though the musical world seemed prepared to consign him to oblivion. His brief appearance during the 1878 Exhibition to play his newly composed *Trois pièces* on the organ of the Trocadéro Palace was not exactly sensational. The following year, he brought his long labour of love, *Les Béatitudes*, to its conclusion. Its subject, Christ's Sermon on the Mount, was a theme very close to his own heart, and he intended the work as a personal statement of his belief in a God of love. The very idealism of its conception immediately roused d'Indy to a high pitch of excitement: here was an epic work in the line of Beethoven's *Missa Solemnis*, Berlioz's *La Damnation de Faust*, and Wagner's *Ring*. Yet the prospect of actually performing an oratorio of such length and scale appeared an utterly daunting proposition to all but Franck himself, who naïvely supposed that the government of the Third Republic might be prevailed upon to sponsor it!

To this end, Franck organized a private performance at his own house in the boulevard Saint-Michel, using singing students from the Conservatoire as soloists, together with members of his organ class and friends for the chorus; he himself was to preside at the piano. Carried away with hopeless optimism, he issued invitations to the Minister of Fine Arts and the directors of the Opéra and the Conservatoire, as well as to leading critics. Once again, his fond desires were dashed. Having sprained his wrist the previous day, he was unable to play the piano and deputed d'Indy to take over at very short notice. D'Indy felt 'somewhat oppressed by the responsibility'. Moreover, the Very Important Persons predictably failed to show up, and even those guests who actually attended gradually drifted away during the course of the evening, leaving only Edouard Lalo and Victorin Joncières in their seats at the conclusion.

Faced with Franck's keen disappointment, d'Indy and his friends were overcome with guilt for not having warned their master that a complete performance of *Les Béatitudes* in such conditions was an impossible venture; in fact, only after Franck's death did it receive an adequately prepared performance, under Colonne.[10] But for d'Indy, the work constituted a milestone of the highest symbolic value in his own spiritual development, which, moreover, helped to engender the myth of Franck as the *Pater Seraficus* over the ensuing years. This seemingly saint-like figure, of an irreproachable purity of spirit, became the beacon of d'Indy's Christian and Catholic conception of art and civilization in a scientific, positivistic age, whose intellectual climate of scepticism constantly undermined belief in permanent religious values.

[10] CF 48–50.

4

Wagnerolatry and Medieval Bells

The decade of the 1880s witnessed the rapid growth of Wagnerolatry in France, which soon reached almost epidemic proportions. Not only the power of the music itself—'bleeding chunks' of which were regularly performed at the Concerts Lamoureux—but also the well-propagated theory of the unity of all the arts provided an extraordinarily potent stimulus in most areas of cultural activity. Indeed, the spell had exerted itself as early as 1861 with Baudelaire's *Essay on Tannhäuser*, his poetic reaction to that work's disastrous Paris première. By the mid-1880s, the cult of Wagner, fostered by *La Revue Wagnérienne*—to which the poets Verlaine, Mallarmé, and Villiers de l'Isle-Adam contributed—was threatening to overwhelm the sense of an intrinsically French cultural identity.

Fully susceptible himself to the enchantments of Bayreuth, d'Indy found a fellow enthusiast in Emmanuel Chabrier, ten years his senior, a wonderfully exuberant character, full of heart and verve, and the most charming friend. His natural milieu was the society of the leading avant-garde artists and writers—Verlaine, Mallarmé, Manet, Renoir, and Degas among others. D'Indy, together with Duparc, Chausson, and de Bréville could frequently be found at Chabrier's apartment at 23 rue de Berne, which was hung with his collection of Impressionist paintings. Throughout the decade, d'Indy and Chabrier were regular visitors to Bayreuth. But it was at Munich in 1880, during a performance of *Tristan und Isolde*, that Chabrier broke down sobbing at the start of the Prelude, to his friend's consternation, and excusing himself, said: 'I know it's stupid, but I can't help it. . . . I've been waiting for ten years of my life to hear that A on the cellos.'

For all his own high seriousness, d'Indy displayed a soundness of practical judgement in relation to Chabrier the composer, to whom he dedicated his early *Poème des montagnes*. He clearly recognized that his friend possessed at bottom a very different musical persona from his own, that of the *musicien cocasse par excellence*, and, as we shall see, he deplored his excursions into the field of serious opera. Despite the incompleteness of Chabrier's basic musical education, d'Indy admired the spontaneous melodic nature of his invention, his intuitive harmonic sense, and especially his abundance of idiosyncratic wit and humour, manifested in the comic opera *L'Étoile*, *Trois Valses romantiques*, *Bourrée fantasque*, and *Joyeuse marche*, the last named dedicated to d'Indy. He did all he could to encourage Chabrier's lighter side, which also appealed to the somewhat repressed boyish instincts in himself. In 1883, Chabrier asked him to play the second piano part of the *Trois Valses romantiques* at the Société Nationale, which compelled him to unbutton himself to an unprecedented degree. During the rehearsal, Chabrier stopped in the middle of the first valse and fixed him with a look of astonishment and cunning: 'This is no good at all, young man— you're playing as if it were written by a member of the Institut!' There followed a splendid lesson on interpretation, bringing in cross-accents, sudden outbursts, and almost inaudible *pianissimi*. As a result, the performance was completely to the composer's satisfaction, and the audience erupted in a gale of laughter; a formidable *succès de fou rire* had been achieved. Long after the event, d'Indy loved to repeat Chabrier's witticisms uttered between performances at Bayreuth and how, while working on *España* he never stopped groaning: 'I fight day and night with a confounded orchestral machine which truly gives me the Devil's own trouble. What can you do? Instrumentation will never be my forte.' Yet, d'Indy concluded with a smile, just think how well *España*'s orchestration sounds![1]

[1] R. Myers, *Emmanuel Chabrier and his Circle* (London, 1969), 7, 26–7, 32, 50. VI, *Emmanuel Chabrier et Paul Dukas* (Paris, 1920), 8, 10. Photiadès, 'Vincent d'Indy', 461.

In July 1882, he travelled to Bayreuth to hear the première of Wagner's final music drama, *Parsifal*. But on his arrival, he was disgusted by the contrast between the outward signs of celebration to mark the great occasion—the long banners in the colours of the new German Empire—and the indifference of the local population. Indeed, a distinct lack of welcome towards the foreign visitors made itself felt, manifest in the poor standard of accommodation, food, and wine provided for them; the 'reign of *ersatz*' had clearly arrived. Moreover, Wagner himself had forbidden any oral communication to take place between the theatre personnel and foreign contingents, and had reserved seats at the general rehearsals and opening performances exclusively for the *patronat*. At this, the French and Belgians protested vociferously.

All these humiliating vexations were forgotten, however, as soon as the great drama of the Holy Grail began to unfold before them. At the conclusion, d'Indy and his friends, overwhelmed by its beauty, abandoned their plans for a late drinking session, and again took refuge in the silence of the surrounding woods. D'Indy had been angered by Delibes's irreverent comment on the Flower Maidens' scene in Act II which he adored, 'because *il y avait des petites femmes*, and young ladies are always entertaining!' On the other hand, d'Indy's searching, erudite mind noticed the close similarity between Klingsor's evocation of Kundry and the apparition of Hélène (Ennoia) summoned by Simon (L'Étranger) in Flaubert's exotic prose poem *La Tentation de Saint-Antoine*, a favourite book of his; these scenes, moreover, were to leave their mark on his own music drama *Fervaal*.[2]

Despite Wagner's rebuff to the French, it may have been on this occasion that d'Indy actually succeeded in meeting the German composer in person, through the ever-helpful Liszt's introduction. To his ingratiating opening gambit that his music was liked and understood in France, Wagner replied: 'Oh, the French understand me very well, but there are *German Jews* who prevent my music from being widely known in your country.' Certainly, it was the case that the third stag-

[2] VI, *Introduction à l'étude de Parsifal de Wagner* (Paris, 1937), 69–71, 74–80, 101–3.

ing of a Wagner opera in Paris, that of *Die Walküre*, did not take place until 1893; but in referring to obstructive German Jews, Wagner must still have been obsessed by his memory of Meyerbeer—d'Indy's youthful idol—the representative demon figure in the Jewish domination of French opera, as he saw it. Such was the spell of Wagner's personality that the impressionable d'Indy could swallow this racialist conspiracy whole.

In his memoirs, the publisher Jacques Durand put forward a different perspective: 'Wagner had been very bitter about the failures of *Tannhäuser* and *Rienzi* . . . and avenged himself with sarcasms about France. After the defeat of 1870, many Frenchmen, taking Wagner's *mélange* of patriotism and art at face value, returned the compliment by banning his works from the theatres and mounting demonstrations during concerts of excerpts. Pasdeloup and Colonne braved the storms, but Lamoureux above all, with his combative nature, held out longest against the public on the basis of *l'Art n'a pas de patrie'*. These ideological battles left a deep impression on d'Indy, for as late as 1930, in his book *Richard Wagner et son influence sur l'art musical français*, he maintained that 'the grave accusation of "excessive Wagnerism" was the main cause of the disastrous performances of Bizet's *Carmen*. How the philosopher Nietzsche would have laughed at this nonsense: for him, *Carmen* provided his way out of stifling, decadent Wagnerism into the clear, lucid Mediterranean air!'[3]

The news of Wagner's death in 1883 came as a shock, but d'Indy and his friends were glad that he had died at the height of his powers and glory: 'We will never again see the huge gnome who brought to life that dead town of Bayreuth,' he exclaimed, 'that fantastic, grimacing face of a man of genius whom we used to cheer in his grand box.'[4]

It is undeniable that d'Indy's posthumous reputation has been damaged by his strong profession of anti-Semitic views during the course of his long life. But, regrettable though it is, it is necessary to see the problem in the wider social and

[3] VI, *Richard Wagner et son influence sur l'art musical français* (Paris, 1930), 34, 56. J. Durand, *Quelques souvenirs d'un éditeur de musique* (Paris, 1924), i. 51–6.
[4] VI to PB, 2 Mar. 1883, BN.

intellectual context of his own age, if he is not to be unfairly judged. Initially, it would seem that he was inflamed by Wagner, a copy of whose notorious 1850 article 'Das Judentum in der Musik' he possessed in a French translation, 'Le Judaïsme dans la musique' (1869); many passages were strongly underlined. Later, in the aftermath of the Dreyfus case in the 1890s, we will see how he became infected by the national paranoia of the Right.

The danger for an intellectually minded Frenchman of becoming totally absorbed by the power and dynamism of German culture was very real. Fortunately for d'Indy, this was counteracted by his loyalty to his roots in the Ardèche and the Vivarais. Every summer he returned to Chabret for spiritual refreshment, embarking on a strenuous programme of mountain walking with family and friends, knapsack on his back. Over the years, his knowledge of the terrain became encyclopaedic, and he always carried· a pocketbook in which he noted down the songs of the shepherds he encountered. In this concern for folklore—itself a manifestation of the legacy of German romanticism—he received encouragement from Julien Tiersot, an expert in the field, whose *Histoire de la chanson populaire en France* (1889) was followed by d'Indy's own *Chansons populaires du Vivarais* in 1892, the musical counterpart of the poet Frédéric Mistral's *Lou trésor dóu Felibrige*, a vast dictionary of Provençal words and proverbs.

The idea of a great indigenous French music drama—apparently suggested to d'Indy by Wagner in person—crystallized in d'Indy's mind during a longer excursion to the Isère. Gazing up at the impressive bulk of Mont Ventoux, there came to him the grand subject of *Fervaal*, the story of a young warrior overwhelmed by the defeat of his country and the loss of his beloved, who, through spiritual illumination, gradually follows the difficult path which leads from egotistical love towards universal love. But neither d'Indy nor his critics seem to have been aware of an extraordinary and meaningful coincidence. Five centuries before, in 1336, Petrarch, together with his brother Gherardo, had climbed that very mountain; for the great Italian humanist scholar and poet, this venture constituted an allegory of a man painfully aspiring to spiritual heights. While Petrarch himself, distracted by the charms of the secular world, sought less steep paths which often led merely downhill, Gherardo reached the summit more rapidly by the harder route. Whether or not d'Indy knew of this, the episode forms the most apt commentary on the course of his life.[5]

With *Fervaal*, a particularly hard and protracted undertaking lay ahead of him, and a full discussion of it will be deferred to a later chapter. At this point, however, certain points need to be made. The subject of this projected music drama originated in *Axel*, a text by the obscure Swedish poet Esaias Tegner; but in his own libretto book, d'Indy transposed the scenario from Scandinavia to the familiar territory of the Cévennes mountains during the early pre-Christian Celtic era of the Saracen invasions. Here, too, was a considerable departure from the Wagnerian mythological sagas with their archetypal situations and essential solipsism, reality being found in the psyche rather than in the external world. *Fervaal*, by contrast, takes place in a definite, if remote, historical time and a specific place; for a Latin temperament like d'Indy's, preservation of a sense of external reality was essential, and indeed, the depiction of nature, drawing on his extensive research into the geography, history, mythology, and language of the region, forms an integral part of the work.

At the same time, his enormously wide-ranging mind impelled him to explore areas of musical history which had fallen into oblivion. Nostalgia for the *ancien régime* was doubtless a factor which drew him to the works of André Cardinal Destouches, Superintendent of the King's Music and Director of the Opéra under Louis XV; the result was an edition of the opera-ballet *Les Eléments*. Likewise, the Italian composer Salamone Rossi received d'Indy's attention, with an edition of a selection of madrigals entitled *Cantiques de S. Rossi*. These comparatively modest beginnings in the field of musicology eventually led to greater things: reconstructions of Monteverdi's *Orfeo* and *L'Incoronazione di Poppea* and

[5] S. Giocanti, 'Vincent d'Indy et le régionalisme musical', *La France Latine*, no. 113 (1991), 81–94. LV ii. 19. N. Mann, *Petrarch* (Oxford, 1984) 89–90.

Rameau's *Hippolyte et Aricie* and *Dardanus*. The comparative austerity and purity of this early music provided another useful antidote to the stimulants of Wagner.

Expending his energies in all directions, d'Indy was nevertheless making enormous strides forward in his mastery of compositional techniques and orchestration. Although his comic opera *Attendez-vous sous l'orme* flopped badly at the Opéra-Comique in February 1882, the later 1870s and 1880s saw such substantial achievements as *La Forêt enchantée*, *Saugefleurie*, *Le Chant de la cloche*, and above all, the *Symphonie Cévenole*.

These years d'Indy would later look back on as his best and most productive, when he worked 'surrounded by my three very young children, laughing, crying, quarrelling under my piano'. For all his need to organize his life, he did not allow any such physical impediments to distract his work. Indeed, over the years, his growing family of two daughters, Berthe and Marguérite, and a son Jean took up a considerable amount of his time. He himself gave the girls piano lessons, from which they would often emerge in tears. Not that he ever exploded in anger; it was rather his inflexible teaching method which involved repeating badly executed passages over and over again until they were almost perfect. Kindly and well-intentioned as he was, he was far from being a permissive parent, and stood ready to impose strict discipline as required. When Jean, at the age of 8, was discovered to have appropriated a broken lead pencil belonging to a schoolmate, d'Indy informed him in no uncertain terms that 'a person who steals a lead pencil is equally capable of stealing money', and proceeded to administer a sound spanking in the time-honoured fashion!

Nor, with such a father standing over him, could there be any slacking in Jean's academic studies. A born teacher, d'Indy supervised his work in Latin, French, geography, and history as he grew older, enabling him to pass his examinations and to enter the army, his chosen profession. His father also communicated his love of all things military, reconstructing with the aid of toy soldiers and boxes slipped under the carpet to represent hills the great battles of the

Napoleonic Empire. It virtually goes without saying that Tolstoy's *War and Peace* was another favourite book.[6]

D'Indy's friends continued to play an essential part in his life, and he was always happy to admit to his circle newcomers devoted to their art. One of these was the young composer Pierre de Bréville. In his relations with him, d'Indy tended to adopt an almost elder statesman-like role, offering advice of considerable wisdom and maturity for his age. He congratulated him by letter on his decision to study with Franck, and recommended that he work assiduously and overcome his negligent, slightly indolent ways; he hoped to see him advance, as he had great confidence in his potential. As for the *Prix de Rome*, he expressed horror at the very idea of years of forced labour at the Villa Medici, with its regular assignments scrutinized by members of the Académie-des-Beaux-Arts, which Berlioz had had to endure, and which Debussy was to undergo likewise in 1885.

Another member of Franck's entourage was Ernest Chausson, a barrister of independent means who had turned to composition. At his home at 22 boulevard des Courcelles could be found many of the élite of the artistic world, including Manet, Renoir, Degas, Rodin, Mallarmé, and Gide, as well as Franck, Fauré, Duparc, Chabrier, and d'Indy himself. Chausson, too, proved to be a great campaigner for justice, setting out in 1884 to obtain the Legion of Honour for Franck, who at last had attained his true stature. Although official acclaim still eluded him, he eventually received the award in August 1885.

Together, d'Indy and Chausson exerted a powerful force for change within the Société Nationale, which increasingly admitted foreign composers to its programmes: Gluck, Bach, Handel, Brahms, Borodin, Glazunov, and Grieg, *inter alia*. This policy created a much more favourable climate for the development of French music, which would have withered in a more provincial atmosphere. In the 'revolution' of 1885, Saint-Saëns resigned, and Bussine was pushed out of the presidency, to be replaced by Franck, who had merely honorary

---

[6] M. de Fraguier, *Vincent d'Indy, souvenirs d'une élève* (Paris, 1934), 70–3. VI to Imbert, 15 June 1887, BN. Jean d'Indy, 'Vincent d'Indy en famille', 326–31.

functions. Thereafter, d'Indy and Chausson effectively ran the society as joint secretaries. Their association was entirely harmonious, with no quarrel or jealousy whatever coming between them. By this time, however, Duparc had contracted the nervous disease which was to bring his creative powers to an end, and compel him to retire to the country, away from active participation in the musical scene.[7]

The medieval Gothic world which had so haunted d'Indy during his tour of Germany in 1873 inspired his ambitious cantata *Le Chant de la cloche*, set in a free town of Switzerland around 1400. Above all, the sound of bells pervades the score, and assumes a special significance; as the cultural historian Johan Huizinger was to write in his classic study *The Waning of the Middle Ages*:

One sound rose ceaselessly above the noises of busy life and lifted all things unto a sphere of order and serenity: the sound of bells. The bells were in daily life like good spirits, which by their familiar voices, now called upon the citizens to mourn and now to rejoice, now warned them of danger, now exhorted them to piety. They were known by their names: big Jacqueline, or the bell Roland.[8]

D'Indy arranged his own text in seven scenes, preceded by a prologue, in which he presents the various stages in the life of the bell-maker Wilhelm, with each stage—from baptism until his final triumph over death—appropriately marked by different bell sonorities. Moreover, in its treatment of the perennial themes of love and art, he was making his own personal statement about these subjects so fundamental to his philosophy of life. Central to the work is the vision of Wilhelm's deceased love, Lénore, urging him to let his soul mount with her to the skies: 'Je suis l'Harmonie éternelle!' As his own death draws nigh, he completes his last bell, praying that it may be a celebration of ideal beauty; indeed, after he passes away, it begins to ring in the market-place of its own accord, with supernatural life.

[7] VI to PB, 2 Mar. 1883, 8 Mar. 1886, BN. J. Barricelli and L. Weinstein, *Ernest Chausson, the Composer's Life and Works* (Westport, Conn., 1955), 34–40, 140. VI to Imbert, 2 July 1893, BN.

[8] Penguin edn. (Harmondsworth, 1955), 10.

The composition of *Le Chant de la cloche* provided d'Indy with a great deal of satisfaction, and he considered that it expressed his own thinking very well. In July 1883, he wrote to de Bréville to tell him that 'the poem, which amounts to about 500 to 600 verses, has given me almost as much labour as the music, and although I can't do the Parnassians' fine chiselling, I believe these verses aren't bad, better in any case than Scribe's or de Jouy's'.[9] The musical score is elaborately constructed, employing a number of Wagnerian-type leit-motifs (or cyclic themes, in Franckian terminology) throughout. Two of the most important of these are first stated in the prologue: the 'masculine' theme representing creative power and the 'feminine' theme the work achieved through love. Although the hand of Wagner lies heavily on the music, both in its style and its conception, the orchestration owes much more to Berlioz in its essentially unblended, linear treatment of instrumental sonority, which preserves individual timbres. A novel feature is the use of two pianos, which add a percussive edge to the scoring, as well as contributing to the production of various bell effects.

D'Indy's mastery of choral writing, gained from his training of Colonne's choir, is first apparent in the baptism scene, in which the priests intone the Credo. Particularly inventive is the orchestral carillon in sextuplet quavers which gradually winds down from high to low instruments (Ex. 2*a*); as regards its conception, a striking comparison can be drawn with the finale of Widor's Organ Symphonie No. 7, published in 1887. D'Indy's beloved countryside forms the setting for 'L'Amour', the meeting of Wilhelm and Lénore, who give voice to their hopes and fears for the future; the distant bell of the angelus brings them back to immediate reality. The world of Wagner's *Die Meistersinger* emerges in 'La Fête', where, with humorous mock-pomposity, the guilds of artisans, tanners, blacksmiths, tailors, and goldsmiths process into the market-place, each with its own special music, capable of combining to some extent with that of the others. Wilhelm is duly admitted as a master-craftsman by the *corporation des fondeurs*, and

---

[9] VI to PB, 2 July 1883, BN.

Ex. 2a. *Le Chant de la cloche*, scene 1: 'Le baptême'

appropriately, an energetic rhythmic idea, once again reminiscent of the forging theme in *Siegfried* pervades the scene.

The heart of the work is the 'Vision', which reveals d'Indy's ability—derived from Franck—to create a series of different atmospheres by means of opposing dark and bright tonalities, together with an extraordinarily imaginative handling of the orchestra. After Lénore's death, Wilhelm sits lamenting, surrounded by his bells, while sombre violas and cellos play the 'theme of sadness' in F minor, characterized by a rising second motive; this is accompanied by the growl of double basses divided into four parts, an effect previously used by Berlioz in 'The March to the Scaffold' of the *Symphonie fantastique*. As Wilhelm's mind becomes absorbed in sad memories, a drooping version of the 'feminine' theme in the cellos is combined with a new Franckian-style theme of love (Ex. 2*b*), while the tonality darkens, moving from a chromatically intensified E major to C minor, in order to underline his feelings of doubt and despair. As he falls asleep, the chimes of midnight ring out: twelve low F sharps *sffz* on the pianos, against long sustained notes in the chorus. Fantastic forms—heraldic animals and gargoyles—appear, and benevolent dream spirits which emerge in the luminous key of E major come to bring peace to his soul with ethereal choral dances. At the stroke of one they vanish, to be replaced by the vision of Lénore offering new hope and rebirth; the 'feminine' theme returns in a more

Ex. 2b. *Le Chant de la cloche*, scene 4: 'Vision'

positive guise, fortified by the increasingly bright F sharp
major tonality.

A very different note is sounded in 'Incendie', a grand operatic crowd scene replete with stirring choruses and brilliant
brass fanfares. A fire has been started by some marauding
travellers, and the ringing of the tocsin creates a general state
of alarm. The 'masculine' theme of creative power in D major
accompanies Wilhelm's restoration of public order and the will

to defend the town with armed force. In the penultimate scene, 'La Mort', he has completed his last bell, and feels the approach of death; he prays that his bell may celebrate ideal beauty.

Finally, in 'Triomphe', this bell hangs in its scaffold in the market-place, upon which four venerable master-craftsmen come to pass judgement. An absurd, pedantic Beckmesser type, Maître Leerschwulst, marches up to the traditional tune 'J'ai du bon tabac', and pronounces his verdict that the bell is badly constructed, contrary to all the rules; no sound, more-over, will come out. The crowd, aroused to fury, demands Wilhelm's presence, but is silenced by the arrival of a priest announcing his death. The singing of the plainchant 'In Paradisum' marks the transmigration of his soul into his bell, which begins to ring spontaneously and with increasing strength. For maximum effect, d'Indy cunningly placed an added sixth note in the massive repeated dominant seventh chord of A flat to reinforce the clash of overtones; but he sub-sequently declared himself to be dissatisfied with the resulting sonority of tubular bells, pianos in their bass register, and *pizzicati* double basses. A profound calm overcomes the assem-bled crowd as the chorus sings the praises of Wilhelm's life and work in a final apotheosis, which combines the 'feminine' theme and the 'In Paradisum'.

From the start, *Le Chant de la cloche* was blessed with good fortune, winning the Grand Prix de la Ville de Paris in 1885. Its première took place at the Concerts Lamoureux in February 1886 to great acclaim; indeed, its success can surely be attributed to its combination of conventional sentiments, picturesque detail, and arresting sound effects, which ensured that it received regular performances throughout d'Indy's life.

5

Morally Bracing Mountain Air

D'Indy was definitely enjoying more success than many of his friends and colleagues, some of whom, like Franck and Fauré, were sorely pressed by their economic circumstances. By comparison with the well-received *Le Chant de la cloche*, Fauré's Symphony in D minor, which d'Indy conducted at Anvers on 14 October 1885, must have been a failure, for the composer destroyed it afterwards; he had doubtless been following a false trail in this instance, but he was by no means alone. Indeed, d'Indy had good cause to be disturbed by the directions which his friends were taking. It seemed patently obvious to him that Franck's genius did not lie in the field of grand opera, yet under fierce pressure from his wife and his son Georges, he had embarked on *Hulda* (1882–5). If they imagined that this would turn out to be a lucrative venture, they were to be sadly disillusioned, for neither it nor its successor, *Ghiselle*, even succeeded in being mounted in his lifetime. D'Indy perceived this state of affairs as a scandalous waste of creative time and energy, all the more so in that Franck had at last got fully into his stride with a series of masterpieces, among them the Piano Quintet, *Le Chasseur maudit*, *Les Djinns*, and *Variations symphoniques*, as yet barely recognized.

D'Indy's views on the subject exacerbated the natural antipathy which existed between Georges Franck and himself. Each represented opposite political polarities. Whereas Georges, a university lecturer, regarded himself as a pillar of the Third Republic, adhering to the principles of the

Revolution and scientific progress, d'Indy, by contrast, appeared as a Catholic reactionary, a member of the aristocracy rooted in the *ancien régime*. In the latter's biography of César Franck, disparaging references to the philosophy of Kant—which the intellectual system of the Republic valued for its establishment of moral law as the principle of certainty, as opposed to Catholic faith and dogma—were surely intended to needle Georges; indeed, the picture of César Franck attempting to read the labyrinthine *Critique of Pure Reason* and finding it a very funny book is truly comic in a Dickensian way.[1]

If Georges was hardly acting in his father's best interests, at least from a purely aesthetic standpoint, the author and dramatist Catulle Mendès, of Jewish origin, found himself cast by d'Indy as Chabrier's evil genius. An enthusiastic Wagnerite who had written a novel *Le Roi vierge* (1881) about Wagner and Ludwig II, Mendès was responsible for persuading Chabrier to attempt serious operas, which, in d'Indy's view, 'absorbed, without any benefit to art, the last creative forces of our poor friend, and led him to the grave'. The first of these, *Gwendoline*, to a libretto by Mendès, is set in Britain during the Middle Ages, and includes battle scenes and tender love duets, with little scope for Chabrier's brand of outrageous humour.

Despite his profound misgivings, d'Indy loyally supported his friend. Cancelling various engagements, he travelled to Brussels for its première at the Théâtre de la Monnaie on 10 April 1886. The audience received *Gwendoline* favourably, but after the second performance, bad fortune struck with the sudden bankruptcy of the theatre's director, and the opera had to be withdrawn from the stage. Although he deemed it 'a commonplace work, rather flat like some Flying Dutchman'—a bizarre pronouncement—d'Indy's heart went out to Chabrier in his bitter disappointment.[2]

A much more positive outcome of his visit to Brussels was his meeting with Octave Maus, a barrister by profession, but

---

[1] J. M. Nectoux, *Gabriel Fauré, a Musical Life*, trans. R. Nichols (Cambridge, 1991), 276. VI, *Emmanuel Chabrier et Paul Dukas*, 9. CF 64.
[2] Myers, *Emmanuel Chabrier*, 63. VI, *Emmanuel Chabrier et Paul Dukas*, 9.

also an inspired and daring promoter of Impressionist and Post-Impressionist painting and sculpture through the Circle XX (1884–93) and its successor, La Libre Esthétique (1894–1914). An ardent Wagnerite, Maus regarded the arts as being in a state of permanent revolution, and considered Franck's music to be the equivalent of modern painting. This initial contact between him and d'Indy quickly ripened into a warm and enduring friendship, which lasted right up to Maus's death in 1918. Within a year, d'Indy became heavily involved with Circle XX, helping to develop its musical side, advising on programme planning, and taking part in numerous concerts as pianist and conductor. It proved to be, as will be seen, a magnificent opportunity for Franck and his disciples, as well as for Fauiré and later Debussy and Ravel; Maus's policy clearly stated that those be chosen 'whose art remains independent and combative'.[3]

Certainly, with d'Indy and Chausson at their head, the disciples were fully prepared to fight for Franck, who still received short shrift from officialdom. There had been great indignation that the Cross of the Legion of Honour had been awarded to him not in recognition of his compositions, but merely in his capacity as professor of organ. A committee, including d'Indy, Chausson, de Bréville, and Pasdeloup, was therefore formed with the object of making his works better known; Pasdeloup accepted a guarantee of 7,000 francs for his expenses in putting on an all-Franck concert at the Cirque d'Hiver on 30 January 1887. The first half of the programme, conducted by Pasdeloup, consisted of *Le Chasseur maudit*, *Variations symphoniques* (with Louis Diémer, d'Indy's old piano teacher, as soloist), and Part II of the early oratorio *Ruth*; Franck himself wielded the baton in the second half, which consisted of the March and Air de Ballet from *Hulda* and the third and eighth *Béatitudes*. In d'Indy's account of the concert:

The performance by an orchestra lacking in cohesion and insufficiently rehearsed was a deplorable affair. Pasdeloup, courageous

---

[3] M. Octave Maus, *Trente années de lutte pour l'art, Les XX, La Libre Esthetique* (Brussels, 1980).

innovator and first champion of symphonic music in France, was
then growing old and losing authority as a conductor; he went
entirely wrong in the tempo of the finale of the *Variations symphoniques*, which ended in a breakdown. As to Franck, he was listening too intently to the vibration of his own thoughts to pay any
attention to the thousand details for which a conductor must always
be on the alert. The interpretation of *The Beatitudes* suffered in con-
sequence, but such was his good nature that he was the only person
who did not regret the wretched performance, and when we poured
out to him our bitter complaint that his works should have been so
badly given, he answered, smiling and shaking back his thick mane
of hair: 'No, no, you are really too exacting, dear boys; for my own
part, I was quite satisfied!'

The young critic and musicologist Romain Rolland also wrote
an unflattering notice of Franck's contribution to the proceedings:

He's a large old man, worn and gaunt, not timid but *gauche*, with
the rather ordinary face of a magistrate set off by white whiskers.
When he wants to be pleasant, an ugly smile, either strained or
embarrassed, opens his mouth and reveals his teeth. There's nothing
at all about him of the salon musician. He conducted the orchestra
in a stiff manner, automatically, like a metronome, with sharp gestures and spare, steady movements. . . . he was extremely well
applauded by almost the entire audience (which surprises me); some
fanatics actually *acclaimed* him.

Perhaps the concert was not, after all, quite such a fiasco as
d'Indy described it. Nor was it ignored by the musical establishment; for among the large turn-out of musicians in the
audience were Saint-Saëns and Ambroise Thomas, Director of
the Conservatoire, neither of whom were well disposed
towards Franck. The positive reception accorded him may
well have been a mere gesture of sympathy towards a poor old
worthy, as he did indeed appear to be.[4]

Increasingly, his disciples came to invest their seemingly
beleaguered and persecuted master with saint-like qualities,
and to conduct themselves as zealots in his cause. But, in the
view of Madame Franck and son Georges, such aggressive mis-

[4] CF 52–3. R. Rolland, *Mémoires et fragments du journal* (Paris, 1956), 166–7.

sionary zeal succeeded only in reinforcing the existing prejudice against him. Nevertheless, the wider Franckian movement, then in its infancy, soon proved to be a fount of energy
which influenced all aspects of French musical life. One of the
most interesting and elusive effects of Franck's character—
charismatic to those who naturally responded to him—was
the way it attracted men of social and cultural distinction; a
significant number of them had studied law—surely some
explanation of the movement's combative nature.

An important group of followers had strong interests in the
field of musicology, exhuming and editing the then forgotten
works of the sixteenth and seventeenth centuries. We have
seen that d'Indy had already resurrected Destouches and
Rossi; he and the other pioneers of the early music revival
looked to the saintly Franck—a throwback to an earlier age
of faith, as he seemed to them—as a beacon in their endeav-
ours, despite his scant knowledge of music before Bach. The
senior figure was the distinguished organ recitalist and composer Alexandre Guilmant, who, like Widor, had trained in
Brussels, under Lemmens. As resident organist of the
Trocadéro Palace, Guilmant had encouraged Franck to write
his *Trois pièces* for its opening in 1878, and had also put on
an enterprising series of recitals entitled 'Summaries of the
history of the organ from 1586 to the present day', which
included long-lost works by Andrea Gabrieli, Merulo,
Titelouze, Frescobaldi, and Clérambault, later brought
together in the published editions *École classique de l'orgue*
(1898–1903) and *Archives des Maîtres de l'orgue des 16ᵉ, 17ᵉ, 18ᵉ
siècles* (1898–1914).

Another crucial figure, Charles Bordes, of a younger generation, was an actual pupil of Franck. Deeply involved with
the music and folklore of the Basque region, he also made an
enormous contribution to the revival of sixteenth-century
Italian and Spanish liturgical music, beginning with his
appointment as choirmaster at the church of Nogent-sur-
Marne. A man of amazing vitality, his future collaboration
with d'Indy and Guilmant in founding the Schola Cantorum
was to provide the Franckian movement with a real focal
point and sense of direction.

Meanwhile, the question of Richard Wagner still loomed large in Paris. It had long been Lamoureux's ambition to give a complete concert performance of one of the operas, and in 1887 he decided on *Lohengrin*, engaging d'Indy to prepare the chorus. Unfortunately, the projected performances coincided with a threat of war with Germany over the Schnaebelé incident on the Alsace–Lorraine border. The situation, blown up by the bombastic huffing and puffing of the Minister of Defence, General Boulanger, thoroughly aroused the populace; the ultra-nationalistic press endeavoured to prevent *Lohengrin* going ahead, in the name of the honour of France. Yet Lamoureux bravely persisted, undeterred by riots outside the Théâtre de l'Eden; and the distinguished audience—which included Boulanger himself, his presence heightening the ambiguities of the situation—was compelled to take cover during the intervals from the barrage of bricks and stones hurled through the windows. The first performance was excellent, and d'Indy's chorus in top form, according to Jacques Durand. Being so busy behind the scenes, d'Indy claimed that he was the only artist in Paris who didn't actually see the performance!

Nevertheless, Lamoureux was unwilling to be responsible for any further provocation and decided to cancel the second performance. He may have been acting on government instructions, for the furious d'Indy exploded to Octave Maus: 'Our government of cowardly cretins has just prohibited the performance of *Lohengrin*. Do you call that the regime of liberty!;;; and, as in speaking of Louis XIV prohibiting *Tartuffe*, one cannot find words sufficiently indignant.' Perhaps his rage prevented him from seeing clearly the full logic of his viewpoint: was the German Wagner really worth such a threat to the social fabric and security of France? It was no longer possible to maintain that 'l'Art n'a pas de patrie', and even d'Indy could not put the blame on a Jewish conspiracy![5]

Like his German near-contemporary Johannes Brahms, d'Indy regarded the symphony as the most daunting compo-

[5] Durand, *Quelques souvenirs*, i. 51–6. Imbert, *Profils des musiciens*, 51. VI to OM, 1887, RBM.

sitional challenge of all. With Beethoven, the form had already been taken to its highest peak of development, a discouraging situation for his successors in the Romantic era, left to wrestle with essentially classical structures which had become the property of theorists. At d'Indy's disposal were the nineteenth-century models of Reicha—passed on to him by Franck—as well as those of the German theorists Marx and Riemann, who conceived these forms in essentially melodic terms, emphasizing the primacy of thematic over tonal structure, and characterizing the opposing main themes as masculine and feminine. This latter idea was eagerly embraced by d'Indy, with his tendency to project symbolic qualities on to women.

For him, indeed, there was a vital psychological dimension to the subject; these symphonic forms were for him invested with a very real intrinsic value, by whose agency a higher organization of experience might be achieved, as well as a rational amendment of the disordered passions. This strong emphasis on the virtues of logic, balance, and proportion owed much to the Thomist doctrines of natural law and Christian humanism embodied in Dante; reason was the essence of man, the divine spark which makes for his greatness, through which he shares with God in the rational order of the universe. D'Indy's fear of the turbulent anarchic forces within him—though contained within his union with Isabelle—corresponded to his awareness of the disintegrative tendencies in the music of Liszt and Wagner: the undermining of tonal structure and coherence through chromatic saturation and constant modulation, and, above all, the subjection of melody *per se* to increased harmonic complexity in the overwhelming desire for heightened expression.

In the face of this inner dissolution of the classical musical language, Franck's teaching and compositional techniques provided a very necessary corrective, with his emphasis on solid tonal architecture and clear deployment of themes. Of particular significance to d'Indy was his master's use of recurring cyclic themes—notably in the early Piano Trio in F sharp minor, the Piano Quintet, and the Symphony in D minor—as a device to unify the different movements of a symphonic or

sonata composition and solve the problem of providing a
properly conclusive finale. In time, d'Indy was to raise the
cyclic method to a quasi-theological principle, just as Franck
himself was to be reborn as the *Pater Seraficus*.

An additional challenge presented itself to d'Indy. As a
highly patriotic Frenchman, he ardently desired to transplant
the symphony, as it were, to the soil of France. He therefore
looked to his own ancestral region of the Ardèche to inspire
what is, by general consent, one of his very finest and most
successful works, the *Symphonie Cévenole*, op. 25, also known
as the *Symphonie sur un chant montagnard français*, for piano
and orchestra, written in 1886. The sheer *joie de vivre* of this
music reflects his active participation in the life of the local
communities during his summer vacations, rather than mere
escape from the pressures of Paris. As well as immersing himself in the history and geography of the region, he would
gather together the local musicians every Friday to coach
them in their instruments, and would take some practices with
the amateur orchestras of Valence and Privas. On Sundays, he
played the harmonium in the church at Boffres.[6]

Not the least remarkable aspect of the *Symphonie Cévenole*
is its superb exploitation of orchestral colour and texture,
entirely consistent with the work's carefully planned structure. The role of the piano has been frequently misunderstood,
for d'Indy did not intend to write a concerto. Instead of
assuming a commanding soloistic role, the piano's essentially
decorative—even impressionistic—textures are designed to
blend with, rather than oppose, the orchestra. Indeed, the
question of balance is crucial, especially in view of the piano's
frequent interaction with the harp, a strikingly advanced
sonorous conception, which anticipates Bartók's *Music for
Strings, Percussion, and Celesta* and Hindemith's *Kontzert-
musik for Piano, Brass, and Harps*.

The first cyclic theme—an actual mountain song heard by
d'Indy in the Cévennes—appears in the introduction, its sense

[6] M. J. Citron, *Gender and the Musical Canon* (Cambridge, 1993), 132–3. A. P.
d'Entrèves, *Natural Law* (London, 1970), 37–49. Holmes, *Dante*, 7–11. J. de la
Laurencie, 'Quelques souvenirs vivarois sur Vincent d'Indy', *Revue du Vivarais*,
Mar.–Apr. 1932, 12.

of pastoral melancholy heightened by the plaintive timbre of the cor anglais; it engenders the opening themes of the three movements. That of the first movement in G major, in classical sonata form, is of a Lisztian grandeur, its rising masculine character contrasting with the lyrical feminine second subject. The latter theme's key of B major (setting up the mediant relationship beloved of Franck) is a positive move into brighter tonal regions, a general direction continued through keys on the sharp side in the ensuing central development. Broken chords in the woodwind, rippling downward, in contrary motion with those of the piano and harp, accompany the first subject, which strides ahead in an expansive mood against the cyclic introductory theme played by oboes, trumpets, and violas, a penetrating combination. The recapitulation arrives in a blaze of colour, with trumpets and cornets blaring as if in the dazzling light of midday.

The slow movement can be considered as a large-scale *Lied* in its structure of three double sections in the main keys of B flat, G flat, and B flat. The initial theme, introduced by the piano, is soon followed by the distinctive and sinister-sounding second cyclic theme (Ex. 3*a*). Subsequently, an urgent, semitonally rising ostinato figure in the bass derived from this theme forms the background to fragments of the first cyclic theme in rustic horn call style, tossed between clarinets, horns, and cornets. In this marvellously evocative hymn to nature, a particularly poetic note is sounded by the piano's passages of liquid impressionistic writing, suggesting mountain streams of crystalline purity.

Village festivities are at the root of the finale's vivid pleinairism and finely contrived rawness of texture; the refrain of this Beethovenian rondo in G major first appears in the sparkling sonority of the piano and harp ensemble (Ex. 3*b*). By contrast, the lyrical second theme is in a more conventionally romantic mould. In the development, the opposite tonal procedure is adopted to that of the first movement: namely, a drift towards the flat side, giving a more sombre colouring. The second cyclic theme eventually reappears in B minor as a sinister witches' dance, its fierce unison string writing accompanied only by low trumpet chords. This gives way

Ex. 3a. *Symphonie Cévenole*, second movement, second cyclic theme

to 'flashbacks' of the slow movement's theme—in a psychological moment worthy of Berlioz in the *Symphonie fantastique*—the remote key of B flat enhancing the sensation of
coming from a distance. Finally, the refrain is treated to some
rhythmic transformations, injecting a burst of energy to bring
the work to its conclusion. The highly successful première was
given in March the following year at the Concerts Lamoureux,
with Marie Bordes-Pène taking the piano part.

On a lighter note, d'Indy was delighted with Chabrier's operetta
Le Roi malgré lui, saying: 'This is real music!' Its première at
the Opéra-Comique received acclaim; yet after the third night
bad luck struck again, with the destruction of the theatre in
a fire, and further performances were postponed for several
months. Some much needed consolation was forthcoming from

Ex. 3b. *Symphonie Cévenole*, third movement, first subject

an altogether different source, the highly cultivated American heiress, Winnaretta Singer, recently married to the Prince Louis de Scey-Montbéliard, her first husband, in what her biographer Michael de Cossart described as 'a marriage of inconvenience'! D'Indy had first met her in 1884 in Munich during rehearsals of Wagner's *Ring*; afterwards, Lamoureux and de Bonnières had taken him to join the *artistes* in the Café Maximilian, amongst whom Madame Singer was already ensconced, and a lively discussion of the merits of the *Ring*'s interpretation took place.

In fact, it was the very Wagnerian aspects of *Gwendoline* which had appealed to her at its ill-starred Brussels première, and, since the Paris Opéra refused to mount it, she suggested that a concert performance be given in her salon. Two evenings were actually held, on 8 and 15 May 1888; the first consisted of extracts from the opera together with new works by d'Indy, Chausson, and Fauré; while the second comprised a complete performance of *Gwendoline* with soloists, chorus, and reduced orchestra. The success of the evenings were assured by the admirable co-operation of Chabrier's friends in their places among the players: Fauré at the harmonium, d'Indy and André Messager in the percussion section, while the composer himself presided at the piano.

Constantly in search of the new and advanced in music, the Princesse Winnaretta and her second husband, the Prince Edmond de Polignac—himself an experimentalist composer and early music enthusiast who was to support the Schola Cantorum—showed little interest in Franck, whom they regarded as an old fogey; indeed, Prince Edmond would refer to *Les Béatitudes* as 'Les belles platitudes'![7] But if the Singer coffers were not forthcoming, Franck's cause received invaluable assistance from a devoted pair of young women pianists, against whom no sexist prejudice can have existed at the Société Nationale under the enlightened secretaryship of d'Indy and Chausson. Marie Poitevin undertook the première of the *Prélude, choral, et fugue* in January 1885, and Marie Bordes-Pène that of the *Prélude, aria, et final* in May 1888. Both works were dedicated to their performers.

Franck was obviously in seventh heaven on these more intimate occasions; Romain Rolland has left a fascinating glimpse of the concert at the Salle Pleyel in April 1888, which featured *Le Chasseur maudit* arranged for two pianos and a version of the early organ *Prélude, fugue, et variation* for harmonium and piano, played by d'Indy and Mademoiselle de Pierpont:

It was amusing to observe [Franck] during the performance of *Le Chasseur maudit*, seated between the two pianos and keeping his eye on his two pupils, passionately interested in his own work, utterly happy: sometimes in sanctimonious bliss, leaning his elbow on one

[7] Myers, *Chabrier*, 65. M. de Cossart, *The Food of Love, the Princesse de Polignac (1865–1943) and her Salon* (London, 1978), 19–20, 38–45. Michael de Cossart to Andrew Thomson, 4 June 1984.

of the pianos, at other times wagging his big red hand, or uttering a disagreeable hissing noise, like certain bad conductors do to calm down unruly elements.

It is impossible to imagine Franck gracing a fashionable salon, completely lacking, as he did, the refined social graces of such as Saint-Saëns, Fauré, and Widor. Even d'Indy, who certainly knew how to behave in polite society—even if he rather despised it—had occasional lapses. Colette described how, reclining on a sofa at a musicians' gathering, 'he would break into an astonishingly vulgar valse, suddenly cutting himself short, struck with shame'.[8]

His innate, though as yet unrealized, pedagogical abilities were about to flower. At de Bonnières's salon, he met a rather dour, self-absorbed youth called Albéric Magnard, son of the wealthy and influential editor of *Le Figaro*, François Magnard. Having, like d'Indy, initially studied law, Albéric was now in revolt against the values of high bourgeois society which his father represented, and was determined to beat his own path through life unaided by the corrupting benefits of influence and nepotism. His passion for music having prevailed over the law, he had enrolled at the Conservatoire in Théodore Dubois's harmony and counterpoint classes and in Massenet's composition class. Another student was the ex-barrister Guy Ropartz, who also became a leading member of the Franckian movement and a composer of five symphonies.

Whereas Ropartz went on from the Conservatoire to study with Franck privately, Magnard at once felt a great affinity with d'Indy, and looked to him as his true mentor. Over the next four years, d'Indy acted as his guide, philosopher, and friend; both felt an acute sense of maternal deprivation, Magnard having lost his mother at the age of 5. A strong consciousness of life and the serious pursuit of art as being fraught with difficulties and dangers formed their outlooks: in d'Indy's case, from the perspective of his Dantesque Catholicism, in Magnard's, from that of the bleak evolutionary philosophy of Darwin and Spenser.

---

[8] Rolland, *Mémoires*, 169–70. E. Lockspeiser, *Debussy, his Life and Mind* (London, 1962), i. 138.

At once, Magnard set to work with an iron determination and commitment; so strong was his self-doubt that he would happily rework any unsatisfactory assignment twice. Already well grounded by Dubois, he was ready for a tough initiation by d'Indy into the workings of fugue and orchestration.

His previous efforts in composition under Massenet, oriented towards the salon and the theatre, had left a profound sense of dissatisfaction, and the challenge of symphonic writing—neglected at the Conservatoire—appealed to his bold, logical character. Under d'Indy's guidance, he wrote, with infinite toil and trouble, his first two symphonies, as well as the opera *Yolande*. Such was the rapport between them that they could also engage in uninhibited discussions, giving free rein to their unbounded enthusiasm. For d'Indy, too, these lessons were an enormously rewarding experience, for they provided the opportunity to try out his ideas of musical pedagogy, which had been gradually forming in his mind in reaction to the Conservatoire's shortcomings. It was his abiding belief that it did 'not concern itself any longer with the *intelligence* of the students, as if they were merely machines for producing notes, and above all, there is no rational and methodical system of instruction. The professors are still stuck in their empirical ways, which loosen the fingers and the voice quite well, but have nothing to do with *Art*.'

His verdict on the performing courses applied equally to the official composition classes, which tended to concentrate on the routines necessary to produce the obligatory cantatas for the Prix de Rome. Within the confines of the organ class, Franck certainly indulged a much more searching conception of composition, unintentionally creating much resentment and hostility among his colleagues. Excellent though his teaching of musical structure undoubtedly was, the wider horizons of historical development eluded him—not surprisingly, considering that his general education had been so neglected. Still vivid in d'Indy's mind was his meeting with Liszt at Weimar in 1873, from whom he had grasped the notion of a chronologically ordered system, by following which, students could discover for themselves the evolution of their art through its successive stages.

The years of intensive study and exploration which d'Indy had himself undertaken in the widest possible range of musical fields available to him at that time—immersing himself in the writings of the German scholars Riemann, Hauptmann, Helmholtz, and von Oettingen—enabled him to apply Liszt's ideas to the teaching of composition. Magnard was privileged to be the first beneficiary of this approach, in which the various epochs and forms were surveyed in the liveliest manner; and, in the words of Magnard's biographer, Gaston Carraud, he 'expressed his sense of wonder like a child, with shouts and wild dancing'. How very different he seemed now from the morose yet docile Conservatoire student!

After four years of these extraordinary lessons, Magnard decided that the time had come for him to proceed alone, taking full responsibility for the course of his life's work. The two men remained on the most cordial terms, their mutual respect for each other as creative artists—like that of Messiaen and Boulez in the present century—surviving diametrically opposite opinions on such burning political issues as the Dreyfus case. However, d'Indy did not seem to be unsympathetic to Magnard's espousal of the feminist cause, in the belief that women's rights would help to solve the social problems of militarism, alcoholism, and prostitution; there was to be no discrimination against women in the educational programmes at the Schola Cantorum.[9]

In Brussels, the musical side of Maus's Circle XX had begun to take off. Concerts in the 1888 and 1889 seasons included Franck's Violin Sonata, premièred by the dashing Belgian virtuoso Eugène Ysaÿe with Marie Bordes-Pène, as well as d'Indy's Trio for clarinet, cello, and piano, *Poème des montagnes*, Suite in D, and *Fantaisie pour hautbois sur les thèmes populaires français*. Fauré's music, too, featured prominently, giving rise to a comic situation in early 1889, when his presence was imperiously requested by Maus at the exact time as he was due to play for a wedding in Paris! Helpful as ever, d'Indy intervened on Fauré's behalf in a caustically worded letter to Maus:

[9] G. Carraud, *La Vie, l'oeuvre et la mort d'Albéric Magnard* (Paris, 1921), 29–36. VI to OM, 10 Oct. 1900, RBM.

Look here, Fauré is landed with a posh wedding at the Madeleine, with orchestra, choirs etc., and everything which makes for a *high life* do. The wedding falls exactly on the 19 February, and the poor chap can't get out of this chore without incurring the anathema of *curés*, vicars, vergers and chair-hirers, and he could lose his job. He won't, therefore, be able to get to Brussels before the evening of the 19th, or the morning of the 20th.

This still left a very tight schedule, yet Fauré duly presented himself as instructed, playing his Second Piano Quartet with the Ysaÿe Quartet on 25 February; on this occasion, d'Indy conducted his friend's *Madrigal, Le Ruisseau*, and the choruses from Act V of *Caligula*. Moreover, d'Indy had had to extricate him from another awkward situation. His bride and bullying parents-in-law took a dim view of the expenses incurred in his visits abroad, and d'Indy's urgent request to Maus on his behalf to recommend 'a very cheap hotel (real or fictitious)' brought an invitation to stay at his own house. This act of charity caused the diffident Fauré considerable embarrassment.[10]

D'Indy in his turn made himself indispensable to Maus, to the extent of arranging loans of pictures for the exhibitions. In October 1889, he wrote: 'You will have for the XX Bonnières's 3 Renoirs and Cézanne landscape . . . the Renoirs are interesting works: 1) the portrait of Mme. de Bonnières, *très curieux*, 2) a life sketch of Wagner, 3) a ravishing still life.' Among the invited artists in these years were his friend Fantin-Latour and Auguste Rodin—engaged in a Dante-inspired project *The Gates of Hell*—with whom he had associated in a Paris dining club named 'Les Prix de rhum', a bad pun on the Prix de Rome.[11] Greatly daring, d'Indy was to sit for the Belgian neo-Impressionist painter Théo van Rysselberghe, the result being a striking likeness in divisionist technique—a rather different proposition from the more conventional, though very fine, studio portrait by the fashionable Jacques-Émile Blanche.

---

[10] Maus, *Trente années*. Nectoux, *Gabriel Fauré*, 39. VI to OM, 26 Jan. 1889, in A. van der Linden, *Octave Maus et la vie musicale belge 1875–1914* (Brussels, 1950).

[11] VI to OM, 1 Jan. 1889, in Linden, *Octave Maus*. F. V. Grunfeld, *Rodin, a Biography* (London, 1987), 267.

The wide-ranging activities of the Circle XX also included authors' conferences, at which appeared such advanced literary figures as Mendès, Villiers de l'Isle-Adam, Verlaine, and Mallarmé, many of whom d'Indy already knew through Chausson. We learn from his correspondence that Mallarmé attended the XX concert on 10 February 1890 in the Grande Salle de l'Exposition de Peinture, at which d'Indy's *Symphonie Cévenole* and Piano Quartet were played. In January the following year, he heard *La Forêt enchantée* at the Concerts Lamoureux. And d'Indy in turn was among the very few at that time who could enter the hermetic poetic world of Mallarmé, the author of *L'Après-midi d'un faune*. This celebrated poem became the literary basis for Debussy's orchestral work of that name—which d'Indy greatly admired and conducted himself with characteristic generosity.

With astonishing literary perceptiveness, he revealed himself to be aware of the poet's employment of musical procedures—sonority, rhythm, and structure—noting the variation technique in *Crise de vers*. And Mallarmé, too, graciously acknowledged the musician's understanding of his work and thought. D'Indy must have taken Mallarmé's dictum to heart: 'Everything sacred which wishes to remain sacred shrouds itself in mystery.' Here, surely, lies the inspiration for d'Indy's sanctification of Franck's cyclic forms as the theological symbol of perfection. Mallarmé's rebirth of the poet's consciousness from sterility had raised the creation of fiction to a supreme metaphysical value, emboldening d'Indy to conceive the myth of Franck reborn from the medieval era.[12]

While a city in the heavens was being prepared for Franck, a monument of a more material nature had arisen in the land of d'Indy's ancestors. Aware that the line ran through him to his son Jean, he deemed it fitting to dignify it by building an impressive château in baronial style at Les Faugs, close to Chabret. Initially, this may have been Isabelle's idea—her husband's life-style being plain and unpretentious—but once the scheme was decided upon, he entered into it with all his

---

[12] Maus, *Trente années*. S. Mallarmé, *Correspondance* (Paris, 1969), iv. 49, 185. S. Giocanti, 'Vincent d'Indy et Stéphan Mallarmé', *Le Coeur de moulin, Bulletin de l'Association Festival Déodat de Sévérac*, no. 10 (1991). Rolland, *Mémoires*, 171.

energy and enthusiasm. No expense seems to have been spared, and Les Faugs is certainly remarkable for its picturesque features, among them a small chapel on the ground floor and Gothic revivalist decoration of the main public rooms, a little incongruously hung with eighteenth-century portraits. At the top of the building, he had his own study, commanding a magnificent scenic vista: on a clear day, the Alps are visible. This room was appropriately hung with musical instruments, and graced with busts of Dante and Beethoven, not omitting a photograph of Franck at the organ. It provided an oasis of quiet amid the turbulence of the ensuing decades.[13]

[13] Laurencie, 'Quelques souvenirs', 9.

6

Dogma and Symbolism

In May 1890, Franck had an accident on the way to visit his pupil Paul Brand. Struck in the side by the pole of an omnibus, he struggled on to Brand's house, but after arriving, lost consciousness. Nevertheless, with great determination, he fought his pain, and carried on with his usual programme of teaching and playing. A serious attack of pleurisy with complications eventually forced him to take to his bed, and he died on 8 November. The effect of his unexpected demise upon his disciples can only be described as shattering, and the students in the organ class—particularly the brilliant Charles Tournemire and Louis Vierne—were devastated. For d'Indy, the shock was like that of losing a dearly beloved parent.

To his infinite regret, he was unable to attend the funeral, considering that first priority should be given to a concert of works by Franck's pupils in Valence, which he had been engaged to direct. He deputed Chabrier to give the funeral oration. The pointed absence of any official reaction from the Ministry of Fine Arts and the Conservatoire was little short of scandalous. Despite his grief, d'Indy could not help viewing with grim humour Georges Franck's vain efforts to persuade Ambroise Thomas, the Conservatoire's director, to be one of the pall-bearers; Maus in Brussels received a lengthy account of Thomas's response, the bureaucratic mind in action:

'No, monsieur, I suffer from colic'—at this point development (the only one which Thomas has ever made) on the appropriate remedies to drive the colic from his foul body—then the peroration: 'Go and see Réty!'—Georges Franck goes and knocks at the Secretary's door, and after waiting for several hours, the latter made this singular reply: 'Very well, monsieur, we will look at your case.'—'But, monsieur, the burial is tomorrow afternoon, I need to know . . .'—'Very well, monsieur, we will look at this business . . . besides, tomorrow afternoon, we have a piano examination . . .' Conclusion, nobody from the Conservatoire at the Service.

This was not exactly true, for Delibes, one of the composition professors, did attend the funeral in a private capacity. Also present were Guilmant and Widor, the latter to be appointed Franck's successor as organ professor. It fell to Eugène Gigout to play at the service at Sainte-Clotilde.[1]

Angered by the attitude towards Franck on the part of the French authorities, d'Indy looked not to Paris but to Brussels for a memorial concert. This took place under the auspices of the Circle XX, with the Ysaÿe Quartet performing Franck's String Quartet. His *Psyché et Eros* was presented in a transcription for two pianos, played by d'Indy and Paul Brand; d'Indy also conducted a female choir in *La Vierge à la crèche*, *Les Danses de Lorment*, *Chanson du Vannier*, and *Soleil*. It seemed, however, that in death, Franck suddenly achieved a status denied him during his life, and inevitably, there were a number poised to profit personally from the new situation. All d'Indy's anti-Semitic paranoia was expressed in a letter to Maus:

There's any amount of filth piling up on poor Father Franck's tomb which is barely sealed, it stabs me to the heart—oh! Artistic TRADESMEN, Jews and others!!! they would count their francs on their fathers' coffins!

Don't set up any Franck society, you and your friends, until I put you in the picture. If you receive any circular on this subject, you may reply that you don't wish to be involved with an association in which Colonne (Judas) is President and Treasurer.

Subsequently, problems arose after Franck's remains had been transferred from the cemetery of Montrouge to Montparnasse. A portrait medallion to be placed on the tomb was commissioned from Rodin by Chausson and Augusta Holmès.

[1] CF 56–60. VI to Paul Poujard, 9 Nov. 1890, AF. VI to OM, 19 Nov. 1890, RBM. C. Tournemire, *César Franck* (Paris, 1931), 74–5. Vierne, *Mes Souvenirs* (Paris, 1939).

'The medallion is a good resemblance,' Rodin wrote to d'Indy, 'and it has cost me a good deal of effort.' Meanwhile, Chausson had changed his mind, and, together with Duparc and certain others, now favoured an unadorned slab with nothing but Franck's name. As a result of Holmès's intervention, however, the original plan was reverted to. Rodin asked d'Indy to make sure that 'our great maître Franck is not placed like a rosette among the acanthus leaves'; he required that the tombstone be raised to eye-level, and that the medallion be placed in an upright position, not 'laid down like a book; it would not get any light'. These stipulations were eventually carried out.[2]

Meanwhile, a more mundane task was waiting: the completion of the orchestration of Franck's opera *Ghisèle* for its première in 1896. In the first instance, Georges Franck had approached Coquard, who was too busy to undertake the entire task himself. Georges' resentment of his father's militant disciples was still very much alive, and he would not countenance any of the members of the Société Nationale or Chausson or Benoît as collaborators—above all, not d'Indy. In a letter to Coquard, Georges fulminated: 'Now, if Vincent d'Indy were to collaborate, he would think himself indispensable, and say so. In spite of all we could do to restrict his assistance to an appropriate part, he would find a way of creating a current, not dangerous but sufficiently uncomfortable.'

Georges continued in a similar vein, even alleging that d'Indy had engineered the rejection of Franck's earlier opera *Hulda* by the Théâtre de la Monnaie in Brussels. However, by January 1896, expediency prevailed: *Ghisèle* had to be completed by the end of February that year. De Bréville promised his help, but expressed his desire that d'Indy be involved. With time rapidly running out, Georges was forced to agree. It was arranged that d'Indy would work on Act II with de Bréville and Chausson. Despite his opinion that the opera was neither homogeneous nor truly artistic, d'Indy, ever a slave of duty, undertook to give it his greatest care.[3]

[2] VI to OM, in Linden, *Octave Maus*, 69. Maus, *Trente années*. Grunfeld, *Rodin*, 329–30.
[3] Dufourcq, *Autour de Coquard*, 46, 49–50, 67–70.

At the same time, the course of the Franck movement took an unexpected turn, one which was to have the greatest consequences for d'Indy. Here, the prime mover was another pupil of Franck's, Charles Bordes, a man of enormous energy and initiative, with an intense interest in early church music and the folklore of the Basque country. In March 1890, he relinquished his post at the church of Nogent-sur-Marne to become choirmaster of the historic church of Saint-Gervais in Paris, where the Couperin family had been organists from the age of Louis XIV until 1826. It was a foundation of some antiquity, with its splendid *chapelle du chevet* dating from the end of the fifteenth century. The vault, of great elegance, rises 30 metres from the ground, providing excellent acoustics.

With the encouragement of the *curé*, the Chanoine de Bussy, Saint-Gervais became the centre of a momentous revival of sixteenth-century church music. At first, however, a more cautious musical policy was adopted. In June 1890, the mixed choir composed solely of amateurs performed Franck's *Messe à trois voix* with the venerable master himself at the organ; on other occasions, Schubert's Mass in E minor, Schumann's *Messe*, op. 147, and Franck's second *Béatitude* were heard. Holy Thursday in 1891 witnessed a more radical programme, with Palestrina's *Stabat Mater* and Allegri's *Miserere*, sung by double choir from opposite transepts of the church. The venture proved successful, attracting good congregations.

The following year, the Société des Chanteurs de Saint-Gervais was formed, with Alexandre Guilmant as president. In addition to d'Indy, the committee included Bordes, Prince Edmond de Polignac, and the musical historians Bourgault-Ducoudray and André Pirro. It was decided to take the risk of presenting an almost entire programme of sixteenth-century a cappella music for Holy Week 1892. At this time in the Church's year, when the organ remained silent, such relatively austere music seemed appropriate, and indeed acceptable. The aim of the Society was to restore this music, hitherto the preserve of academic historians and antiquarians, to its rightful context in the liturgy. Bordes's programme was astonishingly ambitious: Responses by Palestrina, Victoria, and Gallus; *Miserere* settings by Josquin des Prez and Palestrina; Orlando de Lassus's 'Regina Coeli', Victoria's *Passion*, Lotti's Crucifixus, Palestrina's *Improperaria, Magnificat,* and *Stabat Mater*; and in addition, two motets for double choir by J. S. Bach.

Bordes spent the entire winter of 1891–2 preparing this programme with his singers, to whom this music and its stylistic problems were completely unfamiliar. D'Indy was called on to take fifty rehearsals, with Bordes himself in charge of 103. The expense mounted alarmingly, but fortunately at this point François Magnard, Albéric's father and editor of *Le Figaro,* came to the rescue. He instructed his music critic to write a feature article about the Holy Week project at no cost to the Society. It achieved its object: enormous interest was created, and subscriptions poured in from the great names of the social world of Paris. On Wednesday of Holy Week, the nave of Saint-Gervais was full.

For the author J. K. Huysmans, who had embarked on his tortuous journey from artistic decadence towards a life of Christian poverty and subservience, Saint-Gervais's Holy Week presented fashionable concerts, rather than services for the faithful. In *Là-haut*, he complained that 'No meditation is possible in these reunions where ladies swoon behind their eyeglasses; these are frivolous séances of pious music, a compromise between the theatre and God. No, all the same, how it presses on the soul to hear the Virgin's tears falling in the shades, while the *Stabat* weeps beneath the arches.'

Complaints also came from the regular worshippers at the Sunday morning Masses, who found their seats occupied by a growing crowd of aesthetes brought along by Debussy and Mallarmé to hear the Gregorian chants. Although they listened in exemplary silence, their frequent habit of sitting with their backs to the high altar made an unfortunate impression!

The task of the Society was now well under way. Bordes founded a magazine called *La Tribune de Saint-Gervais,* encouraging leading scholars to contribute learned articles. In June 1893, Les Chanteurs de Saint-Gervais performed Bach's *Trauer* Ode at one of Guilmant's organ concerts at the Trocadéro. This was the beginning of the fruitful artistic bond which grew between Guilmant, Bordes, and d'Indy. In November that year, the performance of Palestrina's *Missa Papae Marcelli* constituted another milestone in the Society's progress. Not content with success in Paris, Bordes took the choir on regular *tours de propagande* around the provinces of France, with the aim of regenerating the musical life of the nation. Indeed, even beyond the French borders, the Society made its presence felt: Bordes, together with Guilmant and d'Indy, was in attendance at a *fiesta musical* in Bilbao in 1892, the precursor of the congresses held to revive religious music in Spain.

In retrospect, it can be seen that the Society already contained the seeds of its imminent transformation. In June 1894, a meeting took place at Saint-Gervais with a number of eminent liturgical musicians, including Perruchot of Notre Dame and the Abbé Chappuy of Saint-François-Xavier. The historic decision was taken to establish La Société de Propagande pour des Chef d'Œuvres religieux—better known as the Schola Cantorum. Among other things, it made contact with the Abbey of Solesmes, which throughout the nineteenth century had undertaken valuable reforms and new editions of Gregorian chant, based on the exhaustive studies of early manuscripts on the part of Guéranger, Pothier, and Mocquereau.

An important episcopal letter from Cardinal Sarto appeared in *La Tribune de Saint-Gervais* in 1895, rejecting church music which was light, trivial, and theatrical. 'Plainchant and Palestrina embody the highest qualities,' it said. To the charge that theatrical voluptuousness was necessary to attract people to church, the Cardinal replied that 'people are much more serious and pious than one usually believes'![4]

Such optimistic belief in the fundamental intelligence of mankind and its capacity to participate in the process of God's creation was fully shared by the leaders of the Schola

---

[4] TS no. 3 (Mar. 1900), 77–8; no. 4 (Apr. 1900), 111–16; no. 6 (June 1900), 185–6. J. K. Huysmans, *Là-Haut* (Tournai, 1965), 108–9. R. Nichols, *Debussy remembered* (London, 1992) 39. J. Subira, *Historia de la música Espãnola e Hispanomerica* (Barcelona, 1953), 741–2. A. Nède, 'Pie X et la musique religieuse', *Tribune de Saint-Gervais*, 1895, repr. in *Le Ménéstrel*, no. 32 (9 Aug. 1903), 253–4.

Cantorum. The idea that it could offer itself as a teaching establishment was the next logical step. Bordes, however, did not feel that he had sufficient authority to act on his own, and therefore brought in d'Indy and Guilmant, thereby forming a remarkable triumvirate. For d'Indy, this presented a golden opportunity to harness to the dynamic thrust of Bordes's church music reforms his own conception—already tried out on Magnard—of an historically based course in composition, incorporating Franck's insights and teachings.

His all-embracing mind also worried about the narrow musical education inflicted on instrumental players. In 1892, he had sat on a State Commission charged with drawing up proposals for the reorganization of the curriculum of the Paris Conservatoire. The Minister for Public Education had presided over a predictable gathering of the good and the great: Massenet, Reyer, Thomas, Dubois, Guiraud, as well as various senators and men of letters now long since passed into oblivion. Characteristically, d'Indy submitted his own separate report to the Commission. Its proposals attacked the production of mere musical artisans, unquestioning and uncritical, ignorant of aesthetics beyond the overriding preoccupation with technique. To rectify this situation, each course of study should be divided into two stages, the first concentrating on the technical mastery of an instrument, the second providing 'an artistic education designed to inculcate a complete knowledge of the literature of that instrument, the sense of style appropriate for each work, and the kind of interpretation it called for'.

The Commission as a whole responded with a number of practical objections, rather than total rejection. The sheer expense of its implementation would prove prohibitive, requiring the doubling of most of the existing seventy-five courses, as well as the professors' salaries. Other objections were raised against d'Indy's proposals *per se* by certain professors, who denied the possibility of separating matters of accuracy, rhythm, and agility from those of style and feeling. At this point, the *note annexe* to the report shades into bureaucratic fudge: the proposals were not to be incorporated in the Conservatoire's rules and regulations, but rather put forward as 'recommendations to the enlightened zeal of the *conseil d'enseignement*. It alone, for the most part, could judge the possibility of realizing them without disrupting the organization of the courses, or overloading the students, who regrettably were often obliged to take on paid work on the side in order to survive economically.'

The idealistic d'Indy, who, it must be said, had little experience of being a poor student, was of course not satisfied. On receiving the offer of a composition professorship on the death of Guiraud, his high-minded pride compelled him to decline. It would fall to the newly founded Schola Cantorum to address these problems in due course. But in its first years, its scope was inevitably circumscribed by its strictly limited means. The doors of its premises at the junction of the rue Stanislas and the boulevard Montparnasse—a small, cramped, one-storey house, since demolished—were opened in 1896, although the school's current account stood at a mere 37.50 francs! Bordes took the choral music courses, Guilmant the organ class, and d'Indy the counterpoint and composition studies. Soon, however, the teaching staff grew to include Ropartz and Risler, as student numbers increased.[5]

D'Indy's lectures on the historical development of music were subsequently put in book form by his assistants, and published as the *Cours de composition musicale*. It is a vast, systematic compendium of musical knowledge, theoretical, historical, and analytical, a model of clear exposition. If it is not exactly a literary masterpiece, certain sections achieve a certain rhetorical force. In fact, its schematic nature and presentation give it something of the appearance of a legal textbook. Much of the musical analysis is highly condensed, and appears in note form; on the other hand, d'Indy allowed himself to expand at length when his interest was fully aroused. Not the least part of the value of the *Cours* to his contemporaries was its wealth of musical illustrations.

Fundamentally, the work sets out to reveal the progressive

[5] C. Pierre, *Le Conservatoire National* (Paris, 1900), 382–3. L. Laloy, *La Musique retrouvée, 1902–27* (Paris, 1928), 70. VI, *La Schola Cantorum en 1925* (Paris, 1927), 4–18.

evolution of musical history in highly ideological terms, taking Gregorian chant as the fountain-head of its subsequent developments. Indeed, d'Indy reflected the cultural position of nineteenth-century Catholicism in regarding the Middle Ages as the pinnacle of Christian civilization; he was also strongly attracted by the ideas of Ruskin. The *Cours* therefore gives primacy to the religious creative impulse.

At the same time, he did not remain isolated from the secular philosophies of his time, being far too intelligent and aware of its problems simply to ignore them. Among the various strands of his thought can be found the positivistic philosophy of Auguste Comte. As a former law student at the Sorbonne, d'Indy was bound to have been aware of this heroic attempt to extend the influence of science throughout the thinking of society. Comte's seminal work, the *Cours de philosophie positive*, left its mark on d'Indy's *Cours de composition musicale*. Both books are permeated by the desire to organize knowledge and to reveal unities and connections between parts; as such, they represent a counter-attack on the intellectual anarchy of liberalism and the chaos of individualism, which were also deplored by Ruskin.

Comte imposed a single design on history, in order to reveal knowledge as passing through three chronological phases: namely, the theological, metaphysical, and positive. Likewise, d'Indy, in Part I of his *Cours*, presents the progressive evolution of art in terms of closed historical cycles: the Middle Ages, divided into the 'rhythmo-monodic era' (third–thirteenth centuries) and the 'polyphonic era' (thirteenth–seventeenth centuries), and the Renaissance (seventeenth century). Each cycle has its own distinct and mutually exclusive characteristics.

The 'rhythmo-monodic era' is characterized above all by an *art intérieur*, manifest in the mysterious simplicity of Romanesque architecture and music which is 'purely liturgical, yet infinitely expressive', its Gregorian monody gradually acquiring ornaments and symbols. By contrast, the 'polyphonic era' witnessed an astonishing religious effervescence. The Crusades affected not only the political and social dimensions, but also the artistic world, which 'employed all possible means loudly to proclaim its faith, and to draw the people into

the house of God'. The soaring spires and profusion of ornament of Gothic cathedrals testify to this spirit of exterioriza-
tion, while in music 'the combative spirit forces itself right
into the art of sounds, with polyphony and vocal counterpoint, in which the superimposed parts are in perpetual antagonism, a veritable musical tournament, well conceived to
enhance the brilliance of the religious ceremonies'. Above all,
the constant feature of the art of the Middle Ages was the rôle
of the artist himself, impersonal, modest, and anonymous,
through whose voice countless generations spoke.

However, for all his rhetoric, d'Indy's discussion of music
1300–1500 is remarkably thin and sketchy, confined as he was
by the limited knowledge available to him. A brief review of
organum, cantus firmus, and fauxbourdon is enlivened with
appropriate quotations from Dante's *Divine Comedy*, such as
this:

> And as a voice may be heard through another voice
> When one is persistent and the other comes and goes.[6]

There follows a mere list of names of certain leading composers of the era, among them Pérotin, de Vitry, Dufay,
Ockeghem, and Obrecht.

According to this model of history, the Renaissance represented a marked cultural deterioration—Ruskin's 'foul torrent'—in which the artist lost his anonymity in the pursuit of
personal glory and profit. The spirit of personality and individualism took the place of a simple, robust faith: 'The sculp-
tor will deploy his whole talent in ornamenting façades, the
parts of the monument intended to be seen . . . the aristocracy, intrusive and idle, lose no time in attracting artists as
luxuries to be added to an opulent collection!'

It is generally recognized that the various arts have their
own separate rates of development, and d'Indy had grounds
for maintaining that music did not submit to the influence of
the Renaissance until the very end of the sixteenth century.
By such a convenient stretching of history, the outstanding
masters of polyphonic composition—Josquin des Prez,

---

[6] R. Aron, *Main Currents in Sociological Thought*, vol. 1 (London, 1965), Penguin
edn. (1968), 63–109. CCM i. 144–5, 211–15. Dante, Para. VIII, lines 17–18.

Palestrina, Victoria, and Lassus—could be classed as late medievals. At this point in the *Cours*, musical analysis begins in earnest.

Following this apogee of achievement, the Renaissance brought a general hardening and rigidity to musical thought. Under the influence of the *mensuralistes*, the tyranny of the barline resulted in 'symmetrical and foursquare forms, to which we owe a great part of the platitudes of Italianism in the eighteenth and nineteenth centuries'. Likewise, polyphony was devalued by Vincenzo Galilei and the Florentine Camerata in their quest to reconstruct the music of ancient Greece. The resulting cult of the solo voice 'flattered the vanity of the age, allowing the virtuoso to shine and obtain his desired success'. The polyphonic ideal was further undermined by the rise of the basso continuo and figured bass, which d'Indy deplored; in his view, it encouraged false harmonic theories for its justification: 'Each man tries to classify chords as best he can, laboriously erecting a framework of rules which he is obliged to break in practice.'

Nevertheless, 'all action inevitably provokes a reaction. Out of this ill-fated and troubled period of the Renaissance, a new art was bound to emerge, individual and powerful, which after a long and painful labour, blossomed and radiated throughout Western Europe: in Italy, France and Germany.'

This late Renaissance phase (or early Baroque, as it is termed today) was not to be dismissed *in toto*. As well as the Roman school, represented by Carissimi, d'Indy had a great admiration for Monteverdi, pointing out that his master, Ingegneri, was one of the most expressive of the Italian polyphonists. Acknowledging Monteverdi's debt to the theories of the Florentine Camerata, he also recognized his achievement in creating the *stile rappresentativo*: 'Monteverdi adapted to the voice his manner of feeling the drama, and proposed to make it "the natural expression of human passion in melody".' Moreover, he regarded him as a precursor of Wagner in his employment of instruments for different characters and situations and in his ideas about dramatic production and staging: 'A trumpet signal, curtain open, a hidden orchestra; would one not think of *Rheingold* at Bayreuth?'

Part II of the *Cours* deals in great detail with the rise of symphonic music from its origins in the fugue, suite, and variations. First, d'Indy traced the development of the fugue from the motet, and the suite from the madrigal via the French *musique de cour*; the suite brought forth variation form, 'a logical succession of complete expositions of the same theme, offering each time a different rhythmic, melodic or harmonic aspect, without ceasing to be recognizable'. Sonata form, in its turn, evolved out of the ternary suite, through the works of C. P. E. Bach, Haydn, and Mozart, culminating in Beethoven and Franck.

This part has been considered of particular value for d'Indy's insights into the principles and dynamics of sonata and symphonic composition, which will be more fully discussed later. Quoting extensively from Ruskin's celebrated *Seven Lamps of Architecture*, he strongly emphasized that architectural construction and musical composition obey the same principles. Of fundamental importance are the subtle laws of proportion. Tonality he conceived like a colour spectrum, in terms of distributing light and shade through carefully planned series of modulations. Those moving from the initial tonic key towards the sharp side of the circle of fifths were deemed comparable to an ascent towards the light; conversely, movement toward the flat side symbolized a withdrawal into darkness.

It is noticeable that even in the most rationalist, schematic context, the mystical and symbolic dimension of his mental constitution was liable to break through. Nor can this have been unintentional or unwilled. Certainly, the general positivistic nature and presentation of the *Cours* had much value, both as systematic pedagogy and as providing intellectual and academic respectability in a predominantly secular society. But, for d'Indy, the need to invest his teachings with the faith and authority of Roman Catholicism was equally pressing. To this end, he effectively subverted the dominance of positivism by means of various 'supplements' and 'subtexts' scattered amid the text and footnotes of the *Cours* itself, and also by the essentially mystical portrait of his master in his book *César Franck* (1906).

From these pieces and fragments it is possible to construct an underlying medievalizing mythology, in which the great canonical figures of Palestrina, J. S. Bach, Beethoven, and Franck break out of their closed historical cycles and join hands in a symbolic, transcendental unity; an occult Catholic tradition is hypothesized, running from the early Christian period of Gregorian chant through the hostile Renaissance and Enlightenment to the end of the nineteenth century. In the words of Huizinga's classic *The Waning of the Middle Ages*, 'To the letter of formulated dogma, rigid and explicit in itself, the flowering imagery of symbols formed, as it were, a musical accompaniment, which by its perfect harmony allowed the mind to transcend the deficiencies of logical expression.'[7]

Palestrina, as we have seen, could simply be regarded as a late medieval composer. In the case of Bach, an eighteenth-century Lutheran, d'Indy seized upon the wealth of anachronistic features in his music, pointing out examples of Gregorian melodic formulas as well as his love of musical symbolism, as in the third Kyrie (*Clavierübung*, Part III): here, Bach followed the Gregorian tradition in employing different melodic shapes to represent the persons of the Trinity.

In order to incorporate Beethoven and Franck in the mythology, d'Indy resorted to imaginative analogies and mystical correspondences, linking them with the Italian writers and artists of the—arguably medieval—trecento and quattrocento. Dante still remained very much his guide, philosopher, and friend, but his tastes in the visual arts had undergone a significant change. Partly, no doubt, through Ruskin's pervading influence, his early love of the High Renaissance and its celebration of female beauty gave way to the more austere—even ascetic—pleasures of the 'primitives'. During a visit to Italy in 1894, he had enthused over such painters as Gazzoli, Lippi, and Bartolo di Fredi, finding them superior to Raphael, Correggio, and Guilio Romano. Thus Beethoven's third period inspired this hyperbolic prose:

---

[7] CCM i. 130, 215–18; ii. Pt 1. 10–12; iii. 25–7. Ruskin, *The Seven Lamps of Architecture* (London, 1849; Century edn. 1988), 68. Huizinger, *The Waning of the Middle Ages* (London, 1924), Penguin edn. (1955), 208.

And through this evolution, his spirit seems to compare with the thought of the mystics of the Middle Ages, whose works, both great and simple, remain incomprehensible for him who is not simple like them, inasmuch as this simplicity conceals itself beneath an abundance of detail: such were the French master architects of the thirteenth century; also the admirable Italian decorators like Giotto and Gozzoli: finally, the divine St Francis of Assisi, who related the *Fioretti*, and [Dante] the poet of the *Divine Comedy*, whom we cannot help thinking of when we read these musical marvels.

Dante readily came to d'Indy's mind: the twentieth variation of Beethoven's Diabelli set, op. 120, he described as 'a genial and mysterious paraphrase which one could say was conceived at the threshold of some *città dolente* evoked by the immortal Alighieri'.

> Then the good master said: 'And now, my son,
> We approach the city which takes its name from Dis,
> With its grave citizens and huge armies.'

And in the fugue 'Et exspecto' in the *Missa Solemnis*, d'Indy found 'not the formulas of a choirmaster, but a sacred dance, such as Dante could have described, marvellously symbolizing the universal union'.

Franck, however, with his character so full of natural goodness and humility, lent himself more plausibly to the image of the anonymous medieval craftsman:

Although Franck owed nothing to the Renaissance, he had, on the other hand, much greater affinity, through his qualities of clarity, luminosity and vitality, with the great Italian painters of the fourteenth and fifteenth centuries. His ancestors were Gaddi, Bartolo Fredi, and Lippi, rather than the artists of the later period. Even Perugino's angels, with their somewhat affected attitudes, have already scarcely anything in common with the angels of the *Redemption*; and if we may rediscover the Virgin of the *Béatitudes* in some fresco by Sano di Pietro, it would never enter our heads to invoke Franck's representation of her while looking at La Fornarina, who served Sanzio [Raphael] as a model, or even at some cleverly grouped *Pietà* by Van Dyck, or Rubens.

Above all, how were the nineteenth-century symphony and sonata, with their roots in the Enlightenment, to be reconciled with this medieval vision? According to d'Indy's aesthetic, Franck had brought the form to its highest perfection with the cyclic principle, already found in certain works of Beethoven: the 'Pathétique' Sonata, the Fifth and Ninth Symphonies, and the String Quartet in C sharp minor, op. 131. Not only did this thematic recurrence help to solve the problem of structural unity in an age of disintegrating musical language, but it also served a vital symbolic function: 'The circle (κυκλος) represents the perfect proportion, the Trinity in Unity.'

D'Indy proceeded to draw a bold analogy between the cyclic symphony and the medieval cathedral. Its implications are arresting, for if Ruskin had seen no possibility of a renewal of architecture, but only a return to the past, d'Indy's vision is of a revival of architectural values through the modern symphony. The passage deserves to be quoted at length:

Like a *cathédrale sonore*, [the cyclically constructed symphony and sonata] opens before us a grandiose entrance whose sculptural forms induce us already to sense who is the God dwelling within, who is the Saint to whom it is dedicated. In response to the welcoming gesture of this symbolic door, we hear the call of the introduction made for us: we shall uncover our heads respectfully and enter the immense nave. While the artist's reverent fancy lays itself open again and again to the infinite in each aisle, the central vessel rests, from span to span, on the pillars which the wrought curve of arched vault binds together in harmonious developments. Let us examine more closely these capitals: do not some of them reproduce, in a different attitude, the character, the motive which the entrance originally suggested?

Guided always by these cyclic figures of growing interest, here we are come to the far end of the great nave: the first part of the work is finished. . . . Calm and contemplative, the transept lays out before us its ternary construction. Between its lateral branches, *alpha* and *omega*, beginning and end, the chancel rises, the culminating point of the entire work, from which all brightness shines out, for there everything sings of the glory of God as in a sacred *Lied* whose central phrase, different from the two repetitions which surround it, blossoms in sublime accents where the artist's inspired soul pours itself forth ineffably.

As soon as this slow melody is extinguished, our eyes look up and encounter the upper galleries which wind around the chancel, with their arcades finely carved and grouped in trios: here is, effectively, the normal place for the *Scherzo*, whose delicate traceries will joyously strike our ear and give rest to our heart, still moved by the solemn impressions of the altar where slowly, the sacrifice is completed.

At last, we pass through the chapels of the apse, which follow and alternate regularly like *refrains* and *couplets*, between which ornaments or motives already known to us are set; they are those symbolic characters, those guiding themes which appeared in turn at the entrance, in the developments of the nave, in the varied decorations of the transept. And we salute piously their return in this circular route, in this less severe concluding *Rondeau* . . . 'a last refuge', also, through which the edifice is worthily completed, a monument—sonorous or architectural—a work of radiant beauty, a cyclical work of 'unity in variety', expressing grandeur and order.[8]

Such a powerful myth was to serve a valuable purpose, inspiring d'Indy with the almost superhuman energy necessary to sustain him through the colossal tasks which lay ahead. Over the years, the expansion and ambitions of the Schola Cantorum generated much bitter controversy and antagonism. Moreover, the mounting socio-religious and political problems of the age deeply disturbed d'Indy as a man of the Right. The attack on the institutions of the Catholic Church—the dissolution of the monasteries (1902–5) and the separation of Church and State (1906) by the Third Republic—as well as parliamentary corruption and, above all, the Dreyfus case, must be viewed as the social context of d'Indy's reforms of musical education and its projection of Catholic ideals into the secular world. Behind his disciplined exterior, so carefully maintained and guarded, lay a deeply passionate nature. His intense inner rage at the decadence of national life gave rise to violent diatribes in his letters to close friends of similar persuasions. It is, therefore, little surprise that he eagerly responded to the strident rhetoric of the author, journalist, and politician Maurice Barrès, whose trilogy of social novels *Le Roman de l'énergie nationale*

[8] CCM i. 67–72; ii. Pt. 1. 376–8, 475–8; iii. 275 ff. Dante, Inf. VIII. CF 75–6. Ruskin, *Seven Lamps*, 203–4.

(1893–1902) cogently demonstrated the effects of the enfee-
blement of national energy during this crucial period of
French history. For d'Indy, the tasks which lay ahead indeed
called for Beethoven's force of will rather than the obedience
of the medieval craftsman.

The humiliation of France in the Franco-Prussian War of
1870, the resulting annexation of Alsace and part of Lorraine,
and the continuing German menace constituted a permanent
national disgrace. Soon after the Boulanger crisis, France was
overwhelmed by the Dreyfus case. In 1894, Captain Alfred
Dreyfus, a Jew, was accused of handing over military docu-
ments to the German attaché in Paris. The War Council, in
closed session, found him guilty of treason, and sentenced him
to perpetual imprisonment on Devil's Island.

Subsequently, doubt began to be cast on the correctness of
this verdict, with the discovery of some forged evidence by an
army officer. The resulting ideological civil war—which led
ultimately to Dreyfus's pardon—was waged with the utmost
intensity on both sides. The supporters of Dreyfus, led by the
eminent social novelist Émile Zola—one of d'Indy's *bêtes
noires*—emphasized the overriding importance of liberty and
justice for the individual. But to the Right, the attempt to
defend Dreyfus's innocence at all costs was a veritable act of
treason, bringing the good faith of the army, together with its
officers and legal procedures, into disrepute. The case became
a wider question of national order, with Barrès trumpeting the
principles of authority and discipline, the security of the state
as against anarchy.

D'Indy's aristocratic origins and upbringing, reinforced by
his crucial experiences in the National Guard during the Siege
of Paris in 1871, had made him highly patriotic and conscious
of the military traditions of France, exemplified by the age of
Louis XIV, and, above all, Napoleon Bonaparte (Barrès's *pro-
fesseur d'énergie*). In fact, d'Indy revisited Waterloo in 1897,
during rehearsals of *Fervaal* in Brussels, describing the course
of the battle in precise detail for the benefit of his son, a lieutenant in the dragoons. It was natural for him to identify with
the cause of the army in the Dreyfus case, joining La Ligue

de la Patrie Française. This movement was founded in 1898, to show in the first instance that not all intellectuals were on the same side in the controversy. The anti-Dreyfusard position, indeed, had its supporters among members of the Institut de France and in the universities. Barrès himself was an active member of the committee, and the author François Coppée was honorary president. As well as d'Indy, the literary and artistic members included Jules Verne, Frédéric Mistral, and J. L. Forain.

D'Indy was known to appear on the Ligue's platform, accompanying patriotic songs on the piano. Such was the political intensity of the times that even the Concerts des assises de musique religieuses became the target of Dreyfusard retaliation. On one occasion, Bordes was pursued by a 200-strong rabble, who tore his cassock from top to bottom. To his rescue came d'Indy, laying about him with his fists, and almost strangling two of the thugs!

In the third public lecture of the Ligue in March 1899, entitled 'La Terre et les morts', Barrès maintained that

'The Dreyfus affair is only the tragic signal of a general state . . . Our profound ill is to be divided, troubled by a thousand individual wills, by a thousand individual imaginations. . . . Nationalism is a matter of deciding each question in relation to France. But how is it to be done if we do not have a common definition and idea of France?'

For d'Indy, like Barrès, no contradiction existed between his duty to his country, from which he drew so much inspiration, and the demands of his art. In both cases, the need for order and authority to subdue elements of conflict appeared of paramount importance. Moreover, this climate of nationalism happened to coincide with an artistic reaction against the prevailing obsession with Wagner and the Nordic cult of Ibsen and Grieg. A significant result was a revival of interest in French music of the seventeenth and eighteenth centuries. In an article 'Pour Rameau', published in 1894 in his father's newspaper *Le Figaro*, Albéric Magnard made a plea for a new edition of the complete works of Jean-Philippe Rameau. Taking the point, the publisher Jacques Durand replied to

Magnard, an old college friend, that his firm was willing to undertake the project at the highest level of scholarship.

It could only have been a matter of national pride, rather than profit, which induced Durand—who became a member of the Ligue—to become involved in the rehabilitation of Rameau. Indeed, Rameau's operas, late flowerings of the *grand siècle* of Louis XIV in the eighteenth-century *rococo* period, based on indifferent libretti, seemed at that time to be merely period pieces of the *ancien régime*, despite the outstanding quality of the music.

Under the general direction of Saint-Saëns, the Rameau Edition brought together a number of eminent musicologists and composers: d'Indy, Debussy, Dukas, Guilmant, Hahn, Chapuis, Téneo, and Maurice Emmanuel, while the bibliographic commentaries were provided by Charles Malherbe, who possessed a specialist knowledge of the eighteenth century. D'Indy undertook the editing of the operas *Dardanus*, *Hippolyte et Aricie*, and *Zaïs*. Doubtless, the heroic character of these works, their advanced orchestration, and nature painting appealed strongly to him. The task of reconstruction from the surviving sources proved to be a Herculean labour, as he complained to Ropartz: 'And above all, don't trust the parts held by the Opéra! They have been falsified, perverted, tarted up no more or less than the records of Dreyfus's trial by the good Semites. . . . I have been forced to begin *Hippolyte et Aricie* again *twice*.'

It was far from d'Indy's intention that the Edition should rest in peace upon library shelves: he himself took the initiative to perform Rameau's operas at the concerts of the Schola Cantorum.[9]

---

[9] Y. Chiron, *Maurice Barrès, le prince de la jeunesse* (Paris, 1986), 159–89. Laurencie, 'Quelques souvenirs', 18. Durand, *Quelques souvenirs*, i. 99–104. VI to OM, 18 Aug. 1899, RBM. VI to GR, 22 Sept. 1900, BN.

7

Asceticism Meets the Orient

It is little wonder that Fauré called d'Indy 'the Samson of Music'. In addition to the burgeoning work and scope of the Schola Cantorum, the decade of the 1890s witnessed him equally active as a composer, a conductor, and a tireless champion of French music. He was, indeed, increasingly becoming the pillar of the progressive musical scene, and, at this stage in his life, his generous—even paternalistic—attitude attracted a great deal of goodwill.

His first encounter with Claude Debussy, however, was not auspicious. The Société Nationale had accepted the young *Prix de Rome* winner's *Fantaisie* for piano and orchestra for performance under d'Indy's baton in April 1890. As the programme turned out to be too long, d'Indy decided to play the first movement only; at the end of the final rehearsal, the temperamental Debussy sabotaged the performance by removing the orchestral parts from the stands. Later, he wrote to d'Indy offering excuses for this grossly discourteous act, on the grounds that a false impression of the work would have been created: 'On reflection, I would rather have a passable performance of all three movements than a fine performance of the first through your good offices. It wasn't a rush of blood to the head or any kind of ill feeling that moved me to take such drastic action . . . You still have my gratitude, at least, and my sincere friendship.' Indeed, he was disappointed in the shortcomings of his own work, with its echoes of d'Indy's *Symphonie Cévenole*, and certainly, he always intended to rework it.

Fortunately, d'Indy was prepared to overlook the incident

as an aberration of youth; for, two years later, he commended Debussy's *La Damoiselle élue* to the Société Nationale. After its performance on 8 April 1893, Debussy wrote to Chausson: 'I had a letter from Vincent d'Indy, very friendly, with praises that would bring a blush to the lilies that sleep between the fingers of the *Damoiselle élue*.' Undoubtedly, it was the Pre-Raphaelite aesthetic of this setting in translation of Dante Gabriel Rossetti's *The Blessed Damozel*, exquisitely matched with arabesque-laden music, which so appealed to the gentle, feminine side of d'Indy's nature, as did Debussy's *L'Après-midi d'un faune* the following year.

The symbolist movement, too—the decadent fin de siècle world of the poetry of Verlaine and Mallarmé and the plays of Maeterlinck—had its allure for him, as well as for Debussy. Both were interested in the possibility of turning Maeterlinck's *La Princesse Maleine* (1889)—a drama of fatally interlinked human destinies unfolding amid supernatural storms—into an opera. But neither composer brought this idea to fruition. Debussy, on learning that Maeterlinck had given prior permission to d'Indy, turned to the same author's *Pelléas et Mélisande*, while traces of *La Princesse* are to be found in d'Indy's opera *L'Étranger* (1902). Yet, as we will see, his relationship with the symbolist movement was a problematic one, for its emphasis on intuition and anti-intellectualism conflicted with his increasingly pedagogic activities and academic system building.[1]

Certainly, the academic side largely prevailed in his String Quartet No. 1, performed in Brussels by the Ysaÿe Quartet in February 1891 and at the Société Nationale on 4 April. D'Indy was delighted: 'Ysaÿe is truly a genius. He understands and assimilates instantly any composition put before him, and has the gift of communicating all he feels to his fellow *artistes*, and of giving them precise explanations.' More guarded was Fauré's reaction to the work itself: 'The Andante is extremely successful. I also like the piece in the form of a folksong. But the first movement and the finale please me less:

[1] *Gabriel Fauré, Correspondance*, ed. J. M. Neetoux (Paris, 1980), 184. *Debussy Letters*, 30, 52. *Correspondance de Claude Debussy et Pierre Louÿs 1893–1914* (Paris, 1945), 99.

they are dry, and more interesting for their technical writing than for their ideas. The Andante, on the other hand, is full of feeling, very human.'

The year 1892 brought gratifying and well-deserved recognition, for in January d'Indy was nominated a Chevalier of the Legion of Honour, and two months later *Le Chant de la cloche* received a fine performance in Amsterdam under Viotta. In addition, Magnard's success in having his opera *Yolande* mounted at the Théâtre Royal de la Monnaie in Brussels in December gave credit and satisfaction to his mentor. Indeed, Brussels was to be the scene of many triumphs for d'Indy, and, through his association with Octave Maus, he became very influential in Belgium. Due to his advocacy, such works as Chausson's *Concert pour piano, violon, et quatuor*, Debussy's *La Damoiselle élue*, and Dukas's overture *Polyeucte* featured in Maus's concerts of the Circle XX. With regard to the last-named, d'Indy had written in 1892: 'Dukas has just written an absolutely smashing overture, I've been overwhelmed by it. It's certainly the most beautiful and noble work to have been produced for a long time. *This boy must be pushed*, he is a bear but has some mighty good ideas.' Other letters deal with practical matters in great detail: problems of dates, performers, and rehearsals, even the positioning of the platform. He himself declined to play the demanding piano parts of Franck's trios and quintet. Singers raised questions: 'Another thing: the matter of Dinah. I know her, she is a good musician, sings well, a little *vinaigrette*. . . . Only beware of her repertoire. Would she learn new pieces easily and willingly?' He offered amusingly caustic advice on forming a female chorus: 'Choose eight (at least) good musicians, musicality preferable to virginity.' And when the performance of Chausson's *Concert* on 4 March 1892 nearly foundered with the pianist's withdrawal, d'Indy—who had taken personal charge of the arrangements and was anxious to spare Chausson a bitter disappointment—found a last-minute replacement to join Ysaÿe and the Crickboom Quartet.[2]

[2] A. Ysaÿe and B. Ratcliffe, *Ysaÿe, his Life, Work and Influence* (London, 1947), 171–3. *Gabriel Fauré*, 167. LV ii. 26, 43. Linden, *Octave Maus*, 41, 44. Barricelli and Weinstein, *Ernest Chausson*, 54.

Meanwhile, d'Indy was labouring to bring *Fervaal* to completion for its première in Brussels. But in September 1893 he lost valuable time when his elder daughter accidentally drank from a phial of carbolic acid. For fifteen days she hovered between life and death, and much care and nursing proved necessary to assist her recovery. Determined to finish the vocal score that year, he took himself and his family to the south of France for the winter, to work without the distractions of Parisian life. Dukas wrote to commiserate: 'I understand very well that, to complete *Fervaal*, you're doing without your strides along the boulevards and the excellent music performed here every winter.' The following month d'Indy had achieved his task. There still remained the gargantuan task of orchestration, 'the recreation after the suffering', as he said to de Bréville.

Soon afterwards, he returned to Paris for a soirée at Chausson's house. After dinner, cigarettes, and cigars, he played and sang Act III of *Fervaal* 'like a little schoolgirl reciting her lessons'. At 11.45, Debussy, also present, was prevailed upon to reveal his own work-in-progress, *Pelléas et Mélisande*. Turning the pages for him as he played, d'Indy did not then experience the profound cultural shock which the première of the work was to elicit.

Both *Fervaal* and *Pelléas* presented severe challenges to the prevailing fashions and trends of French opera. Indeed, despite the very different characters of their composers—d'Indy aloof and aristocratic, Debussy surly and self-absorbed—they were effectively united in their contempt for the conventional tastes of the bourgeois public and the socially correct world of the salons. They themselves frequented only the most elevated artistic circles. Pleasing the fickle, entertainment-seeking opera audiences—not to mention the corps of musically ill-informed, self-opinionated critics—presented a daunting task even for such a seasoned professional as Massenet. He, too, had his share of failures, as well as notable successes like *Manon* and *Thaïs*. Moreover, the belated French reception of Wagner's music dramas—the *Ring* cycle, *Tristan und Isolde*, and *Die Meistersinger*, premièred at the Paris Opera between 1893 and 1909—inevitably proved highly controversial. Nevertheless, some ground had been prepared for *Fervaal* by the success of Ernest Reyer's *Sigurd* (1884), based on a text resembling *Götterdämmerung*, and admired by d'Indy for its reproduction of Wagnerian music drama within the French tradition.

During January and February 1894, d'Indy took a working holiday in Italy in the company of his daughters, visiting Rome, Venice, Siena, San Geminiano, Assisi, and Florence, where he enthused over the primitive artists of the quattrocento. 'Gozzoli transports me,' he told de Bréville; 'the Lippis sweep me off my feet, Bartolo di Fredi fills me with joy, in short, all these good people were blindingly superior to the Raphaels, Corregios, and other Guilio Romanos.' The high point of the visit to Florence turned out to be the frescos of Benozzo Gozzoli in the Riccardi Palace of the Medicis: 'The Adoration of the Kings', with their spectacular processions arrayed in exotic costumes. In Venice, he was bowled over by Carpaccio's frescos *San Giorgio degli Schiavoni* in the Schola di San Giorgio; the dramatic slaying of the dragon is enacted against the pageant of Venetian life, teeming with people, animals, and such picturesque details as a band of shawms and tabors. 'C'est tout Venise,' he informed Poujard, 'playing havoc with Giorgione, Bordone, Bellini, and even Titian!'

Installed at the Hotel de la Minerve in Rome, he spent four or five hours each morning on the orchestration of *Fervaal*. In the afternoons, he went out walking. 'A charming life', he wrote to de Bréville, 'with a delightful sun, far from concerts and all the bother involved in *la musique militante*.' He let himself relax a little too much, it seems, for by late July, only Act I had been scored, and time was running short. He would have to push himself hard to get through the remaining acts within five months.[3]

Fervaal has generally been regarded as a Wagnerian music drama, but this is an overstatement of the case. Certainly, Wagner's influence is apparent in the broad conception of the

[3] VI to PB, 27 Sept., 30 Oct. 1893; 1 Feb. 1894, BN. *Correspondance de Paul Dukas, choix de lettres établi par Georges Favre* (Paris, 1971), 18. *Debussy on Music*, ed. F. Lesure (London, 1977), 76. Barricelli and Weinstein, *Ernest Chausson*, 35–6. VI to Poujard, 8 Mar. 1894, AF.

work, in which the music constitutes the vital element of the drama, and the familiar philosophical notions of the denial of the will to live and the regeneration by universal love dominate d'Indy's own text. He also employed a system of leitmotifs representing states of being—love, heroism, vengeance, grief—rather than individual characters. Moreover, the vocal and instrumental lines are intrinsically lyrical in character. The orchestration, too, rejects the Wagnerian technique of a blended mass of timbres in favour of highlighting the individual sonority of each instrument according to Berlioz's procedure.

At the same time, the contribution of Meyerbeer to the dramatic effectiveness of *Fervaal* should be fully recognized, not only in its melodramatic *coups*, but also in the picturesque scenes and local colour. In his opera *Le Prophète*'s contrast between the Anabaptists and the true religion of Fidès, we can see a likely model for Fervaal's conflict between paganism and the new religion of light—in both cases expressed in terms of opposing flat and sharp tonal centres. And the appearance of the Gregorian chant 'Pange lingua' to symbolize this new religion had a certain precedent in *Les Huguenots*, where the Lutheran choral *Ein feste Burg* is sung by the Protestant side in the French civil wars.

Act I of *Fervaal* is set in the south of France during the legendary period of the Saracen invasions, when two religious eras—the indigenous Celtic and the Saracen—were coming to an end. The two principal protagonists occupy special places in their respective societies: Fervaal, the last descendant of the Celtic gods, on whom has been laid the oath to remain pure and untroubled by love, in order that he may best devote himself to the preservation of his country, Cravaan, from the threat of invasion; and Guilhen, a young Saracen princess and daughter of the Emir, who has occupied the surrounding region. By chance, it is she who rescues Fervaal from a band of Saracen maurauders, and takes him to her own gardens to recover from his wounds. The oriental atmosphere of luxury and ease in this idyllic place, where orange, lemon, and olive trees grow amid a profusion of fragrant flowers, is evoked with pleasantly languid music not too dissimilar to Fauré's *Les*

Roses d'Ispahan. Gradually Fervaal succumbs to Guilhen's charms.

The ensuing love scene between them lacks the overpowering eroticism of *Tristan and Isolde*, and emphasizes their essential innocence and chastity. Fervaal's music, in B major, is predominantly heroic in character, as he recounts his life in terms of childhood, war, and religious joy. Guilhen, likewise, is a child of nature, accustomed to a life on horseback in the hunt, expressed with rollicking music in 6/8 or 12/8 metre. Despite the extreme healthiness of their dispositions, both confess that their love for each other has brought enslavement to passion; in an extended duet full of baroque conceits, they discover *la douloureuse joie, joie amère, douleur charmante*. As in *Tristan*, it breaks off in a musical 'coitus interruptus', not with the unexpected return of King Mark, but the distant war-cry of Fervaal's mentor Arfagard. Fervaal, recalled to his sense of duty, cries 'maudit soit amour' as Arfagard drags him away. Thus deserted, Guilhen acts like the archetypal woman scorned, and responds to the demands of her starving fellow Saracens with a proposed attack on Cravaan, Fervaal's country.

Act II, set in Cravaan in the Cévennes region, contains a remarkable melodramatic scene in which the mountain goddess Kaito is summoned by Fervaal and Arfagard to declare the destiny of their country. Whereas d'Indy felt deep-lying inhibitions in expressing eroticism and orientalism—which constituted a threat to his own hard-won self-mastery and control—the chthonic, primeval powers of nature invariably tapped his boldest and most daring imaginative vein. To evoke the *mysterium tremendum*—the sense of daemonic awe and dread which appears in the religions of primitive man—the stage directions prescribe lurid, supernatural imagery derived from Flaubert's *La Tentation de Saint-Antoine*: clouds assume 'primordial forms' upon the altar—a succession of high rocks, trees, giant plants, fantastic animals, and an immense serpent. D'Indy's musical response, moreover, is most apt in its phantasmagoric orchestration (coloured by the addition of a contrabass clarinet, as well as bugles, harps, and gong) and, for its time, its outlandish harmonies—whole-tone chord progressions and triadic chords rising in chromatic steps.

Asceticism Meets the Orient

At length, white female forms embodied in mist slowly revolve around Kaito to a wordless women's chorus off-stage: the effect is worthy of Gustav Holst in its sensation of remoteness, heightened by the doubling of the serpentine-shaped contrapuntal lines by four saxophones. For this idea, d'Indy was indebted to Franck's opera *Hulda*. These voices continue in a sequence of parallel triads rising in semitones as Kaito hierarchically utters her prophecy of the end of the gods in exclamatory minor ninths (Ex. 4*a*):

Si le Serment est violé, si la Loi antique est brisée,
si l'Amour règne sur le monde, le cycle d'Esus est fermé

Seule la Mort, l'injurieuse Mort appellera la Vie
La nouvelle Vie naîtra de la Mort.

Ex. 4a. *Fervaal*, Act II, scene 1: Kaito's prophecy

103

It is essential to realize, however, that these extraordinary sections take their place as tonally unstable episodes within a long-range plan based on the keys of G minor and E flat major, representing *patrie* (Cravaan) and the false light. And when Kaito predicts the new age, the key of love and the true light, D major, shines out resplendently.

At Arfagard's bidding, Fervaal offers himself to the assembled chiefs of Cravaan, and is acclaimed leader. In the ensuing religious ceremony, Arfagard blesses the holy water: the solemn music, played by four saxhorns and tuba, is, in its sequence of chromatic modulations, strongly reminiscent of Amfortas's agony in the Grail scene of *Parsifal* (Ex. 4*b*). Subsequently, d'Indy captured the atmosphere of impending war with a vividness derived from personal experience in the 1870–1 Siege of Paris. A *cornet à bouquin*, played on-stage, sounds the alarm as a messenger announces the massing of the enemy. This scene, overall in B major, which so effectively expresses the fluctuating psychology of the crowd, its feverish anticipation, moments of fear and panic followed by irrational

Ex. 4b. *Fervaal*, Act II, scene 3: Arfagard blesses the holy water

euphoria and false hopes, is constructed in Meyerbeerian fashion from a sequence of linked sections; the handling of the
male-voice choral masses and the inflated brass-dominated
orchestra show a masterly hand. Much of the music, appropriately and unashamedly populist in character, consists of
rousing marches and fanfares—bugles ring out against the
shouts of 'La guerre a frappé sur les boucliers!'—while rising
chromatic scales generate crude excitement at climax points.
At the same time, there is a sophistication in the orchestra's
lean and energetic motivic working which contributes greatly
to the nervous tensions of the situation.

Particularly worthy of mention is d'Indy's effective use of
a melodramatic device used by Meyerbeer and Verdi: the
juxtaposition of public and private domains. During the
tribes' lusty call to arms, Fervaal confesses to Arfagard his
continuing passion for Guilhen in violation of his Druidic
oath, and predicts his impending sacrifice, which the God Ésus
will claim.

Act III opens on a scene of desolation among the mountains
of the Cévennes, the bleak, wind-swept landscape aptly
evoked by bugle and saxhorn sonorities. The army of Cravaan
has been destroyed by the Saracens; but, in the tradition of
Greek tragedy, we see only the aftermath of the battle.
Fervaal is alone in the midst of a ravine; but Guilhen, who
had accompanied the invading army and lost her way, also
finds herself there. Expiring in the extreme cold, she dies in
his arms as they proclaim the eternity of their love.

Overwhelmed by the catastrophe of his country and the loss
of his beloved, he sings 'Ils dorment tous ceux que j'aimais'
with its strange progressions of chords in mediant relationships underlining the dissolution of his life's hopes. In the lowest abyss of despair, however, divine light begins to infiltrate
his spirit, while a veritable Manichean conflict takes place
between the pagan powers of darkness and the new dawning
religion of love. Gradually, the overall tonality changes from
D minor to D major as Kaito's music of parallel triads in the
depths of the orchestra recedes, and a celestial chorus breaks
through with the melody alone of the 'Pange lingua'. The
shining stars and the first rays of an 'ideal sun' are seen to

vanquish the menacing forces of primeval nature, the sombre clouds, thunder, and lightning which obscure the mountain. Bearing Guilhen's body in his arms, he ascends the mountain towards the light, which increases in brilliance, singing, in rising ecstasy, a triumphant wordless fanfare.

Here Fervaal's spiritual journey, like Dante's through Hell, Purgatory, and Paradise, reaches its conclusion. In the absence of words at this point, d'Indy was surely minded of the sublime lines of the final canto of the *Paradiso*:

> O how my speech falls short, how faint it is
> For my conception! And for what I saw
> It is not enough to say that I say little.
>
> O Eternal light, existing in yourself alone
> Alone knowing yourself; and who, known to yourself
> And knowing, love and smile upon yourself![4]

In his personal life, too, d'Indy was being reminded of the impermanence and transitoriness of the world. His old comrade Chabrier died on 13 September 1894, disheartened and in failing health. Deeply moved, d'Indy declared that with him 'everything stemmed from the heart: that is why Chabrier was a great artist.' At the same time, he found himself in an embarrassing position, for Chabrier had hoped that he would complete his opera *Briséis* after his death. We have seen how d'Indy considered his friend to have taken a false turning into serious opera, and *Briséis* he dismissed as a 'religio-erotic conception'. Pressed by Chabrier's son, Marcel, he declined the task in a letter whose tone of academic rhetoric was probably intended to mask his real feelings about the matter.

I consider the completion of a work left incomplete by a man of importance as an utterly anti-artistic enterprise when it is a question of putting *oneself* into it (if it were only orchestration, it would be the equivalent of the repair of a damaged fresco, a slightly reprehensible task, yet possible and sometimes useful) but to draw substance from one's own being to blend with another substance of a

---

[4] G. Flaubert, *La tentation de Saint-Antoine* (Paris, 1874), Flammarion edn. 130–6, 196, 199, 238. Dante, Para. XXXIII, lines 121–6. *New Oxford History of Music, vol. 9: Romanticism 1830–1890* (Oxford, 1990), 92–100.

totally different essence, will never produce anything but a hybrid mixture, and, in any case, a negative artistic result.[5]

There were more deaths that year. Most tragic was that of Guillaume Lekeu in January, at the age of only 24, whose career d'Indy had watched over after Franck's demise. His advice to him had been sound and magisterial: he should get to know himself and his abilities, allot a portion of his time to reading, and induce his friends to give a candid opinion of his work; feelings of impotence were common to all creative artists, to be endured rather than resisted. Suddenly, this exceptionally gifted youth had been struck down by typhoid fever. In a state of shock, d'Indy managed to organize a memorial concert of Lekeu's music at the Salle d'Harcourt.[6]

The passing of François Magnard signalled the end of an era, in which his goodwill towards Franck's movement for the sake of his son Albéric had been manifest with supportive publicity in *Le Figaro*. Albéric's genuine grief found sublimation in the *Chant funèbre* completed the following year, a magnificent funeral march of almost Mahlerian pessimism and intensity, which d'Indy admired and added to his own conducting repertoire. Indeed, the artistic rapport between them was sufficiently strong to survive that terrible year of the Dreyfus case and its protractions, for Albéric Magnard took the side of the Dreyfusards, even sending a letter to Émile Zola supporting his famous counter-attack 'J'accuse' in Clemenceau's journal *L'Aurore* (13 Jan. 1898). These events were to be the inspiration of Magnard's *Hymne à la Justice*. But d'Indy's own sense of justice towards his former pupil was no less laudable; likewise, he did not allow his anti-Semitic views to poison his relations with his cultivated Jewish colleagues, Maus and Dukas among them.

A decidedly unconventional personality, the Spanish pianist and composer Isaac Albéniz made his appearance in Chausson's salon around this time. Such was the vibrancy, simplicity, and openness underlying his fantastic appearance that the circle

[5] VI to Marcel Chabrier, 5 Oct. 1894, BN. Myers, *Emmanuel Chabrier*, 120. VI, *Emmanuel Chabrier et Paul Dukas* (Paris, 1920), 9.
[6] L. Davies, *César Franck and his Circle* (London, 1970), 269–71.

could overlook his tirades and vagabond artistry, and treat him rather like a mascot. While making firm friends with Bordes, Dukas, and Fauré, Albéniz particularly looked up to d'Indy with the awe and humility of a novice. His previous mentor, the distinguished Spanish folklorist Felipe Pedrell, had advised him to follow his own instincts, as another visitor to Paris, the cellist Pablo Casals, recalled. 'Down with rules!' exclaimed Pedrell, 'Burn all the harmony textbooks, the counterpoint ones also, and those on composition and instrumentation which have not been written for you, and would stifle your natural genius.' Yet Albéniz seems to have realized the need to acquire more knowledge and discipline if he were not to remain a mere purveyor of salon trifles. The fruit of his studies at the Schola Cantorum was to be *Iberia*, a masterpiece of Spanish nationalism comparable with that triumph of French regionalism, d'Indy's *Symphonie Cévenole*.

Albéniz's admiration for d'Indy impelled him to attend all the performances of *Fervaal* in Brussels and Paris. He also arranged for him to conduct a series of concerts in Spain, where, in the large cities, audiences for symphonic music were being attracted by the recently formed orchestral societies. D'Indy made a number of guest appearances with La Sociedad Catalan de Conciertos, presenting, in March 1895, a series of five historic concerts in Barcelona. En route, an amusing incident took place at the Spanish border, where he was temporarily detained on suspicion of being an anarchist; it took considerable persuasion to convince customs officials that his conducting scores were not secret codes!

His concert programmes were patently didactic in character—forerunners of those given at the Schola Cantorum—and offered a historical survey of the development of orchestral music from the eighteenth century. Works by Bach, Destouches, Rameau, Gluck, Haydn, and Mozart were played at the first concert; by Weber, Mendelssohn, Schumann, Berlioz, Bizet, and Saint-Saëns in the next. Complete concerts were devoted to Beethoven and Wagner and to the modern French school: Franck, Bordes, de Bréville, Chabrier, Chausson, Fauré, Ropartz, and d'Indy.

His reception by packed houses overflowing on to the staircases was overwhelming in the intense heat, for this audience proved to be unrestrained in its reactions. It demanded encores for the Overture to *Tannhäuser* and the selection from Act III of *Die Meistersinger*. Although it whistled Fauré's *Pavane*, his 'Air de danse' from *Caligula* met with approval, as did the excerpts from Franck's *Rédemption* and d'Indy's *Wallenstein*. Absolute silence surrounded the first two movements of the *Symphonie Cévenole*, but after the finale, thunderous applause broke out, compelling an encore.[7]

Throughout this year, *Fervaal* remained his major preoccupation. With the completion of the full score, there began the trials of its production at the Théâtre Royal de la Monnaie in Brussels; the history of this leviathan of an opera bears some resemblance to the launching of Brunel's monstrous steamship *The Great Eastern*. From the outset, the directors seemed determined upon a policy of obstruction, with the result that the première was postponed from February to the autumn of 1896. In the meantime, d'Indy found distraction in composing *Istar*, a set of orchestral variations. He spent some weeks at Biarritz, where he experienced a storm of terrifying force over the Bay of Biscay. This inspired both his *Lied maritime* and the final scene of his next opera, *L'Étranger*, which he was then planning. Back in Paris, the administration of the Conservatoire ran into rough waters with the sudden resignation of the Director, Ambroise Thomas. Sensibly, d'Indy did not fall for the rumour that the successor might be himself; predictably, a safer pair of hands, Théodore Dubois, was appointed.

Throughout the period of rehearsals of *Fervaal*, which commenced in September, d'Indy remained in Brussels, leaving Magnard in charge of his counterpoint classes at the Schola. His efforts to supervise the production were met with an atmosphere of ill will: 'I won't be able to leave the rehearsals for a day without the risk of seeing everything I've struggled

---

[7] Subira, *Historia de la música Espanola*, 673, 676. S. Giocanti, 'Vincent d'Indy et Isaac Albéniz', *Revue de l'Association* (forthcoming). G. Laplane, *Albéniz, sa vie, son œuvre* (Paris, 1956). P. Gilson, *Notes de musique et souvenirs* (Brussels, 1942), 15–16. J. M. Corredor, *Conversations with Casals* (London, 1956), 45, 163. VI to his daughter (?), 11 Mar. 1895, AF. VI to GR, 1 Apr. 1895, BN.

to build up dismantled,' he complained to Ropartz, later reporting with heavy sarcasm that he was walking on velvet because of a rumour that the directors had almost decided to repaint some old scenery at a cost of 3 francs, 75 cents!

The première was once again postponed, and finally took place on 12 March 1897. By then, however, the attitude of the company had changed completely to one of admiration. Moreover, intense interest and anticipation were building among the public, for d'Indy had taken the unusual step of prior publication of both libretto and vocal score. Would *Fervaal* prove to be the authentic French answer to Wagner's music drama, as many musicians hoped? Certainly, the production proved a triumph, despite some apparent economies in the staging; the artistic commitment of the singers and musicians conducted by Flon, with Jeanne Raunay and Imbert de la Tour in the roles of Guilhen and Fervaal, underscored the work's qualities. Among its greatest admirers was Dukas, who wrote a penetrating account of it, rightly dismissing opinions that it was merely a Wagnerian pastiche. In short, a landmark in French music had come into being.[8]

Dukas's genuine love and admiration for *Fervaal* never left him. D'Indy, on his part, held him in increasing esteem. He was delighted by *L'Apprenti sorcier*, first performed in Paris that year, remarking subsequently that 'the works which established the reputations of Chabrier and Dukas were both big scherzos, *España* and *L'Apprenti sorcier*'. The same year, d'Indy made the acquaintance of Richard Strauss during visits to Frankfurt and Mannheim to conduct *Wallenstein* and the *Symphonie Cévenole*. Their admiration was mutual, and d'Indy found a firm supporter in the brilliant young composer and conductor.[9] The year 1898 opened with the Paris première of *Istar*, on 16 January at the Concerts Colonne under d'Indy's baton. In this orchestral work he turned to an Assyrian theme. The cruel, barbaric civilizations of the ancient world clearly appealed to a repressed vein of sado-masochism in his

[8] LV ii. 35, 36. Carraud, *La Vie . . . d'Albéric Magnard*, 60. VI to GR, 15 Sept., 19 Nov. 1896, BN. *Les Écrits de Paul Dukas sur la musique* (Paris, 1948), 365–73.

[9] VI, *Emmanuel Chabrier*, 23. *Richard Strauss and Romain Rolland, correspondence, diary and essays* (London, 1968), 3.

nature: one of his favourite books was Flaubert's *Salammbô*, a historical and archaeological reconstruction of Carthage in the form of a novel overloaded with lurid—and indeed revolting—detail. On a visit to the British Museum in 1887, he had been captivated by the Assyrian mural sculptures from the palace of King Ashurnasirpal II (883–859 BC) depicting military campaigns and royal lion hunts. In the Assyrian epic poem *Izdubar* he found a subject to appeal to the public: 'To obtain the release of her lover held captive in the Underworld, the Goddess Istar must divest herself of one of her ornaments or one of her garments at each of the Seven Doors of the Dark Abode; at last, triumphant in her nakedness, she passes through the Seventh Door.'

This legend became the pretext for an unusual formal experiment—a set of variations in reverse order, concluding with a bare unison statement of the theme itself, to symbolize the naked body of Istar. The opening *appel* motive G F Db recurs, together with a subsidiary march theme, between the variations to mark her progress past the succession of doors. In variation I, the harmonic basis only of the theme supports a glittering Impressionist orchestration, a sexually tantalizing suggestion of a Salammbô figure, provocatively arrayed in a mass of emeralds and gold, with pearls at the end of her hair.

Subsequently, the musical textures move progressively from complexity towards simplicity and austerity, shedding elaboration and ornament as Istar reveals herself. During the tarantella of variation V, the flowing counterpoint of variation VI and the desiccated two-part writing for flute/piccolo and violins of VII, (Ex. 5*a*), new whole-tone formations, together with rising sequences of falling fourths, begin to crystallize. Finally, the theme itself emerges to integrate these elements into a lengthy, tonally vague melody. This has been described by Vallas as 'un cadavre monodique', on account of its imagined similarity to the shape of a female body; indeed, its marked absence of erotic feeling suggests Baudelaire's line 'La froide majesté de la femme stérile' (Ex. 5*b*). The sensation of sexual anticlimax, moreover, is thrown into relief by the progress of the march theme, a current moving in a contrary direction, as it were, to the increasing asceticism of the

Ex. 5a. *Istar*, Variation VII

Ex. 5b. *Istar*, theme

variations; gathering confidence after a hesitant start, it con-
cludes the work in a blaze of pure radiance in clear F major
tonality, as Istar obtains the release of her beloved.

> Elle a présenté les Eaux sublimes
> et ainsi, devant tous, elle a delivré
> le FILS DE LA VIE, son jeune amant.

Certainly, the serious philosophical nature of the Istar legend precluded the kind of full-blown erotic treatment characteristic of Strauss's 'Dance of the Seven Veils' in his opera
Salomé; the use of a formal, if highly unorthodox, scheme of
variations proved much more appropriate. Yet the work's pos-

1. Vincent d'Indy, aged 7

2. A drawing of Salzburg by d'Indy, 1873

3. A drawing of the building of Wagner's theatre at Bayreuth by d'Indy, 1873

4. A water-colour of Boffres by d'Indy (n.d.)

5. Château Les Faugs

6. Vincent d'Indy
c.1890

7. A portrait of d'Indy by
Jacques Émile Blanche,
1890; from this it appears
that d'Indy was left-handed

8. A portrait of d'Indy by
Théo van Rysselberghe, 1908

9. Vincent d'Indy in his 'famous hat', *c*.1920

10. Villa 'L'Étrave' at Agay

11. Léon Bakst's costume design
for Ida Rubinstein for *Istar*, 1924

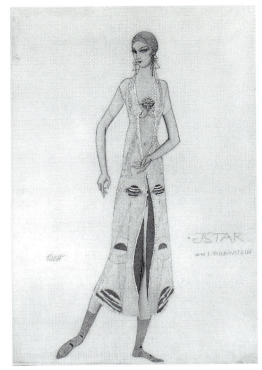

12. Léon Bakst's décor design for *Istar*, 1924

13. Bust of d'Indy by
Bourdelle, 1929

14. Vincent d'Indy in 1930;
this suggests that he may have
been a compulsive smoker!

15. Vincent d'Indy just before his death in 1931

itive anti-eroticism can seem puzzling, especially since it was
subsequently choreographed for the ballet stage with great
success. Light is shed by Roland Barthes's structuralist essay
'Striptease', which presents the very essence of a professional
striptease performance as a meticulous exorcism of sex itself:
'Evil is advertised the better to impede and exorcise it.' The
customary exoticism of décor and clothing transports the
body into the world of legend or romance, which continues to
pervade the woman with their magical virtue even after being
removed. Moreover, the dance which accompanies the act is
in no way an erotic element, consisting as it does of over-
familiar ritual gestures, as if to hide and smother nudity. The
ensuing desexualized nakedness appears as an unreal object,
beautiful and slippery, withdrawn from human use. But how
utterly unexpected that d'Indy, in conceiving this complex
and contrived work, should have crossed forbidden boundaries
into the morally subversive territory of the Moulin Rouge![10]

This, of course, raises intimate—and ultimately unanswer-
able—questions as to his private life. Was this pillar of
Catholic rectitude really an *homme sensuel* in occasional need
of a hedonistic safety-valve? Or is there rather in *Istar* a
Freudian subtext, as it is tempting to see, a coded statement
about sexual repression in respectable bourgeois society?

Any feelings of euphoria after its performance soon gave
way to intense anxiety, as d'Indy's daughter fell dangerously
ill a week later. An immediate change of air was urgently pre-
scribed. The timing, too, proved awkward, since there
remained only a month to the Paris première of *Fervaal* at the
Opéra-Comique on 26 February. Its adventurous director,
Albert Carré, recently appointed, appeared concerned to make
amends for France's neglect of its own contemporary opera; it
had been left largely to the Théâtre Royal in Brussels to pio-
neer the productions of Franck's *Hulda* and *Ghisèle*, Chabrier's
Gwendoline, Reyer's *Sigurd* and *Salammbô*, Magnard's
Yolande, and, most recently, *Fervaal*. Carré's own carefully
prepared production of the last named—conducted by André
Messager with Jeanne Raunay again in the role of Guilhen—

[10] LV ii. 239–40. R. Barthes, *Mythologies* (Paris, 1957; Eng. trans. London, 1972),
Vintage edn. 84–7.

laboured under difficulties through no fault of his own. After a fire at the Salle Favart, the Opéra-Comique had moved temporarily to the Place du Châtelet, a theatre with a constricted stage and tiny wings; when the Celtic warriors entered in Act II, their weapons got caught up in the scenery.[11]

Barcelona beckoned d'Indy back for a concert of French music. 'There was a battle over Chausson's *Soir de fête*', he told Maus; 'in spite of obstinate defenders, the whistles won against the applause.' Indeed, the general atmosphere resembled a bullfight: 'For these Catalans, there is no difference between musicians and matadors, when a bull has been killed with a beautiful sword thrust, and a symphony performed in brilliant style.' In fact, this was to be Chausson's last year; he died on 10 June 1899 on his own estate in a bicycling accident. D'Indy felt the loss keenly: 'Chausson belonged to the strong race of those who suffer through their idea before producing it'—a position with which he sympathized absolutely.

Predictably, the burden of Chausson's musical estate fell upon d'Indy to deal with. In accord with the wishes of the widow, he placed the *Chanson perpétuelle* and the unfinished String Quartet in the hands of Durand. Dutiful as ever, he undertook the completion of the Quartet under pressure from her and Lerolle. 'I always find working *on demand* infinitely difficult,' he told de Bréville—a surprising admission from one so self-disciplined. Nevertheless, the work was ready for performance at the Société Nationale in January 1900.[12]

Despite the loss of Chabrier, Lekeu, and Chausson, Franck's movement continued to gather strength. On 14 May 1899, Magnard conducted his own Symphony No. 3 at the Nouveau-Théâtre in Paris. An outstanding work of enduring value, it received due acclaim from the public and the press. 'It's a terrific thing, I'm absolutely mad about it,' exclaimed d'Indy to Ropartz. 'The last movement in particular is superb in its themes and form.'

New blood was also coming in. Joseph Jongen, a future director of the Brussels Conservatoire and representative of

[11] VI to GR, 23 Jan. 1898, BN. Durand, *Quelques souvenirs*, i. 105.
[12] VI to OM, 25 Nov. 1898, RBM. VI to GR, 22 Nov. 1898, BN. VI to PB, 29 July 1899, BN. Barricelli and Weinstein, *Ernest Chausson*, 140, 203.

Asceticism Meets the Orient

Franck's school in Belgium, became closely allied with d'Indy during his stay in Paris from 1899 to 1902, dedicating his Piano Quartet to him. And two ardent young *Franckistes* of the highest calibre occupied the organ lofts at musically prestigious churches in Paris—Charles Tournemire at Sainte-Clotilde and Louis Vierne at Notre Dame. Both were to be drawn into the work of the Schola Cantorum. Not least significant was d'Indy's discovery of the 16-year-old pianist Blanche Selva. Enraptured by her playing and extraordinary musical feeling, he reckoned that she was the only woman in his experience who played Beethoven well. Very soon, a spiritual father–daughter relationship grew up between them, and, in due course, she became a distinguished professor of piano at the Schola. By no stretch of the imagination, however, could her physical attributes inspire visions of Dante's Beatrice or Fra Lippi's angels: even d'Indy ungraciously referred to her as 'la grosse Selva'.[13]

[13] VI to GR, 10 May 1899, BN. VI to PB, 1 Oct. 1899, BN.

115

8

The Schola Cantorum in Action

The year 1900 represented a landmark in the history of the Schola Cantorum. New premises were urgently required for its burgeoning activities, and an ideal solution, both practically and symbolically, was found with the acquisition of the former English Benedictine monastery at 269 rue Saint-Jacques, beside the great church of Val-de-Grâce.

The monastery had a remarkable history. Its chapel was built in 1674, the foundation-stone having been laid by Henrietta of England, daughter of Charles I. The English Benedictine monks were under the protection of *le roi soleil*, Louis XIV himself; indeed, the Catholic James II of England and VII of Scotland, who fled to France in 1688 from the invasion of William of Orange, was buried there in 1701. Thereafter, the monastery became a refuge for Jacobite loyalists and British Catholic aristocrats. At the end of the eighteenth century, the American diplomat Benjamin Franklin stayed there while he wrote the preamble to the Constitution of the United States. The monastery's fortunes declined with the Revolution, when it was used first as a prison, and then as a cotton mill. During the nineteenth century, it served as a preparatory school for the École Polytechnique.

The building—still the Schola Cantorum today—was designed by the architect Charles d'Avilère, a pupil of Mansard, and is distinguished by its elegant courtyard and interior staircase. The former chapel became the Great Hall of the Schola, in which a Cavaillé-Coll organ was installed.[1]

[1] VI, *La Schola Cantorum*, 16–18, 72–87.

116

Before the official opening ceremony took place in November 1900, the Schola announced its presence and ambitions with a Programme Général des Assises de Musique religieuse et classique from 26 to 30 September, under the honorary presidency of Mgr. Foucault, Bishop of Saint-Dié, and Dom Pothier, a leading authority on Gregorian chant. The sheer scale and scope of these concerts was remarkable for this period, and provided an illustration of the Schola's published aims: namely, the return to the Gregorian tradition, the upholding of the style of Palestrina, the creation of modern religious music inspired by the Gregorian and Palestrinian traditions, and the improvement of the organ repertoire. The choral performances were given by Charles Bordes and Les Chanteurs de Saint-Gervais, and Alexandre Guilmant, too, was active in his capacity of Artistic President, hosting receptions and playing the organ.

Surprisingly, d'Indy—doubtless heavily engaged in the organization of the year ahead, with its schedules of courses and concerts—seems to have played no leading part on this occasion. But it is highly unlikely that he had not been involved in the programme planning, in view of its extreme boldness. As if to emphasize the continuity and evolution of music history from its origins, and to project the traditional music of the Church into the wider public domain, we find the Gregorian 'Alleluia, Salve Virgo', Roland de Lassus's 'Nos qui sumus in hoc mundo', and Victoria's 'Tanquam ad latronem' juxtaposed with arias by Bach and Handel, harpsichord pieces of Rameau, a Beethoven cello sonata, and Schumann's Violin Sonata in A minor, among other works. In a programme of modern religious music, the outstanding young composer-organist Charles Tournemire, who had been appointed to Sainte-Clotilde in 1898, played his own *Pièce symphonique*, de Séverac's *Prélude*, and Ropartz's *Sur un thème breton*; motets by d'Indy ('Deus Israel') and Bordes ('Dialogue spirituel') amongst others were heard together with Saint-Saëns's Cello Sonata and Franck's Violin Sonata.

Other attractions included lectures on Gregorian chant by Gastoué and Pothier's practical classes in plainchant. The music of the seventeenth and eighteenth centuries was not neglected, with performances of the déploration from Carissimi's *Jephthe*, Schütz's *Dialogue on the Passion*, Charpentier's 'O amor, o bonitas, o caritas', and J. S. Bach's cantata 'Bleib bei uns denn es will Abend Werden'. At the formal close, a solemn mass took place at Saint-Gervais, using Palestrina's *Missa salve regina*.[2]

It was most appropriate that it fell to d'Indy, with his breadth of knowledge extending over the entire field of music, to deliver the address at the opening ceremony of the Schola's new home on 2 November 1900. Entitled 'A School of Music Responding to Modern Needs', it proposed very radical solutions to the unsatisfactory state of music in France at that period, by attacking head on the problems of training and educating musicians.

First, he made his diagnosis in colourful terms. 'Art is not a metier': there is more to being a musician than merely playing an instrument or writing a fugue or a cantata correctly. The curse of modern society is semi-education; indeed, many musicians would be better employed as bank clerks, politicians, or representatives of Bordeaux wines. Art is not essentially a profitable occupation: 'Leave such business to the numerous Jews with whom music is encumbered.'

Yet his idealism was tempered with practicality: he strongly emphasized that singers, instrumentalists, and composers alike must first acquire a sound technique, the equivalent of fostering supple movements by military exercises. This was to be the content of the first stages of the course. But, 'where metier ends, art begins.' The second stages, by contrast, offered a spiritual education, concentrating on the areas of history, aesthetics, and their practical applications.

But in order to attain the goal, it is indispensable that these two kinds of teaching be co-ordinated in a logical way: I come thus to the method which seems to me the best and most practical way to obtain the desired result.

Art, in its course throughout the ages, can be reduced to the idea of the *microcosm*. Like the world, like peoples, like civilizations, like man himself, it goes through successive periods of youth, maturity

[2] 'Programme général des Assises de musique religieuse et classique', copy in Archives de la Maison diocésaine, Paris, Dossier 2 G2–1.

and old age, but it never dies, and renews itself perpetually. It is not a closed circle, but a spiral which constantly rises and progresses.

Adapting the same microcosmic system to the organization of my ideal school, I claim to make the students follow the same course which art itself has followed, in such a way that, reliving in their period of study the transformations undergone by music throughout the ages, they will emerge much better armed for modern combat.

There followed a comprehensive plan of d'Indy's fully integrated curriculum for singers, instrumentalists, and composers, based on a thorough historical knowledge of their fields. Moreover, a study of Gregorian and Palestrinian styles was insisted on in all courses, on the presupposition that all art—painting and architecture, as well as music—is of a religious order: 'Students will have nothing to lose and everything to gain from familiarizing themselves with the beautiful works of these ages of faith, which taken as a whole will be for the spirit like a basic stump on to which the branches of a modern social art will be grafted.'

He proceeded to demolish the popular romantic delusion that the burden of historical and analytical knowledge would rob the composer of personality and individualism, a notion surely disproved by the shining examples of Bach and Beethoven, themselves indebted to the works of their predecessors: 'War on *particularism*, that unhealthy fount of Protestantism; "everything for the good of everyone", this is the slogan which the students and professors will endeavour to put into practice.' The so-called Jewish school of nineteenth-century opera was held up as a warning against the abandonment of historical roots and the cult of originality at all costs: ironically, this could only result in a musical style liable to become dated in a short time. Another superficially modern movement, highly suspect in his eyes, was the Italian and French operatic verismo of Leoncavallo, Mascagni, Puccini, and Charpentier. By contrast, the mission of the true artist 'is not to follow the public, but to precede and guide it'.

Finally, after paying tributes to his master César Franck and his colleagues Bordes and Guilmant, d'Indy quoted from the Gregorian gradual:

Maneant in vobis fides, spes, caritas
Tria haec: major autem horum est caritas.

This most positive, forceful speech hardly seems the utterance of a pure Catholic reactionary, as d'Indy has unjustly been branded. The general tone is remarkably progressive, despite passing swipes at familiar pet hates—Jews, commercialization, and Protestantism. If, on the one hand, he condemned operatic verismo, as the musical manifestation of the hated Zola's 'social realism', he referred, on the other hand, to the creation of a modern *social* art through which Christian values would be propagated throughout society. In this, the ideas of Ruskin can be perceived, as well as the doctrine of the 'Common Good' expressed by Pope Leo XIII in his encyclical *Rerum novarum* of 1891.

Above all, it was the medieval world which informed d'Indy's vision of a transformed modernity, and he could not resist introducing some arcane symbolism. The spiral combines the circle, representing perfection, with the straight line, representing progress—one thinks of Dante's Mount Purgatory, with its rising succession of interconnected circular cornices. Even the graded hierarchy of musical courses, comprehensively listed in his speech, evokes the ascending circles of the heavens in Dante's Neoplatonic conception of Paradise; each moving circle represents an area of doctrine, with the highest, the crystalline heaven, controlling the movements of the lower. Likewise, in d'Indy's curriculum, the technical aspects of musical accomplishment were to be subservient to higher aesthetic and spiritual considerations.

The glory of him who moves everything
Penetrates the universe and shines
In one part more and, in another, less.[3]

The same month as the official opening of the Schola, there arose the threat of a rival establishment opposed to its ideals, as we learn from d'Indy in a letter to Ropartz, expressed with characteristic verbal aggression: 'Have you seen the new Dreyfusard Conservatoire under the title of "College of

[3] VI, *La Schola Cantorum*, 60–71. Holmes, *Dante*, 81–3. Dante, Para. I, lines 1–3.

Modern Aesthetics", which Bruneau, Charpentier, Zola, and Banhélier are setting up in Montmartre? Their programme is truly comical. . . . they want war, and they shall have it.' The Conservatoire, too, was up in arms. 'This war amuses me enormously,' he told Maus, 'and I bear up under it vigorously, treating it all as a bit of fun. We've got Widor setting about him and calling the Schola a business venture(!) Oh! la! la! and saying that Guilmant is only there because it brings him in a fat income!!! Now Guilmant hasn't earned five centimes in three years of teaching there, any more than I have.'

Despite d'Indy's relish for it, controversy was not the official voice of the Schola. In February 1902, the *Tablettes de la Schola* announced that it 'will never lower itself to polemics, but will reply to words by facts, and so as not to arouse jealousies, it will concern itself only with matters directly concerning the Schola'. This self-denying ordinance, indeed, was a perfectly sincere statement of its position, and moreover, consistent with that of the Ligue de la Patrie Française, as proclaimed by Barrès: France suffered from 'dissociation', its various centres of energy uncoordinated and uncooperative towards each other. The Schola had been established to effect much-needed reforms in musical education, but it acted towards other institutions in the spirit of persuasion. In fact, from 1896 to 1911, Guilmant held the organ professorships at both the Schola and the Paris Conservatoire concurrently, and in 1912, d'Indy took over the class of orchestral conducting in the latter.

Inevitably, the Schola's Catholic ethos attracted confirmed reactionaries like Léon Bloy, a polemical author and journalist who condemned all forms of modern life. He contributed articles to the *Tablettes* on St Edward the Confessor of England and on d'Indy's book on *Beethoven*. Three of his books he dedicated to d'Indy, whom he regarded as a fitting spiritual and musical director of his two daughters' education at the Schola.[4]

---

[4] VI to GR, 20 Nov. 1900, BN. VI to OM, 16 Nov. 1900, RBM. TS, Feb. 1902. R. Barrès, *Les Déracinés* (Paris, 1897), Gallimard edn. (1988), 277–83. VI, *La Schola Cantorum*, 80. L. Bloy, *Journal* (Paris, 1956–63), iii. 114, 284–7.

Yet the Schola happily avoided becoming a closed shop, for ideology was firmly counterbalanced by the practical concerns of Bordes, Guilmant, and d'Indy himself, together with a wide range of distinguished professors, among them Albéniz, Grovlez, E. Risler, Blanche Selva, J.-J. Nin (piano), de Bréville, Roussel, P. le Flem (counterpoint), Maurice Emmanuel (music theory), A. Pirro (music aesthetics), A. Gastoué (Gregorian and medieval musicology), A. Sérieyx, A. Magnard (composition). A characteristic feature of the Schola was its openness, for it exerted a significant influence on the wider musical world through its concerts and publications; the Bureau d'Édition de la Schola produced both scholarly works like Bordes's *Anthologie des Maîtres religieux primitifs* and such contemporary music as Albéniz's *Iberia*.

Reflecting d'Indy's hatred of bureaucracy, with which the Third Republic was riddled, the Schola was free of the mass of petty regulations, age and nationality limits, anachronistic rituals and even competitions, which dominated the Conservatoire. It proved ideal for late developers and those embarking on second careers, like Satie and Roussel. Despite the formidable hierarchy of the curriculum, the system in practice was operated with considerable flexibility: few students were in a position to complete d'Indy's full course in composition, which lasted no less than nine years! Many students were attracted from Spain, Romania, and South America, where French cultural influence was strong. Interestingly, some English composers considered enrolling, anxious to break free of the stifling environment of Stanford and Parry, with its Teutonic ethos. However, Vaughan Williams decided, on advice from the critic Calvocoressi, to study with Ravel instead, and Cecil Gray was prevented by the outbreak of the Great War.

The social mix of students was remarkably wide, and by no means confined to Catholics. Debussy commented favourably that 'It's a strange thing, but at the Schola, side by side, you will find the aristocracy, the most left wing of the bourgeoisie, refined artists and coarse artisans'. There was none of the snobbery or social exclusiveness of the Paris salons; but the intense devotion to music was liable to be misinterpreted. The novelist Colette, present at a performance of *L'Étranger*, noticed that 'all the Schola were there, listening as if it were the Mass'. Like many others, she found the self-conscious didacticism of the post-Franckian movement rebarbative. The detailed analytical programme note for Ropartz's *Symphonie sur un chant breton* might, she thought, aid comprehension for some people, but it merely made her feel a fool.[5]

With such imposing personalities as d'Indy and Bordes at the helm, it is hardly surprising that tensions—and even conflicts—sprang up between them. Bordes, the original driving force, living on his nerves, was prone to severe fits of Seasonal Affective Disorder brought on by prolonged spells of bad weather. In addition, he and d'Indy had very different conceptions of modern composition, with Bordes envisaging 'a free music in free discourse' according to Gregorian principles, d'Indy holding fast to his own systematic and didactic method.

In 1903, disaster struck, almost bringing about the total shipwreck of the Schola. Its establishment in the rue Saint-Jacques had strained financial resources to the limit, and under Bordes's muddled management the day duly came when a serious deficit could no longer be ignored. Even the indomitable d'Indy seemed to lose his nerve: 'I am rather terrified, I must confess, since I have poked my nose into the Schola's accounts; the situation seems to me, at a single inspection, even worse than it was two years ago!' Later, in January 1904, he confided:

But it is precisely these debts which disturb me, for I see them—I can't understand why—increase rather than diminish! . . . You cannot feel as I feel about it, the bitterness of this situation: to record the almost prodigious artistic achievement of last year and think that this will probably be the end. . . . Ah! . . . I don't suspect anyone of untrustworthiness . . . but surely of absolute incompetence . . . you can judge by these simple figures:

Debts outstanding in October 1903	30,000 fr.
Receipts of 4 November	35,000
Debts of 4 November	38,000

I don't understand.

[5] M. D. Calvocoressi, *Musicians' Gallery* (London, 1933), 283–4. C. Gray, *Musical Chairs* (London, 1985), 97. *Debussy on Music*, 98, 128.

This appalling state of affairs was finally resolved by the *conseil de direction*, which took over the financial management and paid off part of the debt, with help from Maus. Bordes, having declared himself bankrupt, resigned from the Schola and retired to Montpellier.[6]

D'Indy survived fortunately, and assumed the directorship. The alleged military style of the school's organization under his regime provoked comment, but this is only a partial view: he was far from having either the bullying manner of a sergeant-major or the remoteness of high command. His undoubted authority came not from coercion or self-assertion, but from the persuasive strength of reason and tradition. To his student, Mademoiselle de Fraguier, he said that 'one should never wish to impose one's will on others'. Ultimately, artistic disciplines were to be accepted voluntarily in the proper understanding of the tasks to be achieved.

The creation of a genuine musical community based on co-operation and mutual sympathy was fostered by the absence of competitions, compulsory membership of the choir for all students, and the sense of sharing resources, the accessibility of knowledge to everyone. D'Indy himself adopted a plain unostentatious manner, well groomed and impressive in his bearing. He loathed dandyism and affectation. When the Spanish pianist Joaquin Nin arrived for an interview 'all dressed up like a window mannequin' (as his daughter Anaïs Nin recounted), d'Indy was displeased, 'because the other pianists were so ragged, shabby, and soiled'. Yet Nin greatly impressed him with his Bach playing, gaining entry to the Schola despite being overdressed! 'Where did you learn?', asked d'Indy. 'Out of old manuscripts and my own logic', came the answer, with more than a touch of arrogance.

Despite the immense pressures on his time and energy, he cared deeply for the welfare of each individual student, personally welcoming new arrivals and introducing them to their professors. Those with problems could always take them to him and expect a sympathetic response. To Mlle de Fraguier, who was finding her piano professor, Blanche Selva, exces-

[6] Laloy, *La Musique retrouvée*, 78, 134. VI to ?, 30 Oct. 1902, n.d. 1903, 17 Jan. 1904, n.d. 1904, BN. VI to OM, 20 Jan. 1904, RBM.

sively severe, he patiently explained that Selva's attitude was necessary if the difficult gap between amateurism and professionalism were to be bridged. Many such problems were resolved in his office, he sitting at his desk with the student in the depths of a comfortable old armchair. His special affection was for the youngest members of the Schola; indeed, children he always treated with great courtesy. When he visited Strasbourg in 1905, he was taken for a tour of the city by the 14-year-old Charles Münch; the future conductor was pleasantly surprised to receive a note of thanks from the great man on his return to Paris.

For all his kindness and consideration, d'Indy's standards were high and exacting. He himself presided over most of the examinations held in January and all those in June, questioning, listening, and judging with utter impartiality and fairness. Composition students, having first had their works played on the piano, were obliged to answer *viva voce* questions on technique, music history, and *reflexion* (e.g. the future of the string quartet). Nothing was permitted to interfere with these arrangements, even when, in June 1913, he conducted performances of *Fervaal* at the Opéra. After each day's examinations had ended at 6.30, he would snatch an improvised dinner on the premises, jump into a taxi, and arrive on the podium promptly at 7.30![7]

Of integral importance in the curriculum of the Schola were its concerts, held twice monthly, and given not only for the benefit of the students, but also as a means of raising the musical taste of the general public, which was encouraged to attend. The programmes were designed to reveal the extensive panorama of music history and bring to light the then almost totally unperformed music of earlier periods. Artists of the highest distinction gave recitals, while large-scale works were tackled by the Schola's own choir and orchestra, under d'Indy's direction. His policy dispensed with outside 'stiffening' by professionals as far as possible, for he valued above all the students' fresh responses and dedication, which frequently

[7] De Fraguier, *Vincent d'Indy*, 22–3, 35–7, 43–4, 97. C. Münch, *I Am a Conductor* (New York, 1955), 17–18. A. Gabéaud, *Auprès du maître Vincent d'Indy* (Paris, 1933), i. 10, 13. A. Nin, *The Journals of Anaïs Nin 1931–1934* (London, 1966), 249.

brought interpretive results rarely attained by seasoned players.

As a conductor, he was meticulous in his preparation and utterly clear in his intentions and gestures. He searched especially for expressiveness through proper observation of accents and rhythm. If displeased during rehearsals, he would make a courteous reprimand; though occasionally he would lose his temper and break his baton! Viewing his role in military style as the centre of command, he came down heavily on players who failed to come in with leads—'If you had been watching me, that would not have happened!'

The constant theme of the critics was that the Schola's forces attempted works that were too difficult and beyond their resources. Yet d'Indy justified his often unusual choice of programmes in robust fashion. Replying to the demand of *Le Monde musical* that the Schola should celebrate the Berlioz centenary in 1903, he maintained that he was not running a concert society like the Conservatoire, Chevillard, or Colonne, but a school of art dedicated to performing works which students could not hear elsewhere. There was no point in giving symphonies of Haydn, Mozart, or Beethoven, Berlioz's *Damnation of Faust*, or Wagner's operas, which were regularly performed by other organizations, even though they were studied in the composition course.

Nevertheless, comprehensive surveys of the *œuvres* of the established masters were presented: *inter alia*, Bach's cantatas, keyboard music played on the piano by Blanche Selva, all seventeen string quartets of Beethoven, 'The History of the Violin Sonata, Bach—Beethoven—Franck', and Franck's three organ *Chorals* played by Tournemire, interspersed with Schubert songs. In the matter of the use of authentic instruments, the Schola was generally ahead of its time. Basset horns were employed, as the composer specified, in the performance of Mozart's Requiem in April 1902. In the concerts of early music, such as the Première séance de musique française ancienne des XVIIᵉ et XVIIIᵉ siècles in November 1903, the viola da gamba, viola d'amore, and harpsichord found their rightful place. On this occasion, Wanda Landowska played music by Chambonnières, François Couperin, and

Rameau; the programme also included Clérambault's cantata *Orfée*. Curiously perhaps for modern sensibilities, the harpsichord was absolutely proscribed in Bach's music, as Landowska discovered to her chagrin, when invited to play the concertos on the piano. On the other hand, the Schola admitted a Pleyel harpsichord for the French and Italian repertoire.

Some compensation for the lack of a sound French choral tradition was made with selections from Handel's oratorios *Samson* and *Judas Maccabeus* in December 1902. But Bach's Mass in B Minor met with a sour reception from Léon Bloy in March 1907: 'I shall never understand the suitability of counterpoint for the church, and the uproar of a multitude of musicians as an act of faith.'[8]

Without a doubt, the most distinctive contribution of these concerts to the increase of musical knowledge and understanding was made by d'Indy's concert performances of the operas of Monteverdi and Rameau. The researches of Romain Rolland in the libraries of Italy for his Sorbonne doctoral thesis, 'Origines du théâtre lyrique moderne: histoire de l'opéra en Europe, avant Lully et Scarlatti', had brought to light the manuscripts of Monteverdi's works, which, for the previous 200 years at least, had remained totally forgotten except as obscure dictionary references. On his return to Paris, he placed these in d'Indy's hands, a wise move. The latter's revival of Monteverdi's *Orfeo* in February 1904 constituted a landmark in the development of modern musical taste. Acts I and V were omitted on account of their lesser musical interest (in d'Indy's view), and the remaining ones were presented in a French translation. D'Indy himself had reconstructed the score from the original basso continuo, using mainly modern instruments: two piccolos, two oboes, two trumpets (in C and D), five trombones, strings (frequently divided), together with chromatic harp, lute, harpsichord, and two-manual organ (the last named played by the indefatigable Guilmant). Amusingly, the lute, provided by the Paris Opéra, had been made by

[8] De Fraguier, *Vincent d'Indy*, 91, 98. Gabéaud, *Auprès du maître*, i. 12. *Landowska on Music*, ed. D. Restout (London, 1965), 9–10. TS, Nov. 1903; see also TS, 1900–14, *passim* for programme details. Bloy, *Journal*, iii. 42.

Pleyel for Beckmesser in Wagner's *Die Meistersinger*—a connection which d'Indy must surely have relished!

To Ropartz he explained in some detail that

The three repetitions of Orfeo ['s music] could be diversified in their orchestration (*per tutti stromenti* can perfectly mean by all the instruments successively) which is very much in keeping with the spirit of Monteverdi. . . . I would thus propose to you that the eight bars of the first appearance be presented by the strings (very much divided, to give the illusion of violas da gamba written in three parts, with divided first violins singing in octaves), sustained by a gentle combination of foundation stops on the organ. The second time, the same eight bars by trombones and brass alone. The third time at last by the complete orchestra together with the organ's mutation stops.

We have no definite information on the way Monteverdi handled his orchestra, but these repetitions with different instrumentation are frequently found in the works of Italian and German composers, which leads one to think that it was traditional practice.

The symphonist in d'Indy was also fully alive to Monteverdi's dramatic exploitation of tonality, as in Act II, where the Messenger's recitative announcing the death of Euridice and Orpheus's interjections are founded on contrasts of unrelated keys (E major and G minor).

A selection of music from the Prologue and Acts I, II, and III of *L'Incoronazione di Poppea* was heard in February 1905, again in a French translation. Based on Monteverdi's manuscript in the Biblioteca Marciana, Venice (Codici Contarini), d'Indy's edition employed two oboes, strings, chittarone, and harpsichord. It included the great set pieces 'The Death of Seneca' (Act II, scene 1), Octavia's lament (Act III, scene 1), and the coronation scene (Act III). Significantly, the final, luxuriant love duet between Nero and Poppea—representing the triumph of immorality—was omitted, doubtless being inconsistent with the Schola's high ethical tone. D'Indy regarded *Poppea* as 'one of Monteverdi's most interesting works, but it certainly makes no progress on *Orfeo*'. Even here, he was never free of his medievalizing obsession, finding in Nero's recitative a vocalise on the word 'gloire' derived from Gregorian chant—a perverse comment, surely, in view of that character's total corruption! Indeed, his own personal reaction to the opera as expressed to Henri Cochin is highly revealing:

A little marvel, absolutely different from *Orfeo*, but so true in its expression! And extraordinarily youthful despite the composer's old age. There are some comic episodes but always in exquisite taste, and the character of Poppea is marvellously depicted by the composer, more than by the mediocre poet Busenello. . . . Poppea is an adorable Italian coquette of the seventeenth century.

Excerpts from no fewer than four of Rameau's operas were heard at the Schola: *Castor et Pollux* (1903), *Zoroastre* (1903), *Hippolyte et Aricie* (1904), and *Dardanus* (1907). D'Indy considered that this music 'is worthwhile above all for its *expression*, and it is mainly in the accompanied recitative that this expressiveness is remarkable'. *Dardanus* he regarded as perhaps Rameau's masterpiece, pointing out that 'in all the dramatic passages of the opera, one notices a pursuit of effect through oppositions of tonality, by a march towards the light or towards the darkness'. A fine example is the second chorus in Act II, in which a modulation from D minor to C minor corresponds to the words 'gouffres ouverts'.

The performance of the first two acts of *Castor et Pollux* in January 1903 was attended by Debussy in his critical capacity; he wrote an enthusiastic review for *Gil Blas*:

One is forced to admit that French music has, for too long, followed paths that definitely lead away from this clarity of expression, this conciseness and precision of form, both of which are the very qualities peculiar to the French genius. I've heard too much about free exchange in art, and all the marvellous effects it's had! It is no excuse for having forgotten the traditions founded in Rameau's work, unique in being so full of wonderful discoveries.

As a result of the Schola's advocacy, Rameau began to capture the attention of a wider public. *Dardanus* was performed at Dijon in 1907 under d'Indy's direction, and the following year, the Paris Opéra mounted *Hippolyte et Aricie*.[9]

[9] *Debussy on Music*, 111–16. R. Rolland, *Mémoires et souvenirs* (Paris, 1956), 194–6. CCM iii. 25–30, 50–6. VI to GR, 3 Oct. 1900, BN. VI to Henri Cochin, 6 Sept. 1904, AF.

129

In addition to his burden of administration, examinations, and choral and orchestral classes, d'Indy undertook the main part of the teaching of composition. His lectures were held in the elegant Great Hall, which was decorated in the style of the period of Louis XV, with superb wood-carvings and a rose marble fireplace supporting a huge mirror. The surrounding garden, too, contributed to an atmosphere of calm, conducive to concentration and study.

Inevitably, he often arrived late for his classes. Seated at the grand piano surrounded by his students, he expounded his subject with only a small pocket notebook open before him as an *aide-mémoire*. These lectures, according to Alice Gabéaud, were much less dry than the *Cours de composition musicale*, because he allowed himself to indulge in frequent lyrical and subjective flights of appreciation of the music under discussion. This he also illustrated on the piano with magnificent style and feeling. He liked to sing vocal parts, as well as *chansons populaires*; his voice was not devoid of expressiveness, if hardly beautiful.

For all his genuine efforts to put students at their ease, he always maintained the air of a feudal baron. While men were liable to feel a little intimidated, women adored him. If his manner of speaking was *de haut en bas*, the students did not play a passive role, being obliged to participate in the proceedings and attempt analysis on the blackboard. But despite the formidable intellectual apparatus on display, he ultimately favoured the heart above the brain. Musicality was of the essence, and he looked for moral qualities. He made a point of regarding the students' potential as an open question, refusing to prejudge their abilities. Constantly, he encouraged them to press on into more advanced areas, in the hope that they would discover new and unsuspected abilities in themselves. At the same time, he emphasized the importance of organizing one's life in order to avoid unnecessary wastage of time and energy.[10]

At the centre of d'Indy's pedagogy was the Beethovenian type of sonata and symphony, further developed by Franck

[10] Laloy, *La Musique rétrouvée*, 82. De Fraguier, *Vincent d'Indy*, 27–33, 43–7, 70–3. Gabéaud, *Auprès du maître*, i. 5–6.

with four movements interconnected by cyclic themes. Part II of the *Cours* deals exhaustively with this area, in which d'Indy made his most original and significant contribution. His treatment is quite exceptionally lucid, as well as highly schematic; it may well be objected that these works are forced to obey his own a priori formal principles. His teaching of sonata form stressed the tripartite division of exposition, development, and recapitulation; the exposition in its turn was divided into two main contrasting ideas, masculine and feminine in character, exemplified by the subjects of the first movement of Beethoven's 'Hammerklavier' Sonata, op. 106, forceful and lyrical respectively.

In the course of an extensive analysis of this sonata, d'Indy observed that Beethoven's development sections are of such a prodigious richness and an almost infinite variety as to defy rigorous classification.

Each development bears the trace of a ripely pondered plan of construction: to each work corresponds a special plan which one can easily analyse: one discerns there periods of tonal *transition* and *immobility* alternating regularly; stages judiciously determined in keys related one to the other; modulations oriented towards the light or the shade.

As well as prescribing the role of tonality, d'Indy analysed the processes of organic development in terms of amplification, elimination, and superimposition of the elements of rhythm, melody, and harmony. Olivier Messiaen, who, as a student at the Conservatoire in the 1920s, was deeply impressed with this part of the *Cours*, has provided his own commentary on the process of elimination in his *Technique de mon langage musical* (1944):

This procedure is at the basis of all thematic life. It consists of repeating a fragment of the theme, taking away from it successively some of its notes until it is concentrated upon itself, reduced to a schematic state, shrunk by strife, by crisis. Vincent d'Indy explained that very well in his *Cours de composition musicale*.

Nevertheless, there seems to be little place in d'Indy's pedagogic system for spontaneous fantasy, the unconscious, or the unpremeditated. Rather, a pitiless, searchlight glare dispels the darkness and mystery of creative inspiration: 'It is necessary to distrust writing everything which comes to mind. One must make a *very severe* choice, work and rework to the point where one has found what is definitely suitable.'[11]

In practice, however, he did not remain completely imprisoned in his system. When Déodat de Sévérac showed him his four-movement Piano Sonata, it was its total adherence to the sacred principle of cyclic form which met with criticism: d'Indy pencilled in that 'I don't see the *necessity* of bringing all the themes back like this'. Perhaps he considered its charming folk-inspired material not sufficiently weighty to support the full cyclical apparatus, although the transformation of the mercurial scherzo into the finale's choral is an inspired stroke.

The students were encouraged to think for themselves and express their opinions, as long as they were well founded. On one occasion, d'Indy set them a detailed analysis and appreciation of Strauss's opera *Salomé*, although he personally deplored both its vulgarity and the aesthetics of Wilde's play. But he accepted Samazeuilh's praise of the music's dramatic power and mastery of the orchestra. With great humility, d'Indy was even prepared to discuss his own compositions. He admitted that his Second Symphony contained things that he would not do any more, and attributed the success *italianisé* (*sic*) of *Istar* to its final unison passage.

Not restricting himself to a limited canon of acknowledged masterpieces, he ranged over the field of nineteenth-century nationalism, explaining Dargomyzhsky's opera *The Stone Guest* and Mussorgsky's *Boris Godunov* and *Khovantchina* with the help of Laloy, a colleague who understood Russian. Of Grieg, however, he was highly critical—a composer incapable of logic, more sensitive to the charm of a chord than to musical argument in his view.[12]

---

[11] CCM ii, Pt. 1, 240–5, 270–80. O. Messiaen, *Technique de mon langage musical* (Paris, 1944), text 44. *Idem, Musique et couleur, nouveaux entretiens avec Claude Samuel* (Paris, 1986), 191. De Fraguier, *Vincent d'Indy*, 96.

[12] Guillot, Introduction to de Sévérac's Piano Sonata, Éditions musicales du Marais (1990), p. iii. *Richard Strauss and Romain Rolland*, 7. CCM iii. 241. De Fraguier, *Vincent d'Indy*, 95. Laloy, *La Musique retrouvée*, 85.

In his analysis of harmony, d'Indy was almost brutally reductionist. All dissonance he explained as essentially a passing phenomenon, a melodic alteration or decoration of a basic chord progression. In the case of Wagner's celebrated 'Tristan chord', whereas most theorists have offered convoluted explanations (e.g. third inversion of the diminished seventh on G with the alteration of D), d'Indy ruthlessly stripped away the chromatic undergrowth to reveal a simple progression: subdominant to dominant. In trenchant terms, he condemned 'the dangerous aesthetic error of classifying chords and establishing different rules for each of them, thus granting them a distinct reality'. He would certainly have agreed with Ruskin that 'the chords of music, the harmonies of colour, the general principles of the arrangement of sculptural masses, have been determined long ago, and in all probability, cannot be added to any more than they can be altered'.

Indeed, his wrath was truly kindled when a student of mildly revolutionary tendencies brought to the class a sonata composed entirely in 'wrong notes': 'This is not music, this is ugly . . . I do not want anyone who writes in this way to claim my authority.' Again, Ruskin's words from 'The Lamp of Obedience' exactly express d'Indy's own position: 'Those liberties will be like the liberties that a great speaker takes with the language, not a defiance of its rules for the sake of singularity.'

For all his admiration, he could not but regard Debussy as a dangerous model for composers. It was a matter of the overemphasis of the harmonic dimension at the expense of melody and rhythm. D'Indy considered that 'chains of seconds and augmented fifths become dated very easily through abuse. That is not to say that these harmonies should never be used, rather they should not be the goal of composition.'[13]

A number of his more gifted pupils did, in fact, succeed in using impressionistic elements consistently with the approved styles of the Schola. This was the case with Joaquin Turina from Spain, who enrolled there in 1905 on Albéniz's recommendation, in order to acquire a solid technical foundation. In

[13] CCM i. 116–19; Ruskin, *Seven Lamps of Architecture*, 203–4. De Fraguier, *Vincent d'Indy*, 93. Gabéaud, *Auprès du maître*, i. 24.

1907, his cyclic Piano Quintet was performed in the Salle d'Automne, together with three movements of Albéniz's *Iberia*. By the time he left the Schola in 1913, with d'Indy's endorsement of his assiduous attendance in class, he had completed his *Suite Sevillana* and *La Procession del Rocío*, in which he had endeavoured to combine Debussian harmony with d'Indy's teachings on form and counterpoint.

Erik Satie, likewise, had no illusions about his technical shortcomings. A docile student, he graduated from the Schola in 1908 with a diploma in counterpoint (*très bien*) signed by d'Indy and Roussel. D'Indy had set him a series of formal analyses: a motet by Palestrina, Contrapunctus no. 7 from Bach's *Art of Fugue*, and, surprisingly perhaps, Ravel's *Nöel des jouets*. This enabled him to purge his style of its eccentric harmonic idiom, the fruit of his sojourn in Péladan's *Rose + Croix* salon. Orchestration, however, was not Satie's strong point, and a profligate use of instruments in some student exercise drew a caustic comment from his master: 'Three trumpets means the end of the world.'

The author and musicologist Romain Rolland, who admired d'Indy, nevertheless admitted that 'his intelligent eclecticism was perfectly suited to developing the critical faculty, but rather less to forming original personalities'. In this respect, the case of Albert Roussel—doubtless the most outstanding product of d'Indy's teaching—is particularly illuminating. An extraordinarily late developer, he had retired from a career in the French navy in order to study music. A creative conservative, he carried on the symphony as a valid medium of musical expression right through the iconoclastic 1920s and into the 1930s. Although he never rejected the classical values and love of order instilled by d'Indy, the music of Debussy acted as a necessary liberation from the cramping effects of these disciplines; it is significant that his hard-won neoclassical style could absorb both impressionist and oriental influences without disintegration.[14]

On the few occasions when d'Indy was confronted with true

[14] A. Livermore, *A Short History of Spanish Music* (London, 1972), 200–1. G. Chase, *The Music of Spain* (New York, 1941), 175–6. A. M. Gillmor, *Erik Satie* (London, 1988), 134–42. B. Deane, *Albert Roussel* (London, 1961), 8–10, 28–9.

radical genius, the situation became explosive. Béla Bartók, on a visit to Paris, was given introductions to various leading musicians by Busoni and Isidor Philipp. Full of youthful arrogance, he declined to see Widor, and showed little humility in the presence of the director of the Schola.

Vincent d'Indy turned me down completely: *il faut choisir les thèmes*— — — that was really all he had to say. For instance, in the third movement of my *Second Suite*, he didn't feel any key or form!! etc., etc. . . . my meeting with d'Indy was very like when a celebrated professor condescends to receive a beginner and kindly gives him a few hints. *Enfin!* I have had enough of that, and I'm not looking for more.

Similarly, the Italian Edgard Varèse, the future composer of such uncompromisingly modernist scores as *Intégrales*, *Ionisation*, and the *Poème électronique*, very soon formed an intense dislike, amounting to paranoiac hatred, of d'Indy during his year at the Schola in 1904. A man in permanent revolt, his revulsion against his master's Catholic principles, his authority, and paternalism was equalled only by his feelings towards his brutal father, whose characteristics were undoubtedly projected psychologically on to d'Indy himself. The latter's high-minded Ruskinian dictum that 'The aim of art is to teach, and gradually to elevate, the spirit of humanity' can only have seemed pious humbug. After a year, Varèse left the Schola to join Widor's class at the Conservatoire, a move which he subsequently justified on the grounds that d'Indy's idea of teaching 'was to form disciples. His vanity would not permit the least sign of originality or even independent thinking, and I did not want to become a little Vincent d'Indy. One was enough.' Such is the prestige of Varèse in the twentieth century that this blatant misrepresentation has been generally accepted as true.

Yet Varèse had not wasted his time at the Schola, for he was on excellent terms with Bordes and Roussel, with whom he studied medieval and Renaissance music, and counterpoint and fugue, respectively. Among his fellow students, his special friend was Paul le Flem, who was to succeed Bordes as conductor of Les Chanteurs de Saint-Gervais. Above all, it was

the revelation of the wealth of music before Bach, from
Pérotin, Machaut, and Dufay to Josquin, Palestrina, Victoria,
Monteverdi, and Schütz, which inspired him to develop a new
sound world of his own. This was surely a splendid instance of
the continuity between the past and future of which d'Indy
would have approved in principle, even if Varèse's conceptions
were to go far beyond what the older man, by any stretch of
the imagination, regarded as music.[15]

On the question of the education of women, d'Indy and his
colleagues at the Schola operated an entirely enlightened policy. As is well known, prejudice against the idea of the woman
composer was strongly entrenched in the cultural world, and
Saint-Saëns has rightly attracted much opprobrium for
attempting to block female aspirants to the Prix de Rome, as
in the famous case of Nadia Boulanger, a pupil of Fauré and
Widor at the Conservatoire. At the same time, such a phenomenon as Cécile Chaminade certainly did exist, providing
an acceptable stereotype of a purveyor of light-weight salon
pieces of a natural feminine sweetness and charm. Arguably,
this state of affairs reflected the generally prevailing exclusion
of women from the opportunity to acquire the formal skills of
counterpoint and orchestration necessary for the creation of
the large-scale, complex 'higher' structures of the symphony
and opera. At this point, the case becomes entangled in the
thickets of modern feminist theory and politics. According to
Marcia J. Citron, the symphonic aesthetic—exemplified by
d'Indy and the Schola—embodies masculinist values; and
indeed, we have seen how d'Indy, on the level of symbolism,
conceived the tensions and resolutions of sonata forms in
highly sexist terms. Following the German theorists Marx and
Riemann, the *Cours* presents them as a gendered struggle
between two main themes, characterized as masculine and
feminine respectively, the first full of force and energy, the
second entirely gentle and melodically graceful. Very significant for Ms Citron is the hierarchical relationship of tonal

15 *Béla Bartók Letters*, ed. J. Demeny (London, 1971), 96. L. Varèse, *A Looking-glass Diary* (London, 1973), 31–2. F. Ouellette, *Edgard Varèse, a Musical Biography* (London, 1973), 14–15.

functions, with the feminine theme in the recapitulation brought within the tonal sphere of the masculine theme (i.e. in the tonic key): 'It is as if, after the active battle of the development, the being of gentleness and weakness has to submit, whether by violence or persuasion, to the conquest of the being of force and power.' These images 'hint at sexual domination gone awry—possibly rape'.

In defence of the Schola, the counter-example of the Princesse Armand de Polignac, the niece of Prince Edmond and classmate on equal terms with Varèse, can be cited. Enabled by its comprehensive teachings to master the necessary techniques, she became the composer of three operas and the symphony *Les Mille et une nuits*, as well as the first Frenchwoman to conduct professional orchestras in public. Moreover, she established her reputation among the young avant-garde through personal charm rather than feminist aggression.[16]

On the national political plane, the Ligue de la Patrie française, through its lack of clear identity and purpose, soon began to be overshadowed by another more intellectually formidable movement, the Action française, headed by the redoubtable Charles Maurras. He believed in the principle of a strong hereditary monarchy, expressed in dogma of uncompromising precision and clarity. He emphasized the order and discipline which purportedly characterized the Roman Empire, the Middle Ages, and the *Grand Siècle* of Louis XIV. He supported the Catholic Church as a carrier of Roman civilization and of the Latin tradition, with its sense of harmony and measure, as opposed to the Germanic metaphysical passion for the infinite. For Maurras, the integrity of France lay not only in armed defence, but also in maintaining classical traditions.

According to this philosophy, only a hereditary monarchy could provide a better administration of France, and uproot the evils of a centralized bureaucratic state in which powerful minority groups held power disproportionate to their numbers:

[16] Citron, *Gender and the Musical Canon*, 46, 132–41, 186–7. De Cossart, *The Food of Love*, 105–6.

the Jews especially, with their distinctive characteristics and habits of monopolization, speculation, and cosmopolitanism, he regarded as a race without roots, unattached to the French nation. The presence of foreign workers, too, seemed to undermine the country, as well as pose a threat to French workers. By contrast, a restored monarchy would safeguard the autonomy of the regions within a federal state. Thus each region could evolve in its own rhythm, according to its own needs. The true strength of France ultimately lay in the vitality of the provinces.

Although d'Indy did not actually join with Maurras, these ideas did exert some influence in the Schola; an important aspect of its work lay in its concern for the cultural life of the regions, putting out shoots with the conservatoires at Nancy, Bordeaux, Lyon, Avignon, Marseilles, and Montpellier. For his thesis, de Sévérac wrote 'La Centralisation et les petites chapelles en musique', in which he advocated decentralization, urging French composers to draw on regional sources, as he himself did in such piano works as *Languedoc* and *En Vacances*. D'Indy made collections of folksongs from his own Vivarais area, and Canteloube's reputation rests largely upon the *Chants de l'Auvergne*; le Flem's native Brittany inspired his operas *Aucassin et Nicolette* and *Le Rossignol de Saint Malo*. Burgundy was the source of Varèse's very early symphonic poem *Bourgogne* (in which Rolland detected marked traces of d'Indy's style!). Subsequently destroyed, it evoked the church of Saint-Philibert in Tournus; he saw Romanesque architecture as the visual counterpart of the early polyphonic music which he had studied at the Schola.

Concern for the regions was particularly acute with regard to the borders of Germany, where the whole of Alsace and part of Lorraine had been annexed by the victors of the Franco-Prussian War of 1870. The intense desire on the part of France to keep its civilization and ideas alive in the conquered territories was strongly articulated by Barrès, himself from Lorraine. But, as with d'Indy, his Germanophobia took aim specifically at 'The Boche'—Prussian domination under Bismarck and the Kaiser. In his political novel *Au Service de l'Allemagne* (1905), Barrès wrote of the need to 'Romanize the

Germans': in his view, the regions of Trèves, the Saar, and the Rhineland suffered as much as Alsace-Lorraine under the heel of the Prussians. The contemporary mission of France, therefore, should be to infiltrate Germany with its Latin culture.[17]

In 1894, d'Indy's friend and colleague at the Schola, Ropartz, was appointed director of the Nancy Conservatoire in unoccupied Lorraine. Close to the 'frontier', he effected a musical Renaissance with his series of orchestral concerts. D'Indy kept in constant touch, supplying him with a stream of practical advice, ranging from the orchestration of Lully's works to the interpretation of Beethoven's symphonies, and finding a viable substitute for the bells in *Parsifal*. When he was offered the directorship of the Strasbourg Conservatoire in 1907, Ropartz naturally turned to d'Indy, who pointed out the possibilities it provided for an expansion of French influence and sensibility, through the 'exchange of ideas and talents between Paris and Strasbourg, making a counterbalance to the exchange between Strasbourg and Berlin'.

His letter ended with a solemn warning—indeed, a tirade—against Protestantism: 'most dangerous of all from the artistic standpoint'. Even Albert Schweitzer, the celebrated Alsatian organist and theologian whose book *J. S. Bach: le musicien-poète* had appeared two years earlier, in 1905, was accused of reducing Bach's life and work to the level of his own sectarian ideas.

Be very much on your guard against people of this kind, they are cunning, and if some are sincere and convinced, the majority are generally false. In the Dreyfus affair, from which we are dying, they had not been the active element but rather the poisonous channel, and did too much harm to France (they are still at it in the university, which belongs to them) . . . This is the true danger at Strasbourg.[18]

[17] Y. Chiron, *Maurice Barrès, le prince de la jeunesse* (Paris, 1986), 137–50, 212–16. Sisson, 'Charles Maurras', in *The Avoidance of Literature* (Manchester, 1978), 96–103. Varèse, *Looking-glass Diary*, 58–9, 68–9. VI, *La Schola Cantorum*.

[18] VI to GR, 17 Aug. 1894, 1 Nov. 1896, 22 Sept. 1900, 7 Aug. 1907, BN. GR eventually became director of the Strasbourg Conservatoire in 1919, after the return of Alsace-Lorraine to France.

9

Breaking the Boundaries

All his friends could call on d'Indy for fatherly advice at times of difficulty and crisis. He himself well understood the dark night of the soul through which the creative artist must pass in order to arrive at a clearer knowledge of himself and his capabilities. Writing to de Bréville, afflicted by a mood of total discouragement, he advised him that his state of mind seemed to indicate a musical transformation:

You know that no modification of human existence can take place without pain. . . . It is only the feeble and impotent who do not suffer and become discouraged many times in the course of their career. Believe me, there is no such thing as useless suffering—I have indeed experienced it myself, and I'm convinced that you, yes you, are in a period of transition, which, *as long as you don't give up* (as some have done), can—contrary to what you think—be infinitely profitable to you.'[1]

The gestation of his next opera, *L'Étranger*, must, without doubt, have involved d'Indy in some profound self-questioning. His sense of intellectual honesty now compelled him to move away from the congenial areas of history in which his previous works, from *Wallenstein* to *Fervaal*, were set, in order to confront the painful and immediate problems of modern society. Thoroughly disturbed by the increasing acceptance of scientific materialism and its corollary, the pursuit of pleasure and comfort, as fundamental values, his own aristocratic and military background disposed him to assert a contrary posi-

[1] VI to PB, 28 Sept. 1899, BN.

tion: in the words of Léon Bloy, 'A characteristic feature of the bourgeois is a fear of all heroic determination in others, as well as in himself.' Philosophical questions of free will and determinism, freedom and authority, and (in twentieth-century existentialist parlance) authentic and inauthentic human life, constantly agitated d'Indy's mind.

On ideological and personal grounds, he remained totally opposed to Émile Zola—champion of Dreyfus and scourge of the Church—whose *Les Rougon-Macquart* series of naturalistic novels were generally taken to embody crude notions of scientific determinism and a denial of free will and personal responsibility. On the other hand, d'Indy was acutely aware that the religion of light which had triumphed over pantheism in *Fervaal* had degenerated into bourgeois Christian respectability. If the Church still represented the historic principles of order and authority, its moral teachings were all too liable to restrict the flow of dynamic spiritual energy. In this impasse, he discovered in the plays of Henrik Ibsen—which had recently made an impact on French cultural life—symbolic acts of heroic self-realization in confrontation with middle-class Protestant society and its conventions. *Brand* portrays an idealistic, ruthlessly uncompromising reformer of the world; the mysterious stranger in *The Lady from the Sea* offers a respectable woman a chance to escape from the stifling confines of matrimony and live her own true life. These conceptions have indeed left some mark on *L'Étranger*, set in a fishing village, closed and self-preserving, on the south-west coast of France.

The arrival of the Stranger, devoted to the poor and the disconsolate, presents the disturbing force of creative religious inspiration, the transforming shock of universal human morality. He is also the possessor of a magic emerald—a naïve touch of the fairytale world of Hans Christian Andersen, d'Indy's childhood favourite—capable of calming the sea around him. His fate is to be rejected by all except the girl Vita, a complex character who belongs partly to the bourgeois world and is betrothed to an ambitious young customs official, yet has vague spiritual longings, and communes in solitude with the sea. The growing love for each other of the Stranger and Vita, despite its purity and idealism, is ultimately doomed in earthly terms, since it undermines his obligation to remain single and chaste in the pursuit of his mission to mankind. (Again, the obsessive theme of sexual renunciation.)

The heterogeneous nature of d'Indy's libretto, with its eclectic mix of social realism and poetic symbolism, brought into being a corresponding profusion of musical styles, necessitating all his power of will to forge them into a coherent artistic conception. Ibsen's influence is again apparent in the drama itself, much of which takes place on an intimate psychological level. As d'Indy explained to the critic Willy (husband of Colette), 'the action is absolutely *internal* and is only manifest externally at the end of the last Act. *No showy costumes*, no décor—the same thing, a rock in both Acts.' Above all, he attached great importance to the intelligibility of the words; 'but where the sentiment is inexpressible through words, the orchestra comes to assist in all its vigour and passion'. Employing more or less standard orchestral forces, he abandoned the massed saxhorn and tuba sonorities of *Fervaal* in favour of the biting timbres of trumpets and trombones, more appropriate for the evocation of a seascape; the unusual contrabass trombone replaces the tuba as the bass of the brass section, while the piccolo trumpet in D, together with rare trombones *à six pistons*, appear in the final storm scene.

Act I opens with a stoical, folk-style chorus of fishermen, singing a song of toil and unremitting hardship, with which d'Indy's aristocratic paternalism could sympathize. On the other hand, his ideological contempt for the bourgeois order, its materialistic values, and hypocritical manners—manifest in the unedifying courting rituals and silly tactics of arousing jealousy—is reflected in the deliberately banal verismo-style music of André, the customs officer who fulfils his function according to the letter of the law, without feelings of charity; Vita's mother, who encourages the match; and even an aspect of Vita herself in her association with them. In a letter to de Bréville, d'Indy admitted that 'there are some true Opéra-Comique scenes, nothing of Auber, but perhaps much of Grétry with a twentieth-century sauce—you will see—perhaps you will be quite disillusioned with your old friend'. Indeed, one can sense the influence of such despised figures of Zola's entourage as Alfred Bruneau in Vita's light-headed, sentimental effusion of love towards André, with its characteristic triplet phrases.

The triviality of the everyday world, however, serves as an admirable foil to the rarefied dimension of the Stranger, musically characterized by two magnificent liturgical-style themes of assurance and charity, perfect in their expression of his generalized love for humanity, and for Vita as the feminine ideal. As Debussy was to say, 'They illuminate the profound meaning of the drama better than any kind of symphonic commentary.' The tortuous path of love leads these characters through the two great duet scenes in Acts I and II, strongly indebted in conception to Ibsen's conversation dramas. In the second of these the Stranger makes his final decision to leave Vita, despite her pleas that she is doomed to eternal misery. The musical structure shows a high degree of organization and contrivance: its *chiaroscuro*-like trajectory of keys begins in F major, with the motif of charity expanding into the luminous tonal regions of A, F sharp, and D major, as the Stranger expresses his intention to serve the poor and disconsolate (Ex. 6a). However, as he begins to explain to Vita that the hate and scorn he attracts would harm her if she were to follow him, the darker, more profound tonal areas of C and A minor underline the motif of suffering. In thus protecting her, he may be seen to be unwittingly restricting her freedom to discover herself through conflict with the world.

Dominating the entire opera is the mighty Atlantic Ocean, its varying moods from calm stillness in the Prélude to the final raging tempest, depicted in most strikingly original musical imagery—which, moreover, may have acted as a catalyst for Debussy's own singular powers of invention in *La Mer* two years later. In Act II's 'Invocation to the Sea', Vita addresses it fondly as her sole source of love and consolation, just as for Ellida in *The Lady from the Sea* it represented the boundless and the infinite, the expression of a growing urge for freedom. Vita's pantheistic merging into primordial nature is reflected in the music's expansiveness: large intervals characterize her vocal line, which is accompanied by very slow-changing harmonies, harp figurations, and sustained string harmonics.

Ex. 6a. *L'Étranger*, Act II, scene 2: dialogue between the Stranger and Vita, in which he professes his love for the poor and the outcast

Ex. 6b. *L'Étranger*, Act II, scene 3: catastrophe

After her final rejection by the Stranger, she throws the magic emerald given to her as a keepsake, but now devoid of its power, into the sea. Thereupon a great storm arises, and at last the Stranger realizes his mission by setting forth in a small boat to rescue a fishing craft in distress; Vita insists on joining him at the last moment. The assistance of the coast-guard authorities pales into pathetic insignificance, for the Stranger and Vita alone possess the moral strength to enter the maelstrom. Meeting their death, they achieve a symbolic sacrifice for mankind and achieve mystical union with each other, a Christian apotheosis underlined by the Gregorian chant 'De profundis' briefly intoned by an old fisherman.

D'Indy's conception, interestingly, shows some indebtedness to Maeterlinck's play *La Princesse Maleine*, which he had previously considered as a libretto. Its action likewise takes place amid violent thunderstorms of a supernatural force, and, after Maleine's murder, the same chant is heard, sung by the nuns. In *L'Étranger*, the storm, like the avalanche which overwhelms Brand, may readily be conceived in theological terms as a manifestation of the wrath of God ($\dot{o}\rho\gamma\grave{\eta}$ $\theta\epsilon o\hat{v}$); terrible in its overpowering energy and irrational might, it threatens to inundate decadent civilization, together with its ossified religion and morality.[2]

Musically, this scene is a superb example of sustained nature painting and orchestral invention, in which d'Indy drew on his own direct experience of such a tempest while staying at Biarritz. The screaming high register of the piccolo trumpet and the chromatic roaring of the two trombones *à six pistons* admirably evoke the upheaval of the elements. Indeed, he displayed an amazing aural acuteness in capturing the howl of the gale in an extraordinary passage scored for brass; further, its anticipation of a similar passage in the last movement of Debussy's *La Mer* ('Dialogue du vent et de la mer') at figure 43 is remarkable (Ex. 6*b*).

By mid-October 1900, d'Indy had completed the vocal score, having worked relatively quickly. Other commitments,

[2] Bloy, *Journal*, ii, 155. VI to Willy, 31 Aug. 1899, BN. VI to PB, 28 Sept. 1899, 29 Oct. 1901, BN. VI to Calvocoressi, 26 June 1902, BN. *Debussy on Music*, 87–91. R. Otto, *The Idea of the Holy*, Penguin edn. (London, 1959), 32–3.

however, were pressing hard, notably the great move and rein-auguration of the Schola Cantorum, as well as the troublesome realization of Rameau's *Hippolyte et Aricie*. As a result, he had to postpone the orchestration to the following summer vacation. In order to complete it on schedule for Brussels, he forced himself to work on it for fifteen hours each day, a ridiculous ordeal even for the most superhuman of men. These pressures, combined, no doubt, with anxiety about the opera's reception, were hardly calculated to improve his temper. Rather churlishly, he did not visit Rimsky-Korsakov in the green room after a concert of *Sadko* and *Scheherazade* in Brussels. More predictably, he stormed out of the final rehearsal of Charpentier's new Zolaesque opera *Louise*, 'banging the doors in a state of pathological fury', according to Debussy's friend, the poet Pierre Louÿs.

A comparatively light assignment was the performance d'Indy conducted at the Salle Érard of two of Frederick Delius's Danish songs on 16 March 1901, sung in French by Christianne Andray. Debussy found them 'very sweet songs, very pale, music to lull convalescent ladies to sleep in rich districts'. He was probably blissfully unaware of the irony of his facetious observation, for, if he gently mocked the essential passivity of Delius's songs, it was this very same aesthetic sensibility which d'Indy would censure in *Pelléas et Mélisande*, whose long-delayed première took place in April 1902 at the Opéra-Comique. For him, the experience of hearing the work in its entirety came as a profound cultural shock, an implied attack on his own hard-won musical values. His initial reaction was categorical: 'It has no form; it will not live.' Indeed, the music seemed to be merely the slave of Maeterlinck's drama, following the poem word by word.

Confronted by the entirely positive and enthusiastic response of his friends Messager (the conductor), Dukas, and Poujard, he decided to reserve judgement until he had attended a subsequent performance. By June he was prepared to state publicly in an article in *l'Occident* (Brussels) that '[Debussy] has in fact simply felt and expressed *human* feelings and *human* sufferings in *human* terms, despite the outward appearance the characters present of living in a mysterious dream'. And indeed, for all the marked differences in the two composers' aesthetic positions, there do exist some points of convergence in the styles of *Pelléas* and *L'Étranger*, particularly the desire to create musical textures that allow the words to be distinctly audible.

Nevertheless, d'Indy continued to voice reservations about *Pelléas*. It was not precisely a drama, but a suite of *tableaux dramatiques*: 'the musical elements, in pale tints, rather like colours in a Missal, create an atmosphere, but are completely sacrificed to declamation. It is a return—*mutatis mutandis*—to the *stile recitativo* of the old Florentines [Peri and Caccini]. The drama creates the music, not vice-versa.' And 'Debussy's preoccupation with rare harmonies is nothing else but an amplification of Wagner's discoveries'. Ultimately, *Pelléas* constituted 'an aesthetic of sensation, a principle hardly compatible with the true aim of great art'.

How very different from the active, productive, socially engaged philosophy of Ruskin! D'Indy's view of *Pelléas*'s aesthetic seems close to Walter Pater's almost shockingly egotistical vision of ideal beauty in *The Renaissance*, implying a withdrawal from the ordinary world: 'For art comes to you proposing frankly to give nothing but the highest quality to your moments as they pass, and simply for those moments' sake.' Sensing the cultural forces of solipsism and decadence, d'Indy reasserted in his *Cours* the humanistic and ethical values which were embodied in symphonic architecture: 'Reason, will and faith which guide man in the thousand tribulations of life, equally guide the composer in the choice of modulations.' Yet he cannot have remained blind to the dangers of exclusivity, monumentalism, and atrophy of musical language and forms which were liable to result from an excessively rigorous adherence to his pedagogic doctrines. Reading Ibsen's *Brand*, he may well have been disturbed by a reflection of his own shortcomings: the urge to impose his will, a marked tendency to uncompromising dogmatism in the service of God, but to the detriment of love and happiness. Moreover, the fashionable irrationalist philosophy of Henri Bergson was becoming academically respectable: this stressed the primacy of intuition and passivity over reason and analysis, the

Vincent d'Indy and His World

exaltation of the *élan vital* as the creative source of being, in a permanent state of flux and change.[3]

Although Debussy's music was a dubious model for composition students, in the hands of pure genius, d'Indy recognized, unsystematic procedures could justify themselves. Writing about the *Nocturnes* (1899), he pointed out their

> very vague titles, no literary programme, no explanation in terms of dramatic character are forthcoming to justify the strayings of tonality and thematic excursions, pleasing though uncoordinated, of these three movements. So it's a case of the good old *fantaisie*, for one cannot reject these pieces for 'bad craftsmanship', as one would in the case of Bruneau or X. Leroux; they are artistic, they are *alive*.[4]

The première of *L'Étranger* took place at the Théâtre Royal de la Monnaie in Brussels on 7 January 1903, with M. Albert and Claire Friché in the roles of the Stranger and Vita. Much credit was due to the conductor Sylvain Dupuis, an enthusiastic champion of d'Indy's music in Belgium. Present in his new capacity as critic for the daily newspaper *Gil Blas*, Debussy abandoned his habitual morose demeanour, and threw himself into d'Indy's arms at the end of the performance. His review notice expressed his genuine appreciation of the work as a whole, with certain reservations:

> It certainly unfolds in pure and lofty forms, but they have all the intricacy, coldness, hardness, even blueness of a machine of steel. The music appeared to be very beautiful, but it was as if it were veiled; its workmanship struck one so powerfully that one scarcely dared to let oneself be moved—an uncomfortable feeling . . . Let he who will, look freely for unfathomable symbols in this play. I like to see it as a human tale that d'Indy had clothed with symbols only in order to render more deeply the eternal gulf between beauty and the vulgarity of the masses. Without dwelling on technical questions, I want to pay homage to the serenity that runs right through this work.

[3] N. Rimsky-Korsakov, *My Musical Life* (London, 1974), 390. *Correspondance de Claude Debussy et Pierre Louÿs*, 135–6. L. Carley, *Delius, a Life in Letters*, vol. 1: *1862–1908* (London, 1983), 74, 183–4. L. Carley, *Delius, the Paris Years* (London, 1975) 74. LV ii. 49–52. R. Nichols and R. Langham Smith, *Claude Debussy, Pelléas et Mélisande* (Cambridge, 1989), 149. CCM i. 132, iii. 230–1. W. Pater, *The Renaissance* (Oxford, 1986), 153. L. Kolakowski, *Bergson* (Oxford, 1985), 53–65.
[4] *Lettres à Auguste Sérieyx, etc.* (Paris, 1961), 16.

Performances followed soon afterwards at the Paris Opéra, its director, Gailhard, having been persuaded by Durand to mount it. *L'Étranger*'s reputation rapidly reached Berlin, where the celebrated pianist, composer, and conductor Ferruccio Busoni had embarked on an enterprising but controversial series of concerts of contemporary music with the Philharmonic Orchestra in the Beethovensaal. In November 1903, he programmed its Prélude, together with Debussy's *L'Après-midi d'un faune*, and Franck's *Les Djinns*. D'Indy he held in the highest esteem, mentioning him in the same breath as the great Classical and Romantic composers in his *Outline for a New Musical Aesthetics*.[5] With the perspective of time, this valuation seems exaggerated, but there is little doubt about the lofty aspirations of d'Indy's Second Symphony in B flat, completed that year. Whereas the earlier *Symphonie Cévenole* is essentially impressionistic in character, a musical landscape painting, the new symphony stands as a monument to the pedagogic principles which he expounded at the Schola Cantorum; a great cathedral-like sonorous structure employing the full post-Franckian cyclical apparatus in an affirmation of the eternal and absolute values embodied in medieval Christendom.

It is not, however, a purely abstract work of musical architecture, for the argument symbolizes a conflict between the forces of chaos and a higher order, represented by two opposing cyclic themes set out in the introduction. 'Motto A', formed from the notes B♭, D♭, C, E, is stern, almost 'Faustian', with the potential to produce most fantastic outgrowths; while 'motto B' is all feminine sweetness and innocence, possessing powers of integration (Ex. 7*a*).

During the course of the regular sonata-form first movement, 'motto A' infiltrates the transitions between the two subjects and also the central development; having undergone significant intervallic expansion by semitones, it gives rise to whole-tone harmony in shimmering impressionistic textures with harp *glissandi*. Like the roots of an exotic tree growing within the foundations of an imposing classical building, these

---

[5] Durand, *Quelques souvenirs*, i. 118. *Debussy on Music*, 87–91. H. H. Stuckenschmidt, *Ferruccio Busoni* (London, 1970), 35, 137.

Ex. 7a. Symphony No. 2 in B flat, motto themes A and B

Ex. 7b. Symphony No. 2 in B flat, first movement (development)

tonally and structurally disintegrative forces pose a threat to the order and authority of the symphonic ideal (Ex. 7*b*). 'Motto B', on the other hand, takes its rightful place firmly within the structure as the basis of the graceful second subject—in contrast to the muscular, energetic first subject—and of the lyrical main theme of the slow movement, a *Lied* in five sections.

The wild mountains of the Cévennes were the inspiration for the short Scherzo, whose rugged main theme, popular in character with its unexpected flattened supertonic inflection, is transformed into wild folk dances. Whole-tone material reappears with the central theme and the accompaniment motive of rising thirds derived from 'motto A'. In the manner of Beethoven's Ninth Symphony, the Finale brings back the main themes of the work. At last, discipline and order are imposed upon 'motto A', its subversive potential strictly curbed by fugal treatment (Ex. 7*c*), while 'motto B', transformed into an athletic 5/4 rondo theme, receives new momentum. A vast crescendo leads to the peroration, a grandiose chorale, in which the two mottos are contrapuntally combined.

No fewer than three conductors offered to give this symphony its première in Paris on 28 February 1904: George

Ex. 7c. Symphony No. 2 in B flat, fourth movement (fugue)

Marty, for the Concerts du Conservatoire; Edouard Colonne; and Camille Chevillard, for the Concerts Lamoureux. D'Indy chose the last-named, considering him 'capable of working at, and bringing out the difficult details which abound'. Unfortunately, his publisher Durand seemed less than fully enthusiastic about the score. Expressing his intense annoyance to Ropartz, d'Indy reckoned that 'the Durands are truly tenacious in matters of commerce . . . in the end, I shall try to use arguments'.[6]

The year 1904 brought a bereavement and a profound sense of personal loss all the more acute in such an *homme traditionnel* with a highly developed sense of family and ancestral values. In March 1904, his father Antonin died at the age of 82. Inevitably, the ensuing void cast d'Indy's mind back to his other, spiritual father, César Franck. By coincidence, the inauguration of the monument to Franck's memory in the little square in front of the church of Sainte-Clotilde took place the following month, on 22 April. Belated official recognition was now forthcoming, with addresses delivered by Dubois, Director of the Conservatoire, and Henry Marcel of the

---

[6] Gabéaud, *Auprès du maître*, i. 26. LV ii. 53, 58. VI to GR, 16 Dec. 1903, BN.

Académie des Beaux-Arts. D'Indy himself gave an oration glorifying Franck as 'the Saint of Music'. Unhappily, at least to more iconoclastic and unsentimental minds later in the century, Alfred Lenoir's sculpture has the effect of deflating d'Indy's lofty conception; its iconography of Franck seated at the organ, wrapped in thoughts dictated by an angel of inspiration endowed with vast overshadowing wings, has all the maudlin quality of Sullivan's sacred solo 'The Lost Chord'.[7]

Franck's shadow also fell on d'Indy's worthy but rather academic Violin Sonata, op. 59, based on three cyclic themes, composed the same year. Of special note is the slow movement, which gives voice to his intense grief for Antonin, offset by the preceding Scherzo of a folk-style rustic character. The time was also due for an authoritative account and evaluation of Franck's life, which d'Indy undertook with a filial love. The resulting biography, entitled *César Franck*, was published in 1906, and contains purple passages of blatant hagiographic propaganda, such as the following:

His work, like that of the poets in stone, the builders of the French cathedrals, is all a splendid harmony and a mystic purity. Even when he is dealing with secular subjects Franck cannot get away from this angelic conception. Thus one of his works is particularly interesting in this respect; I mean *Psyché*, in which he aimed at making a musical paraphrase of the antique myth. . . . Let us take the principal number in the work, the 'love duet' as we might call it, between Psyché and Eros. It would be difficult to regard it otherwise than as an ethereal dialogue between *the soul*, as the mystical author of 'The Imitation of Christ' conceived it, and a seraph sent from heaven to instruct it in the eternal verities.

The book also contains a hard core of fact, however; d'Indy provides a good deal of valuable information about Franck's life and work from first-hand experience. Tact forbade the revelation of the intimate details of his existence, the family disharmony and temptations of the flesh. But if Franck emerges as a paragon of virtue, d'Indy did not claim a single ray of reflected glory, preferring to remain a mere humble apprentice.

[7] VI to GR, 20 Mar. 1904, BN. De Courcel, *La Basilique de Sainte-Clotilde* (Paris, 1957), 177. LV ii. 60. CF 60, 256.

Breaking the Boundaries

The positivistic dimension of the book is all too easily over-looked. In comparing the life of art to that of a tree in its organic growth from its stem, producing fruits of an infinitely varied nature, d'Indy was in fact using the celebrated illustration of the fashionable positivist philosopher Hippolyte Taine: a magnificent plane tree displaying its 'eternal enigmatic unity, manifesting itself in each form'. And even in his most rarefied flights of rhetoric, d'Indy was concerned to provide an element of objective scholarship; to support the supposition of mystical tendencies in Franck, he cited the authority of another, if lesser-known professor of philosophy, Gustave Derepas, author of a treatise *Les Théories de l'inconnaissable et les degrées de la connaissance* (1883), as well as a book *César Franck, étude sur sa vie, son enseignement, son œuvre* (1897):

César Franck's mysticism is the direct expression of the soul, and leaves him his full consciousness in his aspirations towards the divine. . . . This music, which is truly as much *the sister of prayer as of poetry*, does not weaken or enervate us, but rather *restores to the soul, now led back to its first source, the grateful waters of emotion, of light, of impulse; it leads back to heaven and to the city of rest.*

Particularly susceptible to the legend of the *Pater Seraficus* was the young organist of Sainte-Clotilde, Charles Tournemire. His *Triple Choral* for organ (1910), dedicated to Franck's memory, is reminiscent of the latter's *Trois Chorals* in its title and structure; but a second, and indeed corresponding level of symbolism is indicated by the subtitle *Sancta Trinitas*, the Holy Trinity.

It should be borne in mind that the literary climate at that time was heavily impregnated with symbolism. Marcel Proust, in his great social novel *A la recherche du temps perdu*—then in its lengthy state of gestation—likewise drew resemblances between certain characters and primitive Italian paintings; just as Odette, Swann's mistress, is seen as Jethro's daughter in Botticelli's *Life of Moses*, and a pregnant kitchen-maid at Combray as Giotto's *Charity*, so could d'Indy rediscover the Virgin of *Les Béatitudes* in a fresco of Sano di Petro, and regard Franck's art as like that of the Sienese and Umbrian painters, of a clear truth and luminous serenity.

153

On the other hand, some Proustian characters were modelled on actual artists and composers of the late nineteenth century, such as Elstir the painter, who combined the qualities of the Impressionists and Helleu. And the composer Vinteuil, a shy, noble personality, neglected and unknown, is believed to resemble d'Indy's portrait of Franck, which Proust had almost certainly read. Indeed, Franck had been granted the distinction of a dual persona, both 'primitive' and burningly contemporary. While Maus regarded his works as the musical counterpart of the Impressionist and Post-Impressionist painters, Proust took the Piano Quintet and String Quartet as models for Vinteuil's Septet in his novel. And, according to Proust's biographer George Painter, the very name Vinteuil echoes that of Vincent d'Indy.[8]

Meanwhile, the active schedule of work went on unremittingly. In the late summer of 1904, d'Indy embarked upon a conducting tour of Russia, involving a long train journey of three days and two nights. Fortunately, the carriages were luxuriously appointed, equipped with beds, a restaurant, and a café. On his arrival, there was time for sightseeing, three days of sheer enchantment: the Kremlin and the Novo-Dievitchki Monastery were superb, and Moscow's multi-coloured buildings 'plunge you into dreamlands recounted by certain primitive paintings or tapestries of the fifteenth century, where characters can be seen revolving around rosy palaces, blue churches, and yellowy-green inns'.

From there, he continued on his way to St Petersburg, whose classical eighteenth-century architecture—like 'a large Munich'—pleased him less. But more than adequate compensation was provided by the Hermitage Museum, with its magnificent collection of paintings. At nearby Pavlovsk, he conducted four successful concerts with the Prague Philharmonic Orchestra, although the audiences proved to be disappointingly conservative in their idolization of the soloist and preference for the standard repertoire of Mozart,

---

[8] CF 73–82. Barrès, *Les Déracinés*, 243–4. A. Maurois, *The Quest for Proust*, Penguin edn. (London, 1962), 193–9. M. Proust, *Correspondance* (Paris, 1991), xv. 170. G. Painter, *Marcel Proust* (London, 1965), i. 173, ii. 248. Ysaÿe and Ratcliffe, *Ysaÿe*, 171–3.

Beethoven, and Wagner, rather than Bach, Rameau, Debussy, and Dukas. However, the Russian premières of *L'Après-midi d'un faune* and *L'Apprenti sorcier* did not entirely fall on deaf ears. Of capital importance was the presence of members of Serge Diaghilev's circle, *jeunes Russes* full of burning enthusiasm for new art and young talent. Diaghilev's magazine *The World of Art*—which *inter alia* promoted Impressionist and Post-Impressionist painting—included a review of these concerts by the favourably disposed Alfred Nurok, who commented that 'our musical world can boast total ignorance of the immortal compositions of César Franck'. During his fifteen-day stay in Pavlovsk, d'Indy found Walter Nouvel particularly interesting and charming, and Dmitrievitch Filosofov, Diaghilev's cousin, most sympathetic to his ideas. Unwittingly, d'Indy may well have planted the first seed of the future historic collaborations between Diaghilev's *Ballet Russe* and French composers, resulting in Nijinsky's sexually explicit choreography of *L'Après-midi d'un faune* and the commissioning of Ravel's *Daphnis et Chloë* and Debussy's *Jeux*.

More immediately, d'Indy, together with Fauré, Debussy, and Dukas, among others, sat on the patronage committee which enabled Diaghilev to mount Mussorgsky's opera *Boris Godunov* in Paris in 1908. Appealing as it did to a predominantly aristocratic, cosmopolitan audience, it presented at the same time a necessary counterweight to the ever-growing post-Wagnerian invasion, which did not meet with d'Indy's approval.[9]

The year 1905 opened promisingly with Magnard conducting his Third Symphony at one of Busoni's concerts in Berlin in January. The success of *L'Étranger* set off a vogue for musical seascapes: Paris that year witnessed the premières of Widor's opera *Les Pêcheurs de Saint-Jean* (with Claire Friché taking a leading role), and, more importantly, Debussy's *La Mer*. In the latter, as we have seen, *L'Étranger*'s sea music had set Debussy's own imagination alight, and it is tempting to

---

[9] VI to OM, 14 Sept. 1904, RBM. Lockspeiser, *Debussy*, i. 43. A. Haskel, *Diaghileff* (London, 1935), 170–1. L. Garafola, *Diaghilev's Ballets Russes* (New York and Oxford, 1989), 17, 50–62, 150–1, 283–6.

attribute his creative renewal after *Pelléas* in an orchestral work of symphonic proportions, with two cyclic themes, to the continuing vitality of d'Indy's influence.[10]

During this year he worked on a new orchestral work *Jour d'été à la montagne*, based on a poem by his brother-in-law, Robert de Pampelonne, evoking the mountainous region of the Ardèche. Its general impression is one of a joyful celebration of continuing life, with rustic themes and folk dances, as if his father's death the previous year had brought a heightened awareness of their ancestral home. Moreover, it contains some of his boldest and most forward-looking ideas and sonic inventions. The overall three-movement structure effectively undermines the essentially dynamic and progressivist ethos of symphonic composition by its employment of the non-linear, recurring rhythm of nature itself. Whereas 'De l'aube à midi sur la mer' from Debussy's *La Mer* depicts the volatility of a seascape between dawn and midday, *Jour d'été* went beyond it to portray the course of a complete day in the countryside from dawn to sunset; its opening bars return more or less palindromically at the conclusion of the work to form a large-scale circular structure, in whose end is its beginning. In this, *Jour d'été* is a remarkable anticipation of such quintessentially modern conceptions as Debussy's *Jeux* and Berg's *Wozzeck*. Orchestrally, too, there are some astonishing innovations, above all the use of the piano as a member of the ensemble, adding a percussive edge to the wind and string sonorities, a feature much exploited by Stravinsky, Bartók, Falla, Milhaud, Honegger, and others.

Curiously, there are certain features of *Jour d'été* which resemble the early symphonies of d'Indy's Viennese contemporary, Gustav Mahler—not indeed in their monstrous length and scale, but in their stylized depiction of the sounds of nature, primordial and timeless. The first movement, 'Aurore', commences in the depths of darkness, the note C sounding throughout the seven octaves of the strings; almost imperceptibly, a sense of motion begins to invade this unearthly stasis as, with the first glimmerings of light, poignant bird-calls are

---

[10] Stuckenschmidt, *Ferruccio Busoni*, 35 ff. A. Thomson, *The Life and Times of Charles-Marie Widor (1844–1937)* (Oxford, 1987), 58–9.

heard. The music moves through five rising fifths, from C to remote B major, at which point the day breaks with an astonishing Straussian brilliance; a triumphant-sounding trumpet theme blares forth amid impressionist washes of harps and piano.

A telescoped slow movement and scherzo form the central 'Après-midi sous les Pins'. Into the sultry atmosphere evoked by an expansive melody in E major accompanied by murmuring string figuration, there breaks folk dancing in C major, of an earthy pagan vigour, whose ostinato patterns are worked obsessively to suggest the mad joy of collective excitement. An intervening Trio section in D flat with its poetic horn writing brings a more sombre colouring, a clouding over which culminates in a rumble of thunder. Here, the extraordinarily modern-sounding, almost Bartókian chromatic passage on the piano and timpani shows d'Indy's aural imagination at its most acute (Ex. 8*a*).

In the finale, 'Soir', the gradual encroachment of evening upon the day is achieved within a novel conception of rondo form, which opens ebulliently in B major with another of d'Indy's highly characteristic rough-edged rustic themes; the ensuing episode, by contrast, introduces a paraphrased version of the Gregorian chant belonging to the office of Vespers for the Feast of the Assumption. Time stands still as brief birdcalls reappear in the bright clear mountain air, a superb effect achieved by the brittle Italianate sonority of woodwind, harp, piano in its upper register, and cymbal struck with the wood of the stick. As dusk begins to fall, the recapitulation reverses the order of the principal themes, giving prominence to the Vespers chant in its full, authentic form: Christianity has prevailed over the forces of paganism (Ex. 8*b*). The rustic rondo melody, now transformed, merges into the gentle mood and flow of the chant, in a twilight glow of divided strings. Finally, the coda moves away from the prevailing B major tonality to the comparative darkness of C minor, bringing the descent of mists and darkness, and ending in the mysterious nocturnal abyss with which the work began.

There was then no sign of the impending tragedy which struck d'Indy and his family in the last days of 1905. In

Ex. 8a. *Jour d'été à la montagne*, 'Après-midi sous les Pins'

December, he departed for the United States for a series of concerts with the Boston Symphony Orchestra, visiting Boston, New York, Philadelphia, Washington, and Baltimore. It was, moreover, the first time that a foreign conductor had made a tour with this orchestra, and d'Indy returned the compliment with the highest praise for its truly admirable qualities of discipline and chamber music sensitivity. The

Ex. 8b. *Jour d'été à la montagne*, 'Soir'

programmes consisted of French music: Franck's *Psyché et Eros*, Fauré's *Pelléas et Mélisande*, Debussy's *Nocturnes*, Dukas's *L'Apprenti sorcier*, Magnard's *Chant funèbre*, and Chausson's Symphony in B flat. The last-named was well received, and of d'Indy's own works, *Istar* had a wild success, in contrast to the Second Symphony, which attracted some adverse criticism.[11]

After this artistic triumph d'Indy was plummeted to the depths of despair. On his return to Paris, he found Isabelle dying in agony from a haemorrhage of the brain; a few days later she passed away in his arms. His loss was great, for he had long relied on her as a force for stability and order in his own life and as a fixed point of repose amid the turbulence of the world. His grief and desolation found expression in a new orchestral work entitled *Souvenirs*, a musical recollection of their contented life together amid the mountain scenery of the Ardèche. A theme from the early *Poème de la montagne* reappears, and towards the end the chimes of midnight, the time when Isabelle died, are played by the harp in harmonics above deep string chords, a fitting gesture to an exemplary life.

[11] LV ii. 63–4. VI to OM, 3 Sept. 1905, RBM.

10

Ideological Warfare and Disintegration

It was certainly not d'Indy's way to go into a protracted period of mourning for Isabelle; the active business of his life went on as usual. On 18 February 1906, *Jour d'été à la montagne* received its première at the Concerts Colonne, only six weeks after her funeral. Debussy, whose *L'Après-midi d'un faune* also featured on the programme, remarked facetiously to Raoul Bardac: 'There seemed to be an inordinate amount of work for the bassoon, and I was surprised to hear a piano— I thought you only found pianos on Swiss mountains?'[1] (This is surely a whimsical reference to Rimbaud's *Illuminations*: 'Madame *** établit un piano dans les Alpes.')

The appearances of Richard Strauss in these years proved to be a disillusioning experience for d'Indy, who had begun by cheerfully recognizing his extraordinary gifts at their first meetings during the previous decade. Distaste for the overblown, utterly complacent musical depiction of bourgeois family life in the *Sinfonia Domestica*—which Strauss conducted at the Châtelet in March 1906—was heightened by the steadily rising tide of Germanophobia; d'Indy's friend Rolland, who found the work in extremely bad taste, saw Strauss as the personification of post-Bismarck Germany's vulgarity and megalomania. While such as Colonne, Pierné, and Bruneau gave the *Sinfonia* a rapturous reception, the more aloof d'Indy could only bring himself to say to Strauss afterwards that 'the entry of the double fugue was good'.

---

[1] *Debussy Letters*, 164, 167.

Nevertheless, he felt genuine, if short-lived admiration on reading the score of Strauss's opera on Oscar Wilde's play, *Salomé*. 'A work of the very first order', he told the impresario Gabriel Astruc in a letter of congratulation on its forthcoming production at the Théâtre des Champs Elysées. These performances in May 1907 were not a success, however; even after twelve years the memory still lingered of Wilde's conviction for homosexual offences in 1895, which had led to searing attacks on the aesthetic movement and the cult of decadence in France, led by the critic Octave Mirbeau. Rolland criticized the opera as 'unhealthy, unclean, hysterical or alcoholic, oozing with a perfumed and mundane corruption'. D'Indy's initially favourable reaction soon turned to marked displeasure: at the dress rehearsal, attended by Fauré, in his official capacity as Director of the Conservatoire, and the President of the Republic, d'Indy was heard mumbling with embarrassment that he had little sympathy with the work. In the *Cours*, he maintained that Strauss 'accepts too readily everything which comes to mind—a lack of selection, and an absolute misunderstanding of proportions, from which comes an abuse of vulgarity and *longueurs*'.[2]

Ironically, in Berlin, the heart of the feared and despised German Empire, Busoni continued to feature d'Indy's compositions in his controversial concerts of contemporary music. On 8 November 1906, Busoni himself conducted the Symphony in B flat, while d'Indy took charge of the *Symphonie Cévenole*. Standing in at rehearsal for the indisposed pianist Rudolf Ganz, Busoni showed a much greater understanding of the nature of the piano part—an integral part of the orchestral texture, rather than a dominating solo—than Ganz, who unfortunately recovered in time for the concert. Chauvinism was at the root of the savage critical reception meted out to these works; the Symphony in B flat especially was deemed 'too impotent in its lack of sensibility, this non-music, as hideous as is possible, with its refined

---

[2] *Richard Strauss and Romain Rolland*, 140, 144. N. Del Mar, *Richard Strauss* (London, 1962), i. 192, 196, 283–4. C. van Casselaer, *Lot's wife, Lesbian Paris 1890–1914* (Liverpool, 1986), 6–7. CCM iii. 241. VI to G. Astruc, 6 Apr. 1907, BN.

ugliness of sonority and painful absurdity of harmonic progressions'. The incoherence of the criticism speaks for itself.[3]

Other events brought d'Indy much more satisfaction. Dukas's opera *Ariane et Barbe-bleue*, mounted in 1907, he hailed as 'a major enrichment of French music'. And a signal honour was conferred on him when the Concerts Lamoureux invited him to act as deputy to Chevillard. On the other hand, his relationship with the Opéra-Comique deteriorated rapidly, and ended in near disaster. First, he attacked its performances of Gluck's *Iphigenia in Aulis* publicly for their lack of expression and lifelessness, condemning the director, Carré, as a 'non-musician'. Next, he withdrew from an operatic project *Phèdre et Hippolyte*, destined for the Opéra-Comique, without warning. The situation quickly went out of control, as battle was joined in the pages of *Comoedia* between the aggrieved librettist, Jules Bois, and d'Indy, now deprived of the moderating hand of Isabelle. So acrimonious became these exchanges that the parties finally resorted to the time-honoured, though illegal, method of saving honour. To the astonishment and outrage of d'Indy's friends and relatives, a duel was arranged in the Parc-des-Princes on 11 January 1908. Two shots were fired, but mercifully both men escaped injury. With characteristic sang-froid, d'Indy proceeded on his way to a rehearsal one hour late.[4]

Perhaps nothing contributed to the Schola's reputation for dogmatism more than Pope Pius X's *motu proprio* of 1903, a determined but misunderstood attempt at reform of the music of the Church. A saintly man of the people, Pius was above all a reactionary figure, alarmed by the modern world and its advanced ideas, and concerned to reverse the more open and flexible policies of his predecessor, Leo XIII. Pius's most notorious act was to suppress, with considerable brutality, Alfred Loisy and the Catholic Modernist movement, whose audacious venture to renew Catholic theology drew on Protestant biblical criticism, thereby invoking relativistic concepts to challenge eternal values and unchanging dogmas.

[3] E. J. Dent, *Ferruccio Busoni* (London, 1974), 132, 146. LV ii. 69.
[4] LV ii. 71–3. VI, *Emmanuel Chabrier et Paul Dukas*, 19.

The *motu proprio* effectively sanctioned the work of the Schola in the field of Gregorian chant and sixteenth-century polyphony. To direct the course on Gregorian studies, the Schola had enlisted the Abbé Vigourel, a priest at Saint-Sulpice and an authority on the liturgy; in 1898, the distinguished scholar Amedée Gastoué succeeded him as professor of Gregorian chant and medieval musicology. By upholding the qualities of true sacred music, exemplified above all by Palestrina, the *motu proprio* constituted an attack on the liturgical use of theatre and operatic music so prevalent at the time; the celebrated 'Meditation' from Massenet's *Thaïs*, to cite only one instance, was a popular choice for weddings. Yet it did not disregard the demands of musical progress, even welcoming modern composition in the Church when it offered 'goodness, seriousness and gravity, making it not unworthy of its liturgical functions'.

What Pius X had intended as an 'Instruction on Sacred Music', of persuasive rather than absolute authority, exploded like a bombshell. To the 'rigorists' it seemed almost like a statement of papal infallibility. At ordinary parish level, however, the reaction was entirely negative, even contemptuous; Léon Bloy recorded with horror the view of the *vicaire* of Notre Dame des Champs: 'On the question of plainchant we should disobey for the good of the Church, so as not to make apparent the contradictions of successive Popes. Moreover, it is only a question of artistic appreciation and not dogma. In this matter, we must place ourselves on the level of the average worshipper.' The case of Maurice Emmanuel is particularly illuminating. A product of the Conservatoire, with a doctorate in ancient Greek music, he was also a fervent enthusiast of Gregorian chant and polyphony. As choirmaster of Sainte-Clotilde, he imposed this music single-mindedly upon the congregation, which, perhaps understandably, did not appreciate a diet of such unrelieved austerity. His faithfulness to the provisions of the *motu proprio* cost him his post in 1907. With poetic justice, d'Indy snapped him up immediately for the Schola as professor of the theory of music.

Surveying this disharmonious scene, d'Indy remained secure in his belief in the essential rightness of his cause. In

November 1907, while travelling in Italy, he was granted an audience with Pius X; d'Indy described the occasion to Sérieyx:

He spoke to me about Gregorian chant as if we were on Gastoué's course. Then he made a small profession of faith in tradition and *obedience*. . . . It is pleasing to find—at last—an important person who does not believe himself obliged to do 'what everyone does', following the latest trends, full of intellectual snobbery. . . . Thinking about our little sectarians, I believe I saw them as we see poor human beings in St Peter's Square, from Michelangelo's lantern at the top of the dome.

D'Indy was unlikely to have missed the fiftieth anniversary celebrations of Sainte-Clotilde, the shrine of César Franck and an aristocratic stronghold of the royalist movement. The atmosphere, in the aftermath of Briand's Law of 1906 separating Church and State, was defiantly triumphalistic: in the words of Mgr. Amette, Archbishop of Paris, 'This is not only the patron feast of Saint-Clotilde, it is the feast of Christian France, of her secular vocation to Christianity.' The programme of music performed during the solemn Triduum in May 1908 suggests that, under Emmanuel's successor, Jules Meunier, an acceptable compromise had been reached. While there was a place for Gregorian chant in the Requiem Mass and for the early polyphony of Nanini's *Resurrectio et Vita*, this was balanced by some well-loved examples of nineteenth-century sacred music: Dubois's 'Tantum ergo' and Franck's 'Panis angelicus', Kyrie, and Agnus Dei. Appropriately, the organist, Charles Tournemire, played Franck's *Pièce héroïque* and the *Choral in A minor*.

Later that year, d'Indy witnessed another religious ceremony of medieval grandeur, the burial of the Bishop of Barcelona, conducted with true Spanish majesty and opulence: 'Twelve magnificent bishops in gold and carrying crosiers followed the coffin, then the entire garrison of Barcelona in full uniform, the trumpets of each regiment playing funeral fanfares, the infantry, cavalry, and artillery with all its cannons.' He added sardonically that this could not have happened in Paris, even for Mgr. Amette: 'Impede the circulation of the trams for a miserable bishop!! But if it were Zola, that would be OK!'

We see d'Indy's attitudes manifestly hardening in these years, as he worked on the outline of his new anti-Semitic drama (as he described it to de Bréville) *La Légende de Saint-Christophe*: 'Understand that I'm not making any actual allusions, and that the characters are not called Dreyfus, Reinach, nor even Combes . . . that would do them too much honour.' The aim was to show the nauseating influence of the Judaeo-Dreyfusard faction: ' "Pride"—"pleasure"—"money" in conflict with *les fleurs du bien* = "faith"—"hope"—"charity".'[5]

On a more secular plane, the Schola Cantorum came under a sustained attack initiated in 1905 by the young critic Émile Vuillermoz, a fervent admirer of Fauré and Debussy and self-appointed mouthpiece of a group of radical composers including Ravel, Inghelbrecht, Huë, Roger Ducasse, Casella from Italy, and even de Sévérac, who had treacherously crossed the floor. In effect, a new orthodoxy was growing up around them, exultant after Ravel's Prix de Rome débâcle, which hastened the retirement of that epitome of the *status quo*, Théodore Dubois, Director of the Conservatoire and pillar of the Académie des Beaux-Arts. For the group's self-definition, another adversary was needed, and d'Indy's Schola fitted the bill admirably. Moreover, keen resentment mounted against d'Indy's dominant position within the Société Nationale, which eventually resulted in the breakaway Société Musicale Indépendante (S.M.I.) in 1909/10, led by Ravel. A petty dispute with d'Indy as to whether a low C on the horn could be sounded apparently ignited the tinderbox. There was an irony, too, in the new S.M.I.'s policy of including more works by foreign composers in its programmes, for it will be remembered that d'Indy's similar policy in the 1880s had caused Saint-Saëns's withdrawal from the Société Nationale.

D'Indy's strong emphasis on the teaching of counterpoint—and refusal to regard harmony as a separate subject, as the Conservatoire did—gave Vuillermoz the pretext to launch the

[5] VI, *La Schola Cantorum*, 93–4. A. R. Vidler, *The Church in an Age of Revolution* (London, 1961), 179–89. A. Coeuroy, 'Formes actuelles de musique religieuse', RM, 8 (June 1925), 246–7. Bloy, *Journal*, iv, 23. De Courcel, *La Basilique de Sainte-Clotilde*, 122–3, 175. *Lettres à Auguste Sérieyx*, 18, 22. VI to PB, 17 Sept. 1903, BN.

war of harmony versus counterpoint in the *Mercure musical*. Whereas the Schola turned out 'horizontalists', mere artisans of counterpoint—a dismal science like chess—and fabricators of sonatas ignorant of harmonic developments, the future belonged to the 'verticalists', the new school of Impressionists and harmonic experimenters. Moreover, the Schola was castigated as a hotbed of bigoted Catholicism, anti-Semitism, and extreme nationalism. Added force was given to these accusations by the appearance of Part II of d'Indy's *Cours* in 1909, edited by Sérieyx, a man of the extreme Right and music critic of Maurras's *L'Action française*.

This controversy, based on a false dichotomy, was hardly a novel phenomenon, for French cultural history had been riddled with such ideological conflicts, such as those between the followers of Rubens and Poussin (known as the quarrel between colour and design), Lully and Rameau, Gluck and Piccinni. And the great Rousseau had conceived melody and harmony as being in conflict, for if melody recaptured music's primal nature, harmony was a corruption, 'a Gothic and barbarous invention'. Sensibly, Rolland diagnosed the latest outbreak as a typical case of French anarchy, 'which spent vast resources of talent and goodwill in self-destruction by its doubts and contradictions'. Inevitably, the real musical and aesthetic issues were obscured and distorted.

To the embarrassment of leading figures like Fauré and d'Indy, who had not sought dissension, and found themselves unwillingly forced into opposing polarities, the conflict energized the lesser men and camp-followers on both sides. The numerous little magazines were filled with assertive, half-baked criticism by pundits intoxicated by the novelty of their superficial musical knowledge and semi-education—as Rolland rightly observed, like Molière's *petit bourgeois* M. Jourdain discovering his speech to be prose. This crazy war of harmony versus counterpoint raised the pseudo-question: was music something to be listened to, or merely read? D'Indy's own response was typically robust. When an unfortunate student once referred to 'visual counterpoint', he was marched up to a picture and told that it was an 'aural painting' to which he should listen!

It was not too difficult to caricature the Schola. Its founders had striven for an essentially outgoing, persuasive ethos, but the prevailing atmosphere of Ruskinian high-mindedness and devotion to work as a moral duty unhappily gave the opposite impression of a closed order. Indeed, in Rolland's once celebrated novel *Jean-Christophe*, the character bearing that name perceives the Schola to be like a small Protestant sect with pious, intolerant, aggressive disciples, headed by 'a very pure man, very cold, wilful, and a little childish'. At first, Jean-Christophe, a German musical genius who made France his second home, blamed the French for not liking Brahms; but he soon discovered that 'there were lots of little Brahmses in France. All those hard workers, laborious and conscientious, were full of virtues.'[6]

How d'Indy must have been appalled, as an enemy of mere routine, by the very idea of presiding over such an allegedly inward-looking society, motivated by the Protestant work ethic! It was inevitable that, for every Roussel and Satie, there would be a host of mediocre students, all the more efficient for the clarity of his teaching. Yet he may have felt that, after Isabelle's death, he had lost some of his power to energize and revitalize; isolated and lonely, he may have felt the Schola slipping away from his benevolent paternalism to become the battleground of warring ideologies. The laborious, academic character of his Piano Sonata (1907) expresses well his mood at this difficult time. Doubtless, too, his awareness of the ever increasing anarchic trends in the arts and society tended to reinforce the formalist aspects of his teaching and composition.

In the ongoing battles, the debate became wound up to highly abstract levels, and perceived in theological terms as a conflict between Catholicism and pantheism. Here, the turn of argument reflected the concurrent war against Bergson and his cult of intuition and inner experience, conducted by the neo-Thomist philosopher Jacques Maritain. The latter held that Bergson's anti-scholasticism was essentially pantheistic

---

[6] LV ii. 60–3, 66–8, 78. Fubini, *History of Music Aesthetics*, 209–10. R. Rolland, *Jean-Christophe* (Paris, 1903–12), 'La Foire sur la Place', 70–90. N. Demuth, *Vincent d'Indy* (London, 1951), 10. R. Nichols, *Ravel* (London, 1977), 31–3, 68.

and unchristian, a surrender of the intellect to matter and a denial of a God who can be apprehended in terms of a rational metaphysics. Thus Vuillermoz could write, from the opposite standpoint to Maritain:

The spiritualism and the strong convictions of d'Indy have, quite naturally, led him systematically to reduce the intervention of instinct and aural sensuousness in artistic creation, which are, one and the other, suspected of materialism. [For him] the artist who searches for voluptuous sensations in the field of pure sonority is a kind of latter-day pagan in the Christian world. The harmonic and orchestral refinements of the Impressionists, which appeal directly to the senses, have something blasphemous about them. To protect the laws of spiritual transposition, the creative artist must be inspired by a profound respect for form, which usefully banks up the indisciplines of instinct.

This one-sided categorization of d'Indy as the apostle of strict formalist procedures disgracefully ignored the evidence of his actual music. We have already noted the number of striking, innovative passages of harmonic and orchestral invention in the symphonies and operas, so often directly inspired by nature in all its mysterious chthonic allure. Yet it cannot be denied that he himself, as a strict statement of pedagogic principle, overemphasized the distinction between horizontal and vertical thinking. Certainly, his definition of counterpoint as 'the simultaneous issue of different melodies' was a healthy corrective to both Impressionist tonal drift and post-Wagnerian chromatic saturation, a welcome return to the pure waters of the polyphonists. But d'Indy's apparent conservatism is deceptive, and, paradoxically, remarkably modern in its formulation. As in Bergson's *Evolution créative* the intellect is compared to the cinematograph, which breaks down the perpetual movement and flux of life itself into a succession of static frames on celluloid, so, for d'Indy, 'Music, being an art of movement and succession, chords only appear by the effect of stoppage in the movement of the melodic lines . . . the study of chords in themselves is, from the musical viewpoint, an absolute aesthetic error, for harmony emerges from melody.' Only the necessity to examine the three tonal functions of the common chord—the tonic, dominant, and subdominant—justifies an artificial halt in the melodies which give rise to them.

Tortuous reasoning to express the simple, well-attested truth that good harmony is good counterpoint! It is time to leave this arena of conceptual entanglements, and re-enter the world of practical common sense. Happily, it was Vuillermoz who in effect lost the argument, rather than the Schola, for the reforms at the Conservatoire instigated in 1905 by Dubois's successor, Fauré, included the strengthening of counterpoint and fugue in the curriculum, as well as obligatory history of music classes for composition students. It was surely a tribute to the success of d'Indy's pioneering efforts that Fauré could push through these belated reforms in the face of entrenched resistance. On the other hand, the verticalist party was oblivious to the fact that the most creative Schola students were able to leaven its disciplines with Impressionist elements; more seriously, it had alienated that early champion of Debussy, Vincent d'Indy himself, who from then on regarded Debussy and the Impressionist movement with a suspicion verging on enmity.[7]

Meanwhile, England awaited him. In the 1907 season of Henry Wood's Promenade Concerts, the *Symphonie Cévenole* received a performance by the pianist Carlos Sobrino, and in March the following year, the Society of British Composers held a reception for d'Indy in London. Five months later, it fell to him formally to welcome Edward Elgar at a concert of English music organized by a group of Belgian musicians. Alas, this contact between d'Indy and Elgar, initially promising, was fated to end in disappointment.

Plans were afoot in England for the creation of a Musical League to promote the works of lesser-known composers in the provinces, especially the Midlands and the North. Under the presidency and vice-presidency of Elgar and Delius, the committee at length decided to hold a festival in Liverpool in May 1909, with d'Indy among the enterprising choice of composers

[7] E. Vuillermoz, *Histoire de la musique* (Paris, 1949), 312–15. Kolakowski, *Bergson*, 93–7. VI, *L'Harmonie vivante* (undated pamphlet). R. Orledge, *Gabriel Fauré* (London, 1979), 21–2. CCM i. 116–17.

invited to conduct their own works. Also among the foreign contingent were Debussy, Max Schillings, and Gustav Mahler, the last-named to direct his massive choral Symphony No. 8. Unfortunately, for reasons which remain obscure, they were unable to fulfil their engagements, and the festival, postponed to September, proceeded with works by Ethel Smyth and Vaughan Williams.

A wider variety of entertainment was provided by the London Music Club, whose policy was to invite a series of eminent composers to its evenings of wining and dining, during which their compositions were played. The Club certainly could not be accused of lacking enterprise, for over the years, the guests included d'Indy, Debussy, Sibelius, and even the virtually unknown Arnold Schoenberg, in London for the première of his *Five Orchestral Pieces*, op. 16, under Wood in 1912. However, it was with a sense of apprehension, betrayed by a restless twitching of his face and hands, that d'Indy awaited the post-prandial account of his Piano Sonata by a seemingly inexperienced 19-year-old Jewish pianist called Myra Hess. A potentially difficult situation was rapidly defused as, to his astonishment and relief, she showed herself to be fully in command of the music's complexities. In March 1909, he had made the Channel crossing to conduct the Queen's Hall Orchestra in his *Wallenstein* trilogy; the programme also included Elgar's *Wand of Youth* under Wood. The same month, *Jour d'été à la montagne* was performed by Thomas Beecham, who considered that 'it came off extraordinarily well—and sounded quite remarkable on the band'.[8]

These English visits were a mere pleasant interlude amid d'Indy's sea of troubles, however. The death of Charles Bordes in Montpellier that year brought back poignant memories of the great hopes and aspirations of the Schola. Lecturing in Vienna that summer, d'Indy heard Strauss's latest opera, *Elektra*, and communicated his feelings about it to Ropartz in uncompromising terms:

[8] H. J. Wood, *My Life in Music* (London, 1938), 208. Carley, *Delius, a Life in Letters*, 375–8. P. M. Young, *Elgar* (London, 1955), 143–4. M. McKenna, *Myra Hess, a Portrait* (London, 1976), 50. *Musical Times*, May 1909.

I find it simply hideous—hideous in its subject—hideous in its music—hideous in its orchestra—hideous in its writing. . . . it seems to me the peak of Jewish music, and it is indeed a monstrous successor to the art of Meyerbeer! Truly, all these confusions of vulgar melodies which occur in five or six different keys at once, makes no impression at all. . . . No, decidedly, these modern Germans have nothing to give.[9]

Confronted by the decadence and apparent self-destruction of the great Austro-German tradition, its decline into the emotional anarchy of Expressionism and harmonic disintegration, d'Indy felt all the more determined to keep alive its central canonical masterpieces—above all, Bach's B minor Mass, Gluck's *Iphigenia in Aulis*, and Beethoven's *Missa Solemnis*—in the concerts of the Schola. The Latin tradition, moreover, still showed some signs of life; in April 1910, he contributed a performance of Palestrina's *Stabat Mater* to a concert at the Trocadéro in honour of Dom Lorenzo Perosi, choirmaster of the Sistine Chapel, in which the latter conducted his own symphony *Florence* and the cantata *Dies Irae*. The same month, d'Indy was in Rome to conduct the Italian première of Debussy's *Nocturnes* at the Augusteo in a largely familiar programme consisting of Franck's *Psyché et Eros*, Chausson's Symphony, Roussel's *Soir d'été*, as well as *Istar* and the *Symphonie Cévenole*. 'It went very well,' he told Maus, with wry amusement at the less than fully civilized concert manners of the Romans. 'The orchestra, though not very expressive, could melt in some places. A very funny audience. It's been so criticized for its love of sheer brilliance and melody that now it whistles conscientiously through all the lively bits . . . even Roussel's *Soirs d'été* seemed to them too melodic . . . it reminded them of *Norma*!'[10]

The year 1911 marked the passing of an era. In March Alexandre Guilmant died at the age of 76. His continuing presence to the end as an organist of international standing had brought immense prestige and authority to the Schola. It was entirely fitting that Louis Vierne, organist of Notre Dame, and a pupil of Franck, Widor, and Guilmant, should

[9] VI to GR, 4 Sept. 1909, BN.
[10] Proust, *Correspondance*, x. 67. VI to OM, Apr. 1910, RBM.

have been called to succeed him as organ professor. He was no stranger to the Schola, having been a regular recitalist in its concerts, and hailed by the *Tribune* in 1902 as an artist who 'will certainly be one of the princes of his instrument'. He found d'Indy to be a man to whom he could give his total loyalty and affection; in his turn, the Director of the Schola dedicated to him his organ Prélude in E flat minor (1913). It is very likely that d'Indy's belief in the continuing validity of symphonic forms inspired Vierne to go on writing organ symphonies—six in all—long after Widor had ceased to produce them.[11]

To add to the shock of Guilmant's passing, d'Indy was taken ill with pleurisy. Happily confounding newspaper reports of his death, he spent his convalescence at Tamaris on the Côte d'Azur. Incapable of mental inactivity, he took the opportunity to write a second musical biography, *Beethoven*. Rejecting the intellectually fashionable secular view of his subject, he emphasized the religious, Catholic dimension, but without the extravagant mythologizing of *César Franck*. Indeed, the image of this hero-figure he wished to convey was markedly different from the standard portrait of a tempestuous King Lear, raging against his deafness and defying fate. To Maus he expressed his profound dissatisfaction with the existing studies of Beethoven: those of Rolland, Chantavoine, and Riemann were full of errors, their approach excessively literary, and undermined by failure to look closely at the musical texts. He also said to Labey that 'It is incredible that this inspired figure had become full of grimaces and hatred through the jottings of *musicographes*'. Even Busoni could state that 'It is only through Beethoven that music acquired that growling and frowning expression which was natural enough to him, but which perhaps ought to have remained his lonely path alone'.

By contrast, d'Indy pointed to the serene, fulfilled aspects of his character; in his second period, his soul was filled by his three loves: *la femme, la nature, la patrie*. The author's schematic approach and personal preoccupations obtrude and

[11] L. Vierne, *Mes souvenirs* (Paris, 1939), 48. P. Piédelièvre, 'Louis Vierne à la Schola Cantorum', appendix to the above.

unduly shape the book, which received a eulogy from the big-oted Léon Bloy in *Les Tablettes de la Schola*. But an acid recep-tion came from a more detached source, the American authoress and friend of Henry James, Edith Wharton, who wrote that d'Indy 'demolishes practically the whole of the Beethoven legend, including the identity of the *Unsterbliche Geliebte* and describes his life as a series of artistic and finan-cial triumphs! True to French principles of book-making, he gives no authority whatever for these statements.'[12]

Both creator and destroyer of myths, d'Indy could never resist an opportunity to startle and shock. Something of the rebellious youth always remained in him to *épater les bourgeois*, and to puncture received opinion and *bien-pensant* illusions; it was the reverse side of the conventional respectability he always displayed where his family were concerned. Anything which smacked of the parasitical was fair game; music critics were roundly condemned as practitioners of a useless occupa-tion. Strikingly advanced were his adverse views on art gal-leries which wrenched paintings and sculptures from their intended contexts in churches or domestic interiors to exhibit them flung together *en masse*. Better to hang a single picture in a re-creation of its proper setting, such as a chapel or a bed-chamber.

A holiday in Italy set him back on his feet. Above all, it helped him to distance himself from the feuding factions in Paris. 'I assure you', he informed Maus, 'that in the presence of the temples of Paestum, or the Libreria of Siena, the quar-rels of the S.M.I. and the S.N.M. seem to me like very petty mishaps.' Earlier in the year, there had been a notable scan-dal in the capital, when the Archbishop of Paris forbade Catholics to attend performances of the allegedly blasphemous *Le Martyre de Saint-Sébastien*, a French verse drama by the exhibitionistic Italian decadent poet Gabriel d'Annunzio, with incidental music by Debussy. The transvestite title-role, acted and danced by Ida Rubinstein, a Russian Jewess, portrayed the saint in sexually ambivalent terms as a masochistic

---

[12] VI to M. Labey, 23 ? 1911, BN. LV ii. 82–4. VI, *Beethoven* (Paris, 1911). Dent, *Ferruccio Busoni*, 230. VI to OM, n.d., RBM. TS, Feb. 1912, 68–71. *The Letters of Edith Wharton* (London, 1988), 265.

anti-hero pierced by arrows. It was hardly to d'Indy's taste; yet, on reading Debussy's score, he derived some encouragement for his own work-in-progress: 'I find it abominable music, as old-fashioned as it is pretentious,' he wrote to Maus; but 'all the same, without vanity, *Saint-Christophe* will be better!'[13]

At the very close of the year, on 31 December 1911, a musical event took place in Paris which reassured him that all was not lost in the world of contemporary music: the mounting of Magnard's opera *Bérénice*, based on Racine's classical drama. In a letter to Labey, he enthused: 'It's a beautiful work, very sincere and very French, without affectation and flattery for snobs. I'm happy to see that there are still musicians around who dare to use the common chord. . . . I used to like Magnard a lot—as you do—and I like him even better after *Bérénice*.'

Subsequently, he added that, in his operas, Magnard 'could, without difficulty, have indulged in long and detailed developments, but his very French temperament always curbed the excessively Germanic tendencies of his mind just in time'. Another, rather unexpected admirer of Magnard was the precocious young Conservatoire-trained Darius Milhaud. He had found *Bérénice* impressive despite its lack of refinement—or perhaps for that very reason. And he felt that the harsh, rustic qualities of Magnard's music, with its harmonic sobriety, provided an antidote to the impasse into which Debussy's Impressionism had led French music.[14]

Back in harness at the Schola, he directed portions of Franck's *Béatitudes* and Beethoven's *Missa Solemnis* at its concerts in March 1912, held in the Salle Gaveau. Of the latter work, he wrote perceptively that it is religious music of the highest degree, yet its dramatic qualities make it impossible to conceive as liturgical music. Much as he venerated it, he was aware of weaknesses characteristic of the period, the instrumental treatment of the voices, and the interminable

[13] Van Casselaer, *Lot's wife*, 134–5. M. de Cossart, *Ida Rubinstein, a Theatrical Life* (Liverpool, 1987), 35–43. VI to OM, 22 July, 4 Nov. 1911, RBM.

[14] VI to Labey, 31 Dec. 1911, BN. VI, *Richard Wagner et son influence sur l'art musical français* (Paris, 1930), 70. D. Milhaud, *Notes without Music* (London, 1952), 41–2.

codas—the Amens of the Gloria and Credo. According to Marguérite de Fraguier, he surpassed himself in this work: 'I remember notably the change in his countenance when we sang the Agnus Dei, above all the "Dona nobis pacem". For the first time, we thought he was going to faint. But no, however strong his emotion, it was always governed by the will, and he pulled himself together for the surprising noise of war which interrupts the mystic peace.'[15]

It would be quite wrong to conclude that he had turned his back on the present, even if he deplored many of its manifestations. This was the brilliant era of Diaghilev's Russian Ballet, which brought together the most vital trends in all branches of the arts, and d'Indy was not immune to the dance-inspired climate. He became involved in the enterprising venture entitled 'Concerts des danses' put on at the Théâtre du Châtelet in April 1912 by the Russian ballerina and mistress of Dukas, Natalia Trouhanova, and staged by Jacques Rouché, the future director of the Paris Opéra. A quartet of French composers conducted their own oriental-style compositions. *Istar*, in its new choreographed guise, rubbed shoulders with Florent Schmitt's *La Tragédie de Salomé*, Ravel's *Adelaïde*, and Dukas's *La Péri*. D'Indy found the occasion great fun: 'It went very well, with an audience of idiotic snobs which overdid the applause.' *Istar* seems to have been suitably complemented by Desvallières's scenery, consisting of severe archangels with outstretched wings and large fawn-coloured beards.[16]

D'Indy's own inner daemon drove him to accept an additional responsibility—the class in orchestral conducting for the benefit of the composition students at the Conservatoire. His predecessor was Dukas, who, according to Milhaud, had been a bad conductor, incapable of directing a rehearsal. In response to this invitation, d'Indy wrote to Fauré, his old friend, with heavy humour: 'It is clear as day that I am only

---

[15] De Fraguier, *Vincent d'Indy*, 99–100. CCM iii. 275.
[16] Durand, *Quelques souvenirs*, ii. 13–14. VI, *Emmanuel Chabrier et Paul Dukas*, 19. *Feuilleton du temps*, 30 July 1924, contains a reference to the 1912 production in Henry Malherbe's review of Ida Rubinstein's later choreography. VI to OM, 23 Apr. 1912, RBM.

accepting this class to replace you as Director of the Conservatoire, and to throw you out at the appropriate moment! . . . On the desks I should like 1) Egmont, Beethoven, 2) Symphony in G minor, Mozart, 3) Overture Euryanthe, Weber.' We shall see how, like Franck in earlier days, he was to develop the class as a direct adjunct to the teaching of composition itself.[17]

This vortex of activity brought him due official recognition in the form of the Chevalier of the Legion of Honour. Even more gratifying was the revival of *Fervaal* at the Opéra, conducted by André Messager. Though scheduled for December, it had to be postponed until January 1913, owing to the indisposition of Lucienne Bréval, who sang the role of Guilhen. But any exasperation on d'Indy's part was dispelled by amusement at Magnard's refusal to join him in a box; his retiring friend made the feeble excuse that he would not hear very well!

Dukas's original admiration for the opera had not waned: on the contrary, he told d'Indy: 'Be sure that it is one of the most beautiful works of the theatre of all time. I have rediscovered all my previous emotion, enlarged and deepened. . . . Thank you for having written *Fervaal*!' Ravel, too, rather surprisingly, spoke generously of its nobly sustained musicality: 'We must profoundly admire the example of such integrity. . . . the orchestra gave a perfect rendition of this richly sonorous score, which is complex but always clear.' On the other hand, Reynaldo Hahn expressed himself in a more guarded way: 'Whenever d'Indy allows himself the feeling of expansion, or grants the musical invention a little leisure, his talent attains the richest fullness, assumes a superior fascination and releases a real magnetism.' Hahn's close friend Marcel Proust, who heard *Fervaal* over the *théâtrophone* without stirring from his bedroom, found it 'extremely boring . . . all the phrases 'Le fils de Nuées, s'il n'est pur' etc. seem to me to be of a soporific dryness. I'm of your opinion about the delicious entr'acte (above all when it returns, sung in the last act) . . . I'm crazy about it.'[18]

---

[17] *Gabriel Fauré, a Life in Letters*, 143–4. Milhaud, *Notes without Music*, 24.

[18] *Correspondance de Paul Dukas*, 87. Proust, *Correspondance*, xii. 44, 46, 49. VI to OM, ? Dec. 1912, RBM.

Though disdainful of music criticism, d'Indy could not resist the opportunity to do some himself. Ironically, this was offered to him by the ever-mischievous Vuillermoz, who, doubtless sensing that the war of harmony and counterpoint had been fought to a standstill, sought to rekindle the fires of controversy. His plan was to engage both d'Indy and Debussy to write intermittent concert reviews for the *Revue musicale S.M.I.* at a time of unprecedented developments in the arts. Surprisingly, both accepted; Debussy needed the money, while d'Indy was irresistibly drawn towards centres of activity and energy.

The old warrior appeared to be unwilling to go on record as a sour-voiced reactionary, a role in which many were all too ready to cast him. It was, therefore, in a positive spirit that he listened to the epoch-making scores danced by Diaghilev's Russian Ballet in those years immediately before the Great War. Ravel's *Daphnis et Chloë*, styled as a *symphonie chorégraphique*, largely met with his approval, despite 'incenses of unusual sonorous agglomerations'. As for Stravinsky's *Le Sacre du Printemps*, which had created an almost unparalleled uproar at its première in May 1913, it was 'a work of very great rhythmic, if not musical interest, which indicates a real artistic temperament in its composer'. One senses a strong measure of self-restraint on d'Indy's part in delivering such a bland judgement in the face of this violent onslaught of sound.

He permitted himself to stray into dangerous areas of pure experiment and speculation. While Debussy commented favourably on Russolo's futurist manifesto, *The Art of Noises* (March 1913), which proposed to break away from the limited sonorous range of conventional instruments by means of 'noise intoners', d'Indy was prepared to discuss a novel idea of cinematograph music. This would effectively constitute the triumph of sonority and sensation over the solid virtues of form, requiring the simultaneous playing of a cinematograph to elucidate the diverse phases of the musical flow: 'to present to the eye an agreeable tremulousness which would marvellously harmonize with the tiny orchestral *chichis* and other aural titillations, usually the principal merit of these compositions'. These speculations turned out to be remarkably prescient; for

Diaghilev's ballet production of Stravinsky's *Jeux d'artifice* in
Rome in 1917, the futurist artist Giacomo Balla designed a
light show—beams of coloured light, spirals, and running light
waves—playing on a setting of geometrical solids to harmonize with the composer's pyrotechnical inventions. Similarly,
Schoenberg's Expressionist opera *Die Glückliche Hand* (1913,
but not performed until 1924) used lighting to create crescen-
dos of colour and shifting colour schemes synchronized with
the music, reflecting the emotions of the characters.[19]

From these rarefied heights, d'Indy was brutally brought
back to hard reality. In September 1913 his daughter Berthe
suffered the bursting of a blood vessel in her head, causing a
complete loss of speech. As if in anticipation of her death on
6 December 1913, he directed on 28 November a concert at
the Schola entitled 'La Cantate funèbre', which included
Josquin des Prez's *Déploration de Johannes Ockeghem* and
Bach's Cantata no. 106 (*Actus Tragicus*). At her memorial service at Meudon, a Gregorian Mass was sung by fifty students
of the Schola. Though deeply touched by their gesture of sympathy, he insisted that they receive payment as if it were a
concert. To his dear friend Maus he unburdened himself of his
grief:

You had known her almost as a child, the poor little thing whom I
found on her deathbed with the gracefulness of youth, you would
say that she was 15 . . . and she was smiling, as if she already
glimpsed eternal bliss. . . . If you only knew all the vanities in
moments like these which I'm going through: performances, directing concerts, theatre productions, all that seems empty and useless!
To love an art, to love those who love you, to love the work you do,
these are the things that really matter.[20]

[19] LV ii. 87, 92–3. L. Garafola, *Diaghilev's Ballets Russes* (New York and Oxford, 1989), 79–80.
[20] VI to OM, 27 Sept. 1913, RBM. Gabéaud, *Auprès du maître*, i. 8. TS, Dec. 1913.

11

An Old Soldier Never Dies

The year 1914 began in an increasing mood of tension between France and Germany, even though the war cloud which was to engulf them at the end of the year seemed as yet no bigger than a man's hand. Even on the cultural plane, the prevailing virulent nationalism on both sides diminished each country in the eyes of the other. If Debussy was not properly appreciated beyond the Rhine, Gustav Mahler likewise was rejected by the French, with d'Indy calling his Fourth Symphony 'a piece for the Alhambra or the Moulin Rouge'—fit only for music-halls and sex shows.[1]

In the meantime, the Schola was as active as ever, with a performance of Beethoven's *Missa Solemnis* and a revival of Monteverdi's *Orfeo* at the Salle Gaveau. An unintentional note of humour crept into the concert of the Palestrina Society held at the Schola in February; in response to his advertised talk on 'L'Art spiritualiste', d'Indy was inundated with literature from numerous esoterics, theosophists, yogists, cabalists, and psychists! And in June, a rumour spread that he was about to leave the Schola and replace Fauré as Director of the Conservatoire. Thoroughly stirred up with indignation, the Schola students planned an imposing procession to carry their revered master back from the rue de Madrid to his proper place in the rue Saint-Jacques. Needless to say, the rumour

---

[1] H.-L. de la Grange, *Gustav Mahler* (Paris, 1973), 699, 792.

179

was without foundation, and this extreme course of action proved unnecessary.[2]

The declaration of war by France against Germany aroused d'Indy to a state of high excitement, in which he felt himself about to relive the exertions of his youth in the defence of Paris. Leaving Les Faugs without delay, he rushed to the capital to volunteer for active military service—at the age of 63! To his disgust, he was rejected. Certainly, he was of the same mind as Barrès, who declared the second of August to be *Le Jour sacré*, in which all political disputes fell away before the overriding need to preserve the nation; moreover, there was now a distinct chance of regaining Alsace-Lorraine. And France would at last wake up and rouse itself from its pestilential swamp.

The initial German onslaught, which brought the war to the very gates of Paris, was successfully countered by the Battle of the Marne in September, driving the invader back behind the Aisne. D'Indy felt justifiably proud of his son Jean, a captain in the 18th Chasseurs; writing to Labey about the exploits of Jean's troop, he could not resist indulging himself in a little military romanticism at a time when the doctrine of the offensive at all costs still prevailed, and the fighting had not yet settled into the appalling immobility of trench warfare: 'They have often charged with drawn lances neither more nor less than twelfth-century pikemen, soon they will let them feel their shields, and then the illusion will be complete, and we shall be able to believe that we have returned to the age of Clisson and Desquesclin.'[3]

In the early days of the war, on 3 September, occurred an episode of great symbolic value, which may be crudely described as Magnard's 'last stand'. From his house in Baron, near Nanteuil-le-Haudoin, the composer rashly opened fire on two Uhlans who were about to enter. Soon afterwards, refusing to surrender, he was shot in retaliation, and his house, full of valuable works of art and original manuscripts, destroyed. In practical terms, it was no less than a tragic disaster, an

[2] See TS, Mar. 1914–Nov. 1918, for details of concerts held during the war. Gabéaud, *Auprès du maître*, ii. 14.

[3] Chiron, *Maurice Barrès*, 339–40. VI to Labey, 7 Nov. 1914, BN.

almost Gidean *acte gratuit* of senseless self-destruction. Yet the political journalist in Barrès could work the incident up into a paean of patriotic rhetoric: 'This skilled artist, in the middle of some *petit bourgeois* villas, makes himself, all alone, into the knight of civilization. An immense horizon stretches out before his inspired gaze. He springs forward to cover with his body the cathedrals of France, the French language, the nation-heir of Rome and Athens. See how the sceptic's son has chosen the heroic solution.' Fitting, too, was the comparison made with the Catholic poet Charles Péguy, who, before his death at the Marne, had written the celebrated lines:

> Heureux ceux qui sont morts pour la terre charnelle,
> Mais pourvu que ce fût dans une juste guerre.[4]

Fortified by the prevailing climate of optimism, d'Indy decided that the problems of the war should not prevent the Schola from opening in November for the new academic year. Those professors who had not been called up rallied to his appeal to resume their functions, and sixty-eight students—mainly women—enrolled, a remarkably small drop in numbers under the circumstances. The pages of *Les Tablettes* widened their scope to include lists of professors in active service—*inter alia* Roussel, an inspector of ambulances—and news from the Front. Several concerts were given in aid of the wounded. On 16 January 1915 the programme appropriately consisted of music by Magnard, his Violin Sonata and Act III of *Bérénice*, and Georges Pioche delivered an eloquent address, comparing the monstrous products of modern German *Kultur* unfavourably with the truly great artists, Bach and Beethoven. Happily, there was no proposal at the Schola, however patriotic, for the nonsense of a total ban on German music, as advocated by the National League for the Defence of French Music.

At the same time, more people were being made aware of the sheer labour which lay behind the organization of concerts. While the Schola's students willingly assumed the duties of setting out the platform for the orchestra and stewarding

---

[4] M. Barrès, E. Rostand, and E. Ganche, *1914, Une défense heroïque, Magnard* (Paris, 1915), 11–16.

at concerts, even such a *grande madame* as Edith Wharton,
the American authoress resident in Paris, found herself
approached by d'Indy and others to make her apartment at
25 rue de l'Université available for a small series of concerts
in aid of penniless musicians. Little did she know what she
was taking on:

> I vaguely thought one had only to 'throw open one's doors', as aris-
> tocratic hostesses do in fiction. Oh my! I'd rather write a three-vol-
> ume novel than do it again. . . . I have to be calling on the artists,
> having the programmes printed, reconciling jealous performers, and
> picking up lots of loose threads. However, it's the only chance of
> hearing any really good music this winter, and we *are* hearing it.[5]

Another feature of the times were the reunion dinners held
to cultivate the spirit of patriotism and keep alive the memories of 1870. D'Indy attended many of these, in the company
of the painter van Rysselberghe; the Keeper of the Louvre,
Camille Benoît; the archaeologist Schlumberger; and the
authors Henri Ghéon and André Gide. The last-named, however, had strong reservations about the rash enthusiasms of
this company, yet deemed it prudent to keep silent and devote
his time to refugee work. Indeed, d'Indy seemed to be casting
off his usual self-control and powers of judgement, for, according to Rolland:

> He is full of a mad gaiety. The war (who would have believed it) is
> his element. It is, in his words, the state of nature. . . . he declares
> that if his son is killed, it will be very proper, much better than
> dying in his bed. He is sure of victory, and is getting his motorcar
> ready, he says jocularly, to enter Berlin.

By the end of the year, he could say that

> The Schola is doing better and better, and is overflowing with pupils
> because of the refugees from the North, who no longer have the
> Conservatoires of Lille, Brussels, and Liège. . . . As for the rest, I
> consider this war extremely beneficial since it has forced from the
> depths of our hearts our old French qualities of clarity, logic, integ-
> rity, and uprightness. . . . All these qualities have now come to the
> surface again, breaking through the crust, and I believe that artis-

---

[5] *Letters of Edith Wharton*, 346.

tic progress will take the road of simplicity and beauty instead of seeking the small and the rare as in recent years, at least I hope so with all my heart.[6]

These high-flown sentiments of an Olympian detachment from the very real sufferings of his fellow countrymen would seem merely callous if the veteran of the Siege of Paris had not been prepared to expend himself to the full in the service of his country. For most men of his age, the direction of the Schola under wartime privations would have been sufficiently exhausting; yet a request from the Government to undertake propaganda concerts in allied countries was immediately complied with. It was some consolation for being denied the active military role which he craved.

That year, 1915, he managed to complete his third music drama, *La Légende de Saint-Christophe*, which had occupied him, with many interruptions, since 1908. This work is one of lofty philosophical pretentions, being no less than his profession of faith in the realm of thought, as well as art. The fifteenth-century *La Légende dorée* by Jacques de Voragine forms the basis of d'Indy's libretto, in which the action is transposed to the Ardèche and Vivarais. The opera is thus the ultimate celebration of French regionalism, with Saint-Christophe and even Christ himself present on the soil of the Ardèche. D'Indy also conflated two different legends: in the place of the giant of *La Légende dorée*, he substituted the Giant Ferryman of the Rhône, of local mythology, who lived on the rock of Crussol. Other characters, the lascivious Queen of Pleasure, the grinning King of Gold, and the Prince of Evil, were derived from the carved capitals of the medieval cathedrals.

For all its dramatic aspects, *Saint-Christophe* has features characteristic of the oratorio, not only the prominence of the chorus, but also the employment of a *Historicus* who delivers prologues to each of the three acts and certain scenes, surrounded by a choir in the ancient Greek manner, in front of the curtain; these prologues explain the parts of the action

[6] A. Gide, *Journal 1889–1939* (Paris, 1949), 313. Rolland, *Journal des années de guerre, 1914–1919* (Paris, 1952), 296. *Letters of Composers, an Anthology 1603–1945* (New York, 1946), 282–4.

which cannot be seen or those to be revealed later. In the Wagnerian array of leitmotifs, Gregorian themes play an important part; the deployment of tonality, too, is both complex and flexible, with the key of B major representing Christophe himself. Certainly, this key, which features prominently in many of his works, seems to have possessed special spiritual and psychological resonances for d'Indy.

In Act I, the giant Auférus has sworn on the altar of the God of Thunder to serve the most powerful master in the world. But his successive attendances on three worldly personages—the Queen of Pleasure, the King of Gold, the Prince of Evil—reveal only their weaknesses. The Queen's orgy of sexuality collapses before the King's financial might; he buys up her and her household, but in turn flees before the terrifying apparition of a sneering billy-goat announcing the Prince. A strange parade of false thinkers, scientists, artists, and socialists passes before Auférus, united in their hatred of Christ and charity. But even the Prince quails before the vision of a vast cathedral, confesses his falsehood, and disappears.

Musically, this act is marred by cliché and heavy-handed parody. The element of fake orientalism fails to ignite the orgy scene in which, as in *Istar*, a dancer throws off her transparent body veils to reveal her nudity. Unconvincing, too, is the attempt to evoke the moral hollowness of gold by Impressionist chains of parallel fourths and whole-tone harmonies. More seriously, the scene of 'Les Arrivistes orgueilleux' displays a gross lapse of taste, in the desiccated parody of Debussy's and Stravinsky's stylistic features—independent percussion writing, glissandi, and added second and ninth chords—to accompany the false artists who set the fashion and debunk idealism. In this context, the sublime seven-part chorus based on the Gregorian hymn 'Vexilla Regis', which marks the emergence of the cathedral, brings an abrupt change of tone, heightened by the numinous doubling of the voices by off-stage saxophones, as in *Fervaal*.

Act II takes place on an altogether higher aesthetic plane. Auférus sets out on a long voyage—symbolized by a march theme—in search of the King of Heaven, receiving negative responses from the Kings of the Earth and the Conquerors. On reaching Rome, he interrogates the Pope; but disappointed in the High Pontiff's prophecy, he returns to his native land. D'Indy had the brilliant idea—doubtless inspired by Siegfried's Rhine journey—of executing this scene as a symphonic poem for orchestra, providing a sense of movement in space impossible to represent scenically within a single *tableau*. Most impressive is the joyous representation of the Holy City by an extended section based on the Easter hymn 'Haec dies' (also used by Widor in his *Symphonie Romane*) with a cacophony of bell sonorities produced by clashing harmonies and cross-rhythms in the horn parts.

In the following scenes, Auférus confesses to a hermit, who makes him, as a penance, act as a benevolent ferryman across a raging torrent, the Eyrieux in the Ardèche, evoked in the orchestra by a moto perpetuo of rapid descending chromatic semiquavers. Among those seeking passage is the apparition of a child, whom Auférus takes in his arms; half-way across the torrent, he begins to stagger under the child's weight. But extraordinarily harsh, dissonant chord complexes—anticipating Tournemire and Messiaen—indicate that this is no mere physical discomfort, but rather labour pains in the process of rebirth, the transition from the old to the new life (Ex. 9*a*). The child announces himself to be Christ, as the themes of the Divine Presence and Divine Love, with agonized disjunct contour, are heard in the orchestra. A chromatic chord sequence representing the waters of life, clearly derived from the magic fire music in *Die Walküre*, introduces the baptism of Auférus with the name Christophore (porte-Christ).

This gift of new life, however, brings fresh sufferings and persecution. In Act III, Christophore languishes in prison, awaiting execution. For all its elevated spiritual tone, the scene is obviously indebted in its conception to Massenet's *Thaïs*, in which an Egyptian courtesan attempting to seduce a cenobite is converted to Christianity. In *Saint-Christophe*, Nicéa, the Queen of Pleasure, reappears to offer herself to the prisoner and effect his release. Resisting these temptations, he urges her to repent, singing of the miraculous power of Divine Love to bestow its cure upon those who freely renounce the

Ex. 9a. *La Légende de Saint-Christophe*, Act II, scene 3: 'Le torrent'

evil of their ways: the orchestra plays the gently undulating melody representing miracles, together with the Gregorian 'Qui vult venire' (Ex. 9*b*). The chord sequence of the waters of life is heard again as he pleads with her to think of God. The process of conversion proves to be even more painful and traumatic than that of baptism, as the body of Nicéa is visibly racked with convulsions. Again, d'Indy responded with an astonishing musical paroxysm of harmony; a two-note ostinato motive gradually contracts its rhythm in a mounting

Ex. 9b. *La Légende de Saint-Christophe*, Act III, scene 2: 'La prison'

crescendo, culminating in her triumphant outburst. As the trumpets blast out the miracle theme, she acknowledges the irresistible force of the Word of God which fills her whole being.

After this essentially interior drama, *Saint-Christophe* becomes spectacular grand opera; the execution scene in Halévy's *La Juive* and the auto-da-fé in Verdi's *Don Carlos* are surely the prototypes of the scene of Christophe's condemnation by the Grand Judge, formerly the King of Gold. In the great square, the gathering crowds express their admiration for him as he marches joyously to his death. As in the tradition of Greek tragedy, the actual execution is not played out on-stage, but is related to the audience by the crowd. At first, Christophe seems impervious to the torture of fire and arrows; but with the arrival of the executioner, armed with a long two-handed sword, a melodramatic *coup de théâtre* takes place. As the blade falls, Christophe's triumphant appeal to death is cut short in full cry, only to be taken up immediately by Nicéa, in a wordless vocalise rising in ecstasy. A choral apotheosis brings the work to a close with the transfiguration of Christophe.

Undoubtedly, d'Indy had created a work of monumental stature, yet in comparison with the essential openness of vision and potential at the root of both *Fervaal* and *L'Étranger*, the ethos of *Saint-Christophe* is backward-looking and reactionary. For all its passages of inspired invention, it is hard to deny the sense of a closing of the circle, the construction of a bulwark against the advancing tide of modernism and progressivism, with traditional Catholicism and regionalism pitted against the forces of social and cultural disintegration. As T. S. Eliot was to write in the following decade, 'These fragments I have shored against my ruins.'[7]

The war had become bogged down in the now all too familiar conditions of immobile trench fighting and Flanders mud. In March 1916, a month after the terrible German onslaught at Verdun, Jean d'Indy was promoted to Divisional Head-

[7] Giocanti, 'Vincent d'Indy et le régionalisme musical', 100. Eliot, *The Waste Land* (London, 1922), line 430.

quarters, as his proud father reported to Ropartz. It was at that dark hour that Barrès received the sobriquet 'Le rossignol du carnage' from Rolland for his strident articles in the *Echo de Paris*, which helped to keep the patriotic spirit aflame. It was important, too, that the culture and civilization of France be preserved and transmitted; the condition of the students could not therefore be neglected. In April, d'Indy conducted a concert of French music at the Salle Gaveau in aid of grants for study at the Schola. The wide-ranging programme consisted of Magnard's *Chant funèbre*, Rameau's Overture to *Castor et Pollux*, Franck's *Variations symphoniques*, Debussy's *La Demoiselle élue*, and Act I, scene 1, of Chabrier's *Gwendoline*.

Soon after the Battle of the Somme had dragged out its bloody course from July to September 1916, d'Indy was called to Italy on an important cultural mission to reinforce the links forged by that country's belated entry into the war. Barrès had already made a visit, to take the temperature on the Italian front with Austria, and the resulting newspaper articles made effective propaganda for the new ally. He was received by the poet Gabriele d'Annunzio—now a hero of the air force, wounded in one eye—with a concert of music by Franck and Ravel in his honour. On the day of Italy's declaration of war, d'Annunzio had proclaimed: 'We had two countries, and this evening we have only one, extending from French Flanders to the Sea of Sicily.' How appropriate, therefore, were the productions of Monteverdi's *Orfeo* in Florence and *Poppea* in Turin which d'Indy conducted in October, in addition to *Fervaal* at La Scala, Milan.[8]

While Europe consumed itself in violence unparalleled in the history of the world, the perennial rivalry between the two Paris musical societies, the S.N.M. and the S.M.I., continued to rumble on. To his credit, Fauré, who perceived the utter ridiculousness of the situation, endeavoured to bring them together in a new Société Nationale. But the younger element in the S.M.I. failed to co-operate. 'It didn't work at all,' d'Indy wrote to Sérieyx; 'Ravel, Koechlin, Grovlez, Casadésus

[8] VI to GR, 4 Mar. 1916, BN. Chiron, *Maurice Barrès*, 343–4, 352–3. LV ii. 97–8.

and co. declined in the name of their "aesthetics"??? "which cannot ever be the same as ours". I must say I thought it was extremely funny, and I'm still giggling about it.' Fauré's second attempt was no more successful, as d'Indy could not resist antagonizing the modernists with silly taunts about 'the stuttering cut of their uniform'. Moreover, Ravel took up cudgels with Doire, editor of the *Courrier musical* in February 1917: 'Monsieur d'Indy, in the name of music and the sacred alliance, spreads ironic and spiteful remarks concerning some younger colleagues, most of whom, at the moment, are occupied with other tasks. I am astonished that neither of you realized that the right of reply is forbidden to soldiers, and it would therefore have been better to wait before entering into this polemic.'[9]

The new year had opened with little sign of progress on the military front, although d'Indy derived some measure of satisfaction from the news that Jean took part in an attack with thirty-five men, capturing eighty-two prisoners—all students, as it happened, at the University of Berlin. Meanwhile, the students at the Schola were labouring under conditions of acute discomfort to put on a concert of religious music—Gregorian chants, polyphonic works, and modern pieces by Franck and Bordes. Fuel for heat and light had run out during the long spell of very cold weather, and d'Indy was full of admiration for his young pupils who blew on their fingers during rehearsals in the freezing hall of the Schola. The following month, he directed Bach's St John Passion at the Salle Gaveau, although he was obliged to make cuts, since the police had issued orders that concerts must not be excessively long.[10]

The class in orchestral conducting at the Conservatoire took place, despite the small number of students and available players. Not entirely surprisingly, d'Indy had become frustrated with providing mere technical instruction in beating time. With Fauré's blessing, the composition students were now permitted to direct performances of their own pieces.

[9] Nectoux, *Gabriel Fauré*, 403. *Lettres à Auguste Sérieyx*, 24–5. A. Orenstein (ed.), *A Ravel Reader, Correspondence, Articles, Interviews* (New York, 1990), 180–1.
[10] VI to GR, 7 Feb. 1917, BN.

With assistance and advice from d'Indy, they could gauge the effectiveness or otherwise of their instrumentation. A notable member of the class at that time was Arthur Honegger, from neutral Switzerland, who tried out his first orchestral composition, *Aglavaine et Sélysette*, in April 1917, and one year later, the *Chant de Nigamon*, receiving both encouragement and explanation of the weaknesses of certain passages.[11]

As chance would have it, a decisive change in d'Indy's personal life was on the horizon. Deprived of the opportunity for active service, he felt the need to mix with off-duty soldiers in cafés and restaurants, so that through them he might gain some degree of contact with front-line conditions. On one of these nocturnal forays, he happened to meet up with the daughter of an NCO in a brasserie in Montparnasse. Born in 1887, Caroline Janson turned out to be a musician herself, a former piano student at the Versailles Conservatoire. The rapport between them was immediate, and indeed permanent: with a sensitive understanding of the void in his existence, she became first his confidante, and later, in 1920, his wife. Significantly, he was beginning to forsake Les Faugs with all its old associations, and spend an increasing amount of his vacation time on the shores of the Mediterranean.[12]

His new-found bliss could not blind him to the realities of the times. Much as he suffered as a result of the deaths in action that summer of four of his nephews—one of them an airman shot down by a German masquerading in French colours—his spirits remained hopeful in the face of so much bravery and heroism. Despite the withdrawal of Russia from the war, by the separate treaty of Brest-Litovsk, he remained confident that the end was in sight.

Naturally, there was a musical response to the war on his part, of no uncertain belligerence. He had conceived a new *Symphonie Brevis* back in 1916; writing to Ropartz, he envisaged it as having a classical symphonic time scale of about 40 minutes, in reaction to the modern *Boches* and their *Kolossale-Symphonie* lasting three and a half hours—a swipe at

[11] A. Honegger, 'Souvenirs sur la classe de Vincent d'Indy au Conservatoire', RM, 10 (1951). A. Tappolet, *Arthur Honegger* (Neuchâtel, 1938), 25–6, 33, 40.

[12] LV ii. 101–2. Goichot, article in *Revue Drômoise*, no. 421 (Oct. 1981), 403.

Bruckner and Mahler. Its programme, too, was crudely graphic and jingoistic:

First movement:	Mobilization—the Marne
Scherzo:	Gaiety at the Front
Andante:	*L'Art latin et l'art Boche*
Finale:	Victory, with the hymn of St Michael as peroration

This, however, was to be divulged to friends only, and not printed for the public, for which the following plain titles would suffice: Introduction—*animé*, Divertissement, Lent, Final. He added, slyly, 'there is nothing *Stravinskyste* [sic] about it.' This concealment of the work's programme seems suspicious; perhaps he thought better of mixing the high aspiration of the symphony with patriotic propaganda. In any case, the work is generally considered as comparatively trite, and even unworthy of its composer.[13]

As it happened, a much finer work reflecting the war came from Louis Vierne. A serious operation on his eyes had compelled him to take leave of absence from the Schola and Notre Dame. While convalescing in Switzerland, he wrote his Fourth Organ Symphony, in G minor. Although it has no explicit programme, its character of grim, sombre magnificence seems to stand as a threnody for an entire doomed generation, transcending his own particular, intense grief for his son and brother, both killed in action.[14]

With the launch of the final German offensive along the entire Western front in March 1918, d'Indy's spirits rose to fever pitch. The sense of imminent and increasing danger, the electric atmosphere of suspense, the awareness of great movements of men and armies, all moved him to transports of primitive excitement, heightened by regular attacks from the air. Maus learned that

For the last fortnight, the life of Paris has taken on an excessively picturesque aspect with the bombings by aeroplanes, when the complete blackout of light, even of the slightest gleam turns the boulevards of Paris—especially Montparnasse and Raspail, which are in

---

[13] VI to GR, 4 Jan. 1918, BN.   [14] Vierne, *Mes Souvenirs*.

the direct path of the moon—into absolutely fantastic landscapes
that have to be seen to be believed. There's nothing more terrific
than a walk in these abandoned places where you see *nothing* but
indistinct monuments looking like Cyclopean dwellings, while, near
and far, incendiary bombs explode, and the rumbling of the defend-
ing guns goes on like an organ pedal-point. You have missed a lot if
you haven't seen Paris like this.

Neither did he flinch when the bombardment intensified,
and the 'Big Berthas' fired on the city from a distance of 75
miles. In an almost foolhardy manner, he expressed his contempt for the *Kolossal Kanon* [sic] for which each shot cost
22,000–24,000 francs, just to make little holes of 80 centi-
metres in the public parks! He loved to boast about a shell
which burst near him in the Square de l'Observatoire; quite
unperturbed, he proceeded to measure the hole—4 or 5 metres
in diameter, he recorded with evident self-satisfaction.
Naturally, it was business as usual at the Schola. His soldier's
ability to contemplate death calmly made him unsympathetic
to the nervousness of others. He would remonstrate with students exhausted after nights spent in underground shelters:
'You would be much better off in your bed. At least there's
no risk of getting rheumatism!'

Despite the breakdown of tram and metro services in the
course of a day of severe air raids, the students began to arrive
on foot at the Salle Gaveau, together with a sizeable audience,
for a scheduled performance of Beethoven's *Missa Solemnis*.
But at the last moment the police intervened, insisting that
the concert be postponed to the following week. D'Indy was
quick to see the irony of the situation: 'The sabotage of
Beethoven by the Boches, that's original.' On 29 March, however—four days after the death of Debussy—there was no
longer any place for bravado and grim humour. Saint-Gervais
was directly hit by a shell while a concert was in progress.
Among those who died was a student of the Schola; and
another was wounded.

Shaken by this shocking turn of events, d'Indy realized that
he had been assuming excessive powers and responsibilities
with regard to the lives in his charge. He decided that further
actions be taken in consultation with his staff, and called a

special meeting on 24 April, at which the decision was taken to keep the Schola open, following the example of the university and the schools. The precedent of the Siege of 1870–1 was also cited, during which the musical life of the city had continued. D'Indy duly expressed his appreciation of those colleagues who had bravely remained at their posts, while others who took the safe option of fleeing Paris were considered to have resigned, their positions being filled immediately. Likewise, absent students—if not called up—were liable for payment of fees in full, having placed themselves in breach of contract.

The end of the war was imminent; divisions from the United States were pouring in, and, as from July, the Allies began their final, successful thrust against the German armies. To mark the Armistice in November, the *Tablettes* carried a victory notice: 'Let us take strong resolutions that there will never again be any *neurasthenia*, that destructive scourge, among us, so that nobody can wrongly make it out to be the perquisite of artistic spirits!' D'Indy was to be found among the crowds in the Place de la Concorde, watching 'all the German artillery and tanks rolling along at liberty throughout Paris, the American soldiers mounted all along the Big Berthas, and talking gibberish with clownish gestures'.[15]

[15] VI to OM, 29 Mar., 19 Nov. 1918, RBM. Gabéaud, *Auprès du maître*, ii. 15–17. TS, June, Nov. 1918.

12

Mediterranean Summers

With the end of the Great War, d'Indy's exhilaration knew no bounds. At last, it seemed that the German menace was a thing of the past, and the question of Alsace-Lorraine resolved. To add humiliation to defeat, Clemenceau insisted that the peace treaty be signed in Louis XIV's Palace of Versailles, where, in 1871, in the same Hall of Mirrors, Bismarck had proclaimed William I Emperor of Germany. But if d'Indy had regarded the war itself as a terrible though necessary purgation of the corrupt state of France, he was painfully to discover that its aftermath would fail to bring the expected moral and cultural regeneration. Indeed, the chief political preoccupation was with the disastrous state of the economy and galloping inflation. At the same time, the ongoing thrust of technological change and materialism continued with alarming intensity, to the detriment of traditional values; and the corresponding obsession with the 'machine age' and industrial processes which characterized this post-war era clearly affected the artistic world.

Particularly disturbing for d'Indy was the realization that tendencies towards irrationalism and disintegration which had emerged before the war, far from proving ephemeral, were becoming entrenched in the Dada and Surrealist movements. Hardly more welcome was the pervasive influence of Jean Cocteau, that arbiter of Parisian chic, whose concept of 'lifestyle modernism', the art of the sophisticated commonplace reflecting the consumer styles of the French upper classes, left its mark on many ballet productions in the 1920s. The forerunner of these was *Parade* (1917), with cubist décor by Picasso and music by Satie, the latter not alone among d'Indy's former students in becoming absorbed in this novel aesthetic world. Georges Auric—a renegade Schola student—and Honegger were now members of the group known as 'Les Six', together with Milhaud, Poulenc, Tailleferre, and Durey. D'Indy was especially quick to disown Auric, whose *Foxtrot* he called 'the most foolish effort I have seen since the works of Th. Dubois!' Auric, moreover, soon found himself Cocteau's favourite among Les Six, as fully at home in the world of the circus, jazz, music-hall, and cinema as in the contrasting 'retrospective classicism'—the *grand siècle* of Louis XIV superficially restyled for modern tastes—the very idea of which would have made d'Indy feel physically sick. Both life-style modernism and retrospective classicism were exemplified in Diaghilev's ballets *Les Fâcheux*, *Les Matelots*, and *La Pastorale*, of which Auric's slick pastiche scores formed an integral part.

To the younger generation, d'Indy seemed merely an unwelcome survivor from an obsolete past, the epitome of pedantry; the domineering Catholic poet Paul Claudel expressed himself to Milhaud concerning incidental music to a play of his: 'I am very interested in what you've written to me about *Protée*. Well up to time! It's a pleasure to work with you. You don't take seventeen years like M. Vincent d'Indy to get a score ready.'[1]

From a not entirely unexpected quarter came an attack on d'Indy's *Cours*, rather late in the day, but couched in the most elegant and civilized language. At the very end of his long life, the embittered veteran Saint-Saëns—who himself complained of being treated like mere scrap iron—produced a short book entitled *Les Idées de M. Vincent d'Indy*. He maintained that d'Indy's ideas were not his own, but were heavily indebted to the German theorists Riemann, Hauptmann, Helmholtz, and van Oettingen. D'Indy was also castigated for drawing upon corrupt Bach editions for his musical illustrations, instead of Peters' *Bachgesellschaft*. Saint-Saëns went on to assert that

---

[1] Garafola, *Diaghilev's Ballets Russes*, 98–143. *Cahiers Paul Claudel* (Paris, 1961), iii. 54–5. VI to GR, 20 Sept. 1920, BN.

music is an *art plastique* composed of forms, whereas 'Like Tolstoy, like M. Barrès . . . M. d'Indy seems only to see expression and passion in art'. This eternal quasi-theological argument was still going round in circles; Dukas had earlier contributed the view that 'the error of all the neo-classicists is precisely that of attributing a value to form independently of ideas'. Certainly, d'Indy always firmly held to the doctrine— which vaguely resembles the scholastic notion of substance and accident—that 'Franck never considered that manifestation of a work which we call *form* as anything but the *corporeal* part of the entity of an art work . . . destined to serve as the visible outer covering of the *idea*, which he called "the soul of music" '.[2]

Unlike the proverbial old soldier, d'Indy had no intention of fading away on reaching the age of 70. On the contrary, finding himself seriously affected financially by the economic crisis, and to avoid selling Les Faugs, he accepted a punishing schedule of conducting engagements in France and abroad. On 14 May 1919 he directed the première of Fauré's *Fantaisie* for piano and orchestra with Alfred Cortot at an S.N.M. concert at the Salle Gaveau. He also regularly appeared with Casals's orchestra in Barcelona.[3]

Student numbers at the Schola were keeping up well, with an enrolment of almost 600. But throughout 1919, the untimely indisposition of his assistant Lioncourt obliged d'Indy to teach all twelve courses of composition, in addition to the orchestral class. Another blow, which he felt keenly, was a quarrel and complete break with Blanche Selva; history does not relate why this happened, but could it have been jealousy on her part of Caroline Janson's entry into her beloved master's life? But if he had lost a distinguished piano professor, he at least had the consolation of welcoming back Vierne, now sufficiently restored to health to resume the organ professorship.

The great pioneering days of the Schola were now undoubtedly in the past. Exorbitant costs had reduced the scope of its

[2] C. Saint-Saëns, *Les Idées de M. Vincent d'Indy* (Paris, 1919), 8–11. *Les Écrits de Paul Dukas*, 610. CF 75.

[3] Nectoux, *Gabriel Fauré*, 522. H. L. Kirk, *Pablo Casals* (London, 1974), 339.

concerts, and the brightest students were going to the Conservatoire, which had benefited immensely from the reforms carried out by Fauré. Nevertheless, the Schola continued to attract sizeable contingents from South America, whose members returned to make significant contributions to the culture of their own countries. From Columbia came Guillermo Uribe-Holguin, later Director of the Conservatorio Nacional, and Antonio María Valencia, founder of the Conservatorio de Cali; from Argentina, Juan José Castro and Juan Carlos Paz, the former to become a leading figure in the nationalist movement of the 1930s, the latter an outspoken critic of nationalism and founder in 1944 of the Agrupacíon Nueva Musica which promoted the music of Schoenberg, Webern, Varèse, Cage, and Messiaen.

Among the post-war influx of students from the United States was one Cole Porter. Feeling the need of some solid grounding in composition, the future writer of the famous American musical *Kiss me Kate* enrolled in d'Indy's class at the Schola. But before long he dropped out, finding the regime too academic for his particular kind of talent, which needed to blossom spontaneously. Yet he did not repudiate his brief time there, as it proved to be a useful badge of respectability back home in the States.[4]

Depressed as he was by the wholesale adoption of modernist innovations by young composers, d'Indy forced himself to keep abreast of current developments and to attend a Dadaist séance. This was probably the 'Manifestation Dada' held at the Maison de l'Œuvre on 27 March 1920, featuring Tristan Tzara's *La Première Aventure céleste de M. Antipyrine* and André Breton reading Francis Picabia's *Manifeste cannibale* in total darkness. He came away from this descent into the depths of cultural nihilism relieved to find that he still retained his intellectual faculties and sanity! On the other hand, Satie redeemed himself in his old professor's eyes on the occasion of the public première of *Socrate* at the S.N.M. on 14

[4] *Lettres à Auguste Sérieyx etc.*, 25–7. G. Béhague, *Music in Latin America, an Introduction* (Englewood Cliffs, NJ, 1979). G. Eells, *The Life that he Led, a Biography of Cole Porter* (London, 1967), 55. C. Schwartz, *Cole Porter, a Biography* (London, 1978), 56–7.

February 1920. Commissioned by the Princesse de Polignac, this *drame symphonique* consisting of extracts from the dialogues of Plato was performed by the sopranos Jane Bathori and Suzanne Balguérie to a mixed reception from the audience. Its simple austere textures and severe classical spirit appealed to d'Indy, who discovered in it passages of true poetry and musical feeling.[5]

At last, the Paris Opéra had girded itself up, under Rouché's directorship, to mount *La Légende de Saint-Christophe*. Preparations for its production did not run smoothly, however, and it seemed that the troubled history of *Fervaal* in Brussels was about to be repeated. D'Indy complained to Sérieyx about wasted time in rehearsals, and the need for him to be always on hand to save what had already been achieved from being ruined; and rising costs and union obstructiveness added considerably to the problems. Despite the efficiency of Ruhlmann's musical direction, preparations came to a standstill with the failure of the chorus to learn its music, and further rehearsals had to be postponed. The otherwise suitable month of May proved impossible, for not only would Ida Rubinstein be in the midst of rehearsals for Florent Schmitt's *Antoine et Cléopâtre*, but Diaghilev, too, was scheduled to mount the premières of *Pulcinella* and *Le Astuzie Femminili*. Understandably, on this occasion, d'Indy was in chauvinistic mood, grumbling to Sérieyx that 'Right through this pretty month of May, the Académie *nationale* de musique has become the exclusive property of the [Russian] ballets . . . so that the French can't use the stage for a day, not *an hour*'.

The première of *Saint-Christophe* finally took place in June, with the role of Nicéa sung by the great soprano Germaine Lubin. It was greeted with respect for its qualities of austerity, sobriety, and religious strength, not normally found in theatre works. To the distinguished critic Henri Prunières, writing in *La Revue musicale*, it was 'a vast fresco in sound, comparable to church mural paintings'. He added that 'D'Indy has never written anything stronger or nobler than the symphonic introduction of the second act, "La Queste de

[5] W. S. Rubin, *Dada and Surrealist Art* (London, 1969), 457–8. *Lettres à Auguste Sérieyx*, 26. De Cossart, *The Food of Love*, 136–8.

Dieu", and the prison scene in the third act'. Unfortunately,
Rouché found the scene of Nicéa's conversion distasteful, and
used all manner of subterfuges to induce d'Indy to cut it—
without success, needless to say. But in a performance later in
the month, Rouché took advantage of an indisposition in the
cast to make this cut on his own authority; however, the pan-
demonium which broke out in the audience persuaded him to
restore the scene forthwith.[6]

These years of unremitting professional toil might well have
taken their toll on his health and morale if d'Indy had not
been recharged physically and psychologically by his engage-
ment and marriage to Caroline Janson on 26 October 1920. It
was as if he had finally shed the burden of sorrow and loneli-
ness after Isabelle's death, together with the mental armour
of defiance which he presented to the world in those disturbing pre-war days of ideological conflict. To his life Caroline
brought fresh experiences which, dare one say, he perhaps
never really enjoyed before: a sense of fun and playfulness, a
certain irresponsibility, even full sexual surrender to a woman
representative not of family piety and self-sacrificing devotion, but of the very pleasure principle itself.

In the face of his family's objections to this supposed mis-
alliance, his will remained as firm as ever. Nor did his practical judgement desert him in his determination not to build his
new life with Caroline amid the ghosts of Les Faugs. Making
over the property and estate to his son Jean, he had a villa
built at Agay on the Côte d'Azur, near the sea and surrounded
by maritime pine-trees and red-coloured rocks of porphyry.
There, together with his new wife, he spent his periods of
vacation, composing and frequently bathing in the transparent waters of the little creek nearby.[7]

This change in his personal life brought about a corresponding creative renewal. Just as Franck's deep love for
Augusta Holmès had inspired the astonishing series of masterpieces of his final decade, so it was much to Caroline's credit

---

[6] *Lettres à Auguste Sérieyx*, 28–9. De Cossart, *Ida Rubinstein*, 79–80. Garafola,
Diaghilev's Ballets Russes, 407–8. Prunières, RM, 1 (1920), 47–8.

[7] C. Boller, 'Quelques souvenirs sur Vincent d'Indy', *Feuilles musicales* (Lausanne),
no. 3 (1951), 63.

that d'Indy in his own last years could compose what are arguably his finest works, the orchestral *Poème des rivages* and *Diptyque Méditerranéen*. In these, the pleinairism of the earlier *Symphonie Cévenole* and *Jour d'été à la montagne* has been transferred from the bleak, chill Ardèche to the brilliant sensuous climate of the Mediterranean shores. Indeed, at this point in his life, there is a certain similarity to the poet Paul Valéry, for whom the Mediterranean provided a permanent source of inspiration; like d'Indy, he was very Latin in his temperament, lucid thought, and disciplined rigour. By a nice coincidence, his great poem *Le Cimetière marin* appeared in *La Nouvelle Revue française* in 1920, the year *Poème des rivages* was completed; both works exult in the primitive pagan elements of nature, the sea, the sky, and the sun, symbolizing life and creative rebirth.

> Non, non! . . . Debout! Dans l'ère successive!
> Brisez, mon corps, cette forme pensive!
> Buvez, mon sein, la naissance du vent!
> Une fraîcheur, de la mer exhalée
> Me rend mon âme . . . O puissance salée!
> Courons à l'onde en rejaillir vivant!

(No, no! . . . Up! Into the coming era! My body, shatter this pensive shape! My breast, drink the wind's birth! A coolness breathed forth by the sea gives me back my soul . . . O salt power! Let us run to the waves and spring from them again alive!—*The Penguin Book of French Verse* ed. A. Hartley, Harmondsworth, 1959), p. 71)

The four movements of *Poème des rivages* evoke places dominated by the sea—Agay, Miramar de Mallorca, both on the Mediterranean, Falconara on the Adriatic, and the Bay of Biscay looking out to the Atlantic Ocean. D'Indy's totally assured handling of a large orchestra is breath-taking; essential to the score—obligatory, as he insisted to Ropartz—is the ensemble of four saxophones (alto, two tenors, and baritone) blended into the textures with incomparable finesse and aural imagination. The work's effectiveness also owes much to his control of structure, regard for symmetries, and balance between static and dynamic elements. Indeed, these classical principles of organization are handled with such freedom as to dispel finally the image of the pedagogue.

Notable, too, is the very considerable part that expansive melodic and polyphonic invention plays in this glistening, Impressionist-sounding score, apparent in the first movement, 'Calme et lumière'. After an initial Debussyan broken chord formation in rising open fifths, gently undulating waves are depicted by a developing six-note phrase (reminiscent of the opening of Debussy's *Nocturnes*), above which the first violins gradually unfold an endless, almost Wagnerian melodic line. At the same time, there is a vividly pictorial feeling for the effects of light, realized in sonic terms; in the reprise, the saxophone quartet contributes to the remote, sensuously pagan atmosphere, ruffled by the lightest of breezes, suggested by rapid rising scales in the violins.

The sparkling play of the wind and the waves in the brilliant sunlight is heard in 'La joie de bleu profond', which is characterized by expansive string melodies of energy and warmth, accompanied by almost 'technicolour' arpeggio figuration in the woodwind and saxophones. But for sheer inventiveness of texture, most remarkable is 'Horizons verts', a scherzo and trio. Here, modern civilization breaks in on the natural world with the precursor of those celebrated musical railway journeys—Honegger's *Pacific 231* and Villa-Lobos's 'O tremzinho do Caipira' from *Bachianas brasileiras* no. 2. D'Indy's little train, chugging round the Adriatic shores, is affectionately evoked with the utmost economy of means, using ostinato patterns in the lower strings and bassoons and single notes on piano and timpani, tellingly placed. Again, the effects of light are stunningly realized in an extraordinary whole-tone section of 'staggered' string entries—a device subsequently exploited and popularized by Mantovani—producing the effect of a shimmering heat-haze (Ex. 10a). A slow passage of multiple string harmonics is also very striking, an effect taken up by Honegger in his 1926 score for Rubinstein's ballet *Phèdre*.

It was entirely characteristic of d'Indy that he should bring these picturesque musical evocations of enclosed, land-locked seas into a wider, almost philosophical perspective. Thus the finale, 'Le mystère de l'Océan', with its vision of immeasurable expanses and unfathomable depths, gathers up these

Ex. 10a. *Poème des rivages*, 'Horizons verts'

Ex. 10b. *Poème des rivages*, 'Le mystère de l'Océan'

individual phenomena, as it were, and merges them into a symbolic totality of existence. To this end, the cyclic principle is at work, for the various interrelated ideas which played a subsidiary part in the previous movements are now the main thematic material, powerfully stated by the trumpet (Ex. 10*b*). Yet d'Indy's ocean is no mere metaphysical abstraction; among its varied moods are brooding menace, furious onslaughts of wind and tide, as well as lighter passages of spray and dancing waves, where the pert rising third motive— a feature of the previous movements—reappears. Echoes of Wagner and Franck are to be heard in the moving outbursts of passionate melody; yet, at the same time, the depth of orchestral sonority and dynamic rhythmic thrust points the way towards Honegger's mature symphonic style. It is small wonder that d'Indy told Ropartz he was very pleased with the work, which achieved what he wanted.

At the end of the year, in December 1921, he undertook a demanding tour of North America, conducting, lecturing, and playing the piano. To Sérieyx he enthused about the excellent qualities of the orchestras—above all their attention and discipline in varied programmes, including music by Bach, Lalande, Le Flem, and Roussel. Most important, the world première of *Poème des rivages* took place on 1 December in New York, where it had a very favourable reception. Yet he felt that a glut of music was to be had in the New World, with at least two concerts each day.

The tour, organized on a tight schedule, kept him on the move, with little free time in which to recover from concerts or meditate. But in Boston, he had the opportunity to hear two works from the feverish twilight world of Central European expressionism. Schoenberg's *Five Orchestral Pieces*, op. 16, came across to him as joyless, expressionless, purposeless music. He had even less time for Korngold's opera *Dïe todte Stadt*, which he deemed '*very bad* music . . . mere sub-Puccini, a quintessence of Leoncavallo, with an orchestra à la Darius Milhaud! . . . It's grotesque.' In fact, these works gave him more nausea than the tempestuous return crossing of the Atlantic on board the *Paris*: the damage to the furniture caused by the rolling of the ship he found perversely amusing! And, on his arrival home, there was a mountain of work awaiting him.[8]

The year 1922 brought commemorations and retrospectives. On 22 June, in the Amphitheatre of the Sorbonne, in the presence of President Millerand, there was a national homage to Fauré, now very old and suffering from acute deafness, and with only two years of life left to him. As one of a distinguished line-up of musicians, numbering Cortot, Casals, and the soprano Claire Croiza, d'Indy was present to direct a per-

---

[8] *Lettres à Auguste Sérieyx*, 29. VI to GR, 20 Sept. 1920, 2 Sept., 8 Dec. 1921, BN. The reference to Schoenberg's 'dernière suite' must surely be to the *Five Orchestral Pieces*, op. 16 (1909).

formance of Fauré's *Cantique de Jean Racine*. In the same
month, a Congress of Church Music was held under the presidency of Cardinal Dubois. Together with the leading authorities on Gregorian chant, Dom Mocquereau and Gastoué,
d'Indy took a leading part in the proceedings. In his lecture
'Cantiques et motets grégoriens', he roundly condemned most
of the religious music of the nineteenth century as *chansons de
cabaret*, and defended the purportedly authentic Vatican edition of the plainchant against other modern editions which
obscured the melodic lines with a profusion of additional symbols and supplementary indications.[9]

Meanwhile, the late developer Albert Roussel, a kind of
musical Joseph Conrad, was truly getting into his stride. Two
years after the première of his formidable Second Symphony
(the last of his works indebted to d'Indy's conceptions), his
opera-ballet *Padmâvati*, based on an Indian legend, reached
the stage of the Opéra. Its lengthy gestation had begun in
1908 with a performance of Lalo's *Namouna*, when d'Indy
pronounced that 'something worthwhile could be done with
the ballet nowadays'. After a visit to India, Roussel began
work on *Padmâvati*, on which the subcontinent left its mark
in the form of Hindu scales.[10]

From exotic climes in the Western hemisphere, a youthful
Brazilian composer, Heitor Villa-Lobos, arrived in Paris to
seek a European platform for his folk and ethnically inspired
works, such as the *Nonet*, subtitled *Impressão rápida do todo o
Brasil*, which received a performance there in 1924. Entirely
self-taught, he had nevertheless made a thorough study of
d'Indy's *Cours*, for Brazil was then strongly under the cultural
influence of France. Indeed, according to Milhaud, who had
spent some of the war years there as secretary to the French
consul, Paul Claudel, concerts in Rio de Janeiro frequently
programmed music by d'Indy, Debussy, Chausson, Dukas,
and Roussel. In the judgement of Villa-Lobos's biographer
Vasco Mariz, d'Indy's technical influence is apparent in the
early symphonies, nos. 1 and 2, and the Second Cello Sonata.
In Paris, the Brazilian searched out the French master, who

[9] Nectoux, *Gabriel Fauré*, 425. RBM, no. 4 (Feb. 1923), 70–1.
[10] Deane, *Albert Roussel*, 85.

offered encouragement for his projects, and suggested changes
to the symphonies, nos. 3 and 4, then in progress. These, however, were not to be completed. At this time, Villa-Lobos was
seriously pondering whether composing in traditional classical
forms was still a viable proposition; at the same time, his stay
in Paris provided a necessary distancing perspective on Brazil.
The fruits of these reflections were to be the cycle of nine
Bachianas brasileiras (1930–45), a true synthesis of Brazilian
and European musical language. On his return to his own
country in 1930, he carried with him the torch of didacticism
and educational propaganda, seemingly lit by d'Indy. As
director of the Superintêndencia de Educação Musical e
Artistica under the benevolent dictatorship of Getulio Vargas,
Villa-Lobos instigated ambitious programmes, including mass
choral rallies for the singing of patriotic songs and hymns,
intended as a moral and civic training; the Brazilian premières
of Bach's B minor Mass, Palestrina's *Missa Papae Marcelli*,
and Beethoven's *Missa Solemnis*; and a flood of writings on
teaching methods underpinned by philosophical and historical
theorizing. It was as if the Schola Cantorum were operating as
the cultural arm of authoritarian government policy.[11]

The autumn of 1923 had promised to be particularly oner-
ous for d'Indy, but even his summer vacation at Agay was not
without incident. Forest fires raged in the vicinity, but not
sufficiently to keep him from working on his new but unsuc-
cessful *drame-bouffe Le Rêve de Cinyras*. True to form, he relished the excitement, while his keen visual sense was
fascinated by the curious tints which the burned countryside
displayed and the quality of the sunlight through the intense
smoke, as with an eclipse.[12]

After supervising the examinations at the Schola in
October, he set off directly for a concert tour of Eastern
Europe, visiting Bucharest and Riga, and returning to Paris
in November in time for the start of the Conservatoire's conducting class. The following month was marked by the death

[11] D. Milhaud, 'La musique en Brésil', RM (1920), 60–1. V. Mariz, *Villa-Lobos, Life
and Work* (Washington, DC, 1963), 10, 18. S. Wright, *Villa-Lobos* (Oxford, 1992), 41,
78–9.

[12] *Lettres à A. Sérieyx*, 30.

Mediterranean Summers

of Barrès, whose state funeral took place at Notre Dame in the presence of President Millerand, with Vierne playing the great organ of the cathedral.[13]

The opera and ballet season of 1924 consisted of a most interesting series of premières and revivals, among them Widor's *Nerto* and Tournemire's *Les Dieux sont morts*. Diaghilev's Russian Ballet mounted Milhaud's *Le Train bleu*, Poulenc's *Les Biches*, and—sandwiched between Stravinsky's *Petrushka* and *Les Noces*—Auric's *Les Fâcheux*, whose lack of nobility and introduction of 'wrong notes' into a pastiche of old music aroused his old professor's ire. Two considerably risqué pieces, very much of their pre-war, symbolist period, were boldly revived by Ida Rubinstein: Debussy's *Le Martyre de Saint-Sébastien* and d'Indy's *Istar*. It was not the first time that the latter had been choreographed, but at her charity gala at the Opéra in February, Rubinstein, renowned for the shapeliness of her legs as much as for her statuesque figure, certainly made *Istar* her own, even christening her private yacht after it! Unfortunately, the production made excessive demands on the celebrated designer Léon Bakst, who died at the end of the year.

Further performances, using his sets and costumes, took place at charity events in 1926 and 1927, where, according to her biographer, Michael de Cossart, Rubinstein's 'high-class striptease act' was much appreciated by the war veterans! The reactions of the critics were in a more intellectual vein. André Levinson considered Leo Staat's choreography to be entirely perverse and contrary to the work's hierarchical and monumental character; for Rubinstein's role consisted of a long promenade on points, whereas the heavy step on the entire sole of the foot of the Chaldean figures in the Louvre would have been more appropriate. On the other hand, Bakst's massive décor, though departing from the lively pictorialism and movement of Assyrian sculpture, rightly concentrated on the fierce grandeur of the metaphysical conflict: 'This system of wide, eccentric curves, of rounded areas, encircles the protagonist like a prison without an exit. Istar's anguish hugs the

[13] Chiron, *Maurice Barrès*, 384.

circular wall, enclosed and implacable like the parade of the Hache in [Flaubert's] *Salammbô*.'

Another critic, Henry Malherbe, observed that, although her technique was not beyond reproach, Rubinstein was strange, slight, and beautiful: 'Few ballerinas could disrobe on the stage of the Opéra with such aristocratic nonchalance as not to offend decorum.' He went on to state that Bakst had resolutely discarded the subject and sense of the Chaldean epoch in favour of the Catholic occultist symbolism of Joséphin Péladan, citing the designer's own words:

I applied myself to treating this subject in an astrological and cabbalistic sense—Istar's vestments are, moreover, embroidered with the different emblems of the Cabbala—and these are the astral forces which encircle the unsatisfied soul to prevent it from attaining the desired end. . . . At the seventh door, her nudity, her earthly beauty, triumphs, the forces of darkness are repelled, Paradise collapses, and the Son of Life appears and leads her away, who sought him so obstinately.

Did these occultist elements in the production have the blessing of d'Indy himself? Although he appears not to have played any part in it (the orchestra being in the capable hands of Philippe Gaubert), he had had at least a passing acquaintance with the outlandish Péladan, who combined a pseudo-Assyrian cult with a hermetic mysticism; at his soirées of the Rose + Croix in 1892, d'Indy had directed works by Franck and his pupils.[14]

The Mediterranean continued to be a source of inspiration to him. In 1926, he completed his last orchestral work, the *Diptyque Méditerranéen*. Though rather less ambitious in scale than the *Poème des rivages*, it is nevertheless outstanding in its melodic invention, and imbued with a deep poignancy of feeling as if, at the age of 75, he realized that his days on earth were numbered. In keeping with this valetudinary atmosphere, the score is suffused with a more mellow light, by con-

[14] De Cossart, *Ida Rubinstein*, 100, 112. A. Levinson, *La Danse d'aujourd'hui: études, notes, portraits* (Paris, 1929), 197–200. *Feuilleton du temps*, 30 July 1924. N. Wilkins, *The Writings of Erik Satie* (London, 1980), 128.

trast with the brilliant—even glaring—clarity of the previous work. Originally entitled *Matin et soir sur la mer*, its inherent nature mysticism received an implicit Christian sanction from its definitive title, the two movements corresponding to the panels of an altar-piece. These, 'Soleil matinal' and 'Soleil vesperal' respectively, illustrate the sacred rhythms of nature during the course of a day; thus there is a similarity with *Jour d'été à la montagne* written twenty-one years earlier. Likewise, the *Diptyque* opens with a vast six-octave span, from low double basses to high violins, on the note E, an invocation to nature in all its fullness and mystery, gradually illuminated by the rising sun at dawn.

There emerges a descending melody of rare warmth and tenderness on woodwind and horns, characterized by the intervals of a second and a third. Its development is abruptly broken off by an insistent chorus of cicadas on the flutes, oboes, and clarinets, chirruping in a boldly conceived modernistic section of repeated whole tones and semitones derived from the previous melodic material; rapid broken chords on harps and celesta provide flashes of glinting sunlight. It is as if d'Indy is thumbing his nose at the young Turks, effectively showing them what an ageing, but still creatively active, master can achieve, using their own harsh, restrictive vocabulary. Soon afterwards, the tradition of Franck asserts itself with a superbly expressive B major brass chorale; such was d'Indy's understanding of instrumentation that the flexible trumpet melody is entirely free of brass band style vulgarity (Ex. 11*a*). Towards the end of the movement, this chorale melody reappears, played by strings and harp, a moment of heart-rending candour uttered without reserve and encouraged by the warmth of the midday sun.

A subtle change in the atmosphere is felt at the opening of 'Soleil vesperal'; a sustained superimposed fifth chord in the wind (C♯, G♯, D♯) against shimmering upper strings creates a momentary mood of exotic enchantment, reflecting an awareness, perhaps, of the proximity of North African shores. With the fading of the light appears a new theme, characterized by a rising fifth, its mood of melancholy enhanced by the sonorities of cor anglais, bassoon and horn (Ex. 11*b*). After the

Ex. 11a. *Diptyque Méditerranéen*, 'Soleil matinal'

chorus of cicadas have made a brief return, a chill in the air can be sensed as this theme undergoes an austere transformation, its contours starkly outlined in bare octaves on strings and harps against a background of ostinato horn figuration. A brief, tender brass chorale signals the imminent conclusion. The sense of finality is almost palpable; yet there is not the slightest trace of morbidity, only a stoic resignation in the face of the inevitable.

Some reservations, however, were expressed after its première on 5 December 1926 at the Concerts du Conservatoire. Maurice Boucher, writing in *La Revue musicale*, complained that 'the two parts are too similar, as if a single piece had been cut with scissors in the middle'; the work oscillates between music and description, and 'les cigales sont bien impertinentes'. D'Indy must have felt some degree of discouragement, for he wrote to Daniel Gregory Mason, stating that 'there is no use making orchestral pieces as there is a whole

Ex. 11b. *Diptyque Méditerranéen*, 'Soleil vespéral'

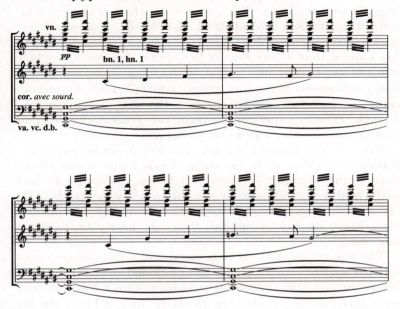

nursery of orchestrators both skilful and amusing, so far as the
sonorities are concerned, while few are able to make chamber
music, a genre that requires a particular way of writing, very
strict and intimate'.[15] In fact, these last years saw the production of an impressive list of chamber works, among them
the Third and Fourth String Quartets, the last left incomplete.
A lightly worn academicism characterizes the String Sextet,
remarkable for the translucence of its part writing; the central
Divertissement stands out with its amusing mock choral in
string harmonics.

A representative group of his chamber works received an
entry in the English publication *Cobbett's Cyclopedic Survey of
Chamber Music*, written by Calvocoressi. D'Indy himself contributed the section on Franck, analysing the Trios, Piano
Quintet, Violin Sonata, and String Quartet. Few, however,
have expressed the essential difference between Franck and

[15] Boucher RM 8 (Jan. 1927), 78–9. *Letters of Composers*, 282–4.

d'Indy with such insight as the future feminist and psychological author Anaïs Nin, whose brother, Joaquin Nin-Culmell, was then a student at the Schola. Untrained but highly intuitive regarding music as she was, she confided to her journal that 'César Franck had unity, coherence, a whole personality. D'Indy was varied, multicoloured, moved by too many influences, broken, scattered, contradictory. *Le premier chant, le deuxième cherche.* I prefer the simple assurance of Franck. D'Indy expresses, instead, the general character of French intelligence, which sees too much.'

Yet, as she listened to her brother Joaquin practising d'Indy's *Le Chant de la montagne*, Anaïs found it one of the most beautiful things she had ever heard. And, after he had performed it marvellously at her studio party in March 1928, she and her Scottish banker husband—emotionally drained by their brave display of Spanish dancing—nearly broke down and cried.[16]

The reputation of the Schola could still attract progressive-minded students from abroad, among them the young Turkish composer and ethnomusicologist Admet Adnan Saygun, sent on a government scholarship to study with d'Indy. On his return to Turkey, he devoted himself to the study of its folklore, accompanying Béla Bartók on a musico-ethnological journey round Anatolia. Moreover, he became the first of his country's opera composers, with *Kóroglu* (1973).

Despite the inner serenity which had come with his second marriage, the old Adam in d'Indy was still liable to break out from time to time. Of the younger composers, only Honegger could stimulate his interest and approval, on account of the sheer solidity of his idiom, seriousness of purpose, and involvement with symphonic structures. On his side, Honegger professed endless admiration for d'Indy, but at the same time loved to provoke friendly debates with him. 'I told him . . . that to me the dogma of tonality seemed an entirely outmoded notion (like the unities of time and place in classical

---

[16] A. Nin, *Journal of a Wife, the Early Diary of Anaïs Nin, 1923–27* (London, 1984), 261. A. Nin, *The Early Diary 1927–31* (London, 1994), Penguin edn. (1995), 46, 64. *Cobbett's Cyclopedic Survey of Chamber Music*, 2nd edn. (London, 1963), i. 418–29, ii. 1–8.

tragedy). . . . What gives unity to a piece of music is the totality of melodic and rhythmic relationships.' Moreover, for Honegger, it was essential to come to terms with the modern world of technology and increased speed, reflected in his depiction of a locomotive in *Pacific 231*. The mechanization of music itself was a burning question, which he addressed in an article in *Comoedia* in 1926: in his view, the future lay with the mechanical piano. Indeed, the very anti-romantic depersonalization of this instrument had appealed to Stravinsky, who had used it in his *Étude pour pianola* (1917) and in the first version of *Les Noces*. It featured, too, in Milhaud's score for Rubinstein's ballet *La Bien-aimée* (1928), enabling him to exceed the virtuosity of Liszt's transcriptions of Schubert's valses!

D'Indy viewed these developments with horror, as the negation of human expression. In a riposte to Honegger, courteously but trenchantly put, he stoutly refuted his pupil's argument that the organ is essentially mechanical in character: 'I can assure you that it wasn't difficult—even when I was only an ignorant young student—to tell whether a certain piece of Bach was interpreted by Father Franck, or by Guilmant, or Vierne, or whether it was being carried off at 120 miles per hour by some virtuoso.' In an interview two years later, he cast doubts on the artistic validity of gramophone recordings, contradicting the widely held view that eventually they would come to replace live concert performances. 'What we seek above all in art is emotion, and we are only moved if we find ourselves in direct communication with the interpreter. No emotion can be drawn from these mechanisms, and so I don't believe that their hegemony can last.'[17]

On the subject of Edgard Varèse, he was scathing: a dishonour to the teaching of the Schola who, moreover, had never come up with a musical idea in his life. He recalled the occasion when, on asking him what he was working on, the student Varèse replied, 'a choral piece in 32 real parts'. At this his master looked a little perturbed, as he himself found eight-part writing sufficiently difficult! Doubtless, this total

[17] Honegger, *I am a Composer*, 82–3. Milhaud, *Notes without Music*, 213. VI to GR, 8 July 1926, BN. *Comoedia*, undated cutting, 1926.

dismissal of Varèse's compositions—of which to date only *Octandre* had been heard in Paris—had its basis in a deep-rooted mutual antagonism, on which further light is cast by the psychoanalytically minded Anaïs Nin's description of Varèse as 'a very fearless, strong, tremendous tempered man with great force; he even looked like a Corsican bandit. But he had no power over the inner forces that were pushing him.' Maybe d'Indy saw in him a reflection of himself as he might have been, without his hard-won power of self-discipline.[18]

A name on the lips of all the young progressives was that of Arnold Schoenberg, whose portentous discovery of the twelve-note serial method of composition had been announced to the world in 1923 as guaranteeing the supremacy of German music for the next hundred years. At the beginning of 1928, a series of concerts of his music were given in Paris, featuring *Pierrot Lunaire*, the Suite op. 29, the Wind Quintet, and *Pelleas und Melisande*. D'Indy proceeded to sound off about the man and his work in absurdly derogatory terms:

'He is a madman', he told *Comoedia*; 'Schoenberg teaches nothing except that you should write everything which comes into your head. This isn't teaching, it's just an opinion! His work, interesting at first, is no more than a mass of meaningless notes. . . . Art demands thought, construction, rhythm, form, equilibrium. . . . Despite that, I understand his success. A theory which recommends writing anything at all is bound to please the new generations of musicians.'

Such prejudiced, uninformed criticism is on a par with the then common failure to recognize that Picasso was a draughtsman of outstanding ability. Likewise, d'Indy showed himself unaware that Schoenberg insisted on his pupils mastering traditional harmony and counterpoint; the Austrian master had himself written a harmony treatise *Harmonielehre* (1909), a fixed point of stability against which he made his daring new departures into free atonality, as in the expressionistic *Five Orchestral Pieces*, *Erwartung*, and *Pierrot Lunaire*. D'Indy moved on to firmer ground in his reply to Honegger's contention that Schoenberg's twelve-note music was intended to

---

[18] Ouellette, *Edgard Varèse*, 98. A. Nin, *A Woman Speaks* (London, 1992), 113. *Comoedia*, 21 Feb. 1928.

be *read*, rather than *heard* (a worn-out cliché from the war of harmony and counterpoint).

These noises don't interest me on paper any more than they do in the atmosphere. Whatever there may be in the interval processes, 'crab canons' or 'retrograde inversions' leave me profoundly indifferent; but if these canons and devices, without seeming to do so, contribute to the general effect of beauty, which my auditory sense leads straight to my heart, then I shall love and adore them.

The astonishing contrapuntal combinations of Bach's *The Art of Fugue* were a case in point.

Nevertheless, at times he could be surprisingly undogmatic on this subject. Writing to Casals in 1930, he expressed his approval of the way his old friend had used atonality in his *Sardanas* for thirty-two cellos as a means of creating an impression of the noise of the fair and the rumbling of the processions during the annual feast of Vilafranca del Panades in Spain.[19] The same year also brought some cheer in the form of Roussel's participation in the fiftieth anniversary celebrations of the Boston Symphony Orchestra with his Third Symphony specially commissioned by Serge Koussevitsky, together with Stravinsky's *Symphony of Psalms* and Honegger's First Symphony.

The old enthusiasms of d'Indy's youth suddenly resurfaced on being invited to contribute to a series of books on composers in popular format; the result was *Richard Wagner et son influence sur l'art musical français*. Wagner's stock had fallen low in the eyes of intellectuals and progressives since the heady days of the 1880s. But not entirely; bizarre as it seems, the young Spanish director Luis Buñuel—who had once considered becoming a student at the Schola Cantorum—made use of Wagner's music in the sound-tracks of his surrealist films *Un Chien andalou* (1928) and *L'Âge d'or* (1930)! In its own way, too, d'Indy's little book is idiosyncratic. Strongly anti-Semitic in tone, it makes much of Wagner's conflicts with the entrenched Jewish school of opera composers, Meyerbeer, Halévy, and Offenbach, while the nationalist perspective is

---

[19] RM, 9 (Feb. 1928), 64–5. *Comoedia*, 21 Feb. 1928. Corredor, *Conversations with Casals*, 172.

apparent in the way Debussy is perceived in relation to the master of Bayreuth: 'The triumph of *Pelléas* does not seem to me to be a destructive agent of the Wagnerian influence, nor, above all, the point of departure of a new musical era . . . but, on the contrary, as the *terminal point* of the fecund and magnificent productive epoch to which Wagner's art has contributed.' Certainly, to d'Indy, Debussy's preoccupation with rare harmonies was nothing but an amplification of Wagner's discoveries, rather than the beginning of the modern French school.

Another volume in the series was devoted to Franck. Its author, Charles Tournemire, took d'Indy's mythologizing to even greater lengths: 'Miraculously, the perfume of the thirteenth century has not evaporated. . . . it was breathed by Frescobaldi, Wagner, Paul Verlaine, César Franck, and certain others.' It was as if Tournemire was asserting himself to be Franck's true spiritual heir, as against d'Indy, whom he regarded as a very cold musician. The organist of Sainte-Clotilde's great Gregorian-based liturgical cycle *L'Orgue mystique* undoubtedly remains an outstanding contribution to the modern revival of church music, embodying, in the words of the 1903 *motu proprio*, 'goodness, seriousness, and gravity'.[20]

In the bestowal of honours, d'Indy was not overlooked. On 10 January 1931, he received promotion to Grand Officer of the Legion of Honour. 'I don't attach much importance to these distinctions,' he told his friend Langrand; 'yet I've been rather pleased to get the *heavy grade* in the Legion of Honour, that poor legion which grows more and more decrepit.' To mark the occasion, a reception was held at the Hotel Lutétia, attended by more than 400 well-wishers. On 23 March he conducted his *Le Chant de la cloche* at the Salle Pleyel, mounting the podium only five days later to direct *Le Camp de Wallenstein* in the course of an all d'Indy concert given by Pierné and the Concerts Colonne. His eightieth birthday did not go unnoticed by the town council of Valence, which made him an *illustre concitoyen*, as well as organizing a gala concert

---

[20] VI, *Richard Wagner*, 12–14, 84. L. Buñuel, *My Last Breath* (London, 1984), 52, 219. C. Tournemire, *César Franck* (Paris, 1931), 9–10. Tournemire to Felix Aprahamian, 28 Mar. 1934, denying that he was ever a pupil of d'Indy.

in his honour on 1 April. The programme included a fragment of Franck's *Rédemption*, d'Indy's *Choral varié* for saxophone, the Prélude to *Fervaal*, and the *Symphonie Cévenole*. Indefatigably, he conducted throughout, before an audience of 1,500.[21]

On his return from Agay in November for the new academic year at the Schola, a marked deterioration in his health and condition could not be concealed. Yet he soldiered on, with a reduced number of classes, looking pale and worn out, prey to memory lapses, and sometimes even absent. On 23 November, one of his students, Alice Gabéaud, knowing that he had completed two choral pieces for schoolchildren that summer, offered to return with him after class to the avenue de Villars, and deliver them herself to Roger Ducasse. On their arrival, it struck her forcefully that d'Indy had the greatest difficulty in climbing the stairs, stopping frequently and complaining about his legs. He did not want any assistance, but she insisted on carrying his heavy briefcase. Courteous to the last, he charged her to convey to Ducasse his complete confidence in him, and that he might suggest any changes to the pieces he wished. D'Indy was concerned, too, that the inspectors for singing in schools should receive his thanks for having invited him to compose them.

Thereafter, things took their inevitable course. A few days later, it was learned that he had been ordered a period of complete rest for a month or six weeks, and that, during his absence, Lioncourt, the Secretary-General, would take over his classes. A nightmarish feeling of foreboding gripped the Schola, for without d'Indy its *raison d'être* was inconceivable. To the news of his death on 2 December 1931, the response was one of stunned disbelief. The immediate reaction of Alice Gabéaud was to hurry over to the avenue de Villars. There a poignant sight greeted her: on a table, a notebook for the composition class lay waiting, ready for use as if nothing had changed. But stark reality could not be avoided. In death, the master appeared utterly calm and dignified, as white as the shrouds in which he had been laid out. In the pallid glow of

---

[21] Goichot, article in *Revue Drômoise*, no. 421 (Oct. 1981), 404–5.

Vincent d'Indy and His World

an electric lamp, there hung above him a great ivory Christ with outstretched arms.

His funeral on 5 December befitted a Grand Officer of the Legion of Honour, with a turn-out of several military detachments lining the entire length of the boulevard des Invalides. Among the enormous crowd which filled the parish church of Saint-François Xavier were many former students of the Schola. The Requiem Mass was solemnly and with deep emotion chanted by those in attendance, who afterwards followed the cortège to his final resting-place in the cemetery of Montparnasse. In that hallowed ground, the remains of Vincent d'Indy at last joined those of his spiritual father, César Franck.[22]

[22] Gabéaud, *Auprès du maître*, ii. 31–3. Photiadès, 'Vincent d'Indy', 458.

Epilogue

The decades after d'Indy's death dealt harshly with his reputation, and only in recent years has there been any real sign
of revived interest or comprehension of his achievements.
Whereas his pupils Roussel and Honegger achieved lasting
international acclaim, d'Indy himself was consigned to the
shades as the one-work composer of the *Symphonie Cévenole*.

With his demise, the Schola Cantorum inevitably suffered a
grievous loss of vitality. Fortunately, the appointment of the
young Olivier Messiaen and Daniel-Lesur to its staff in 1935
brought a much-needed infusion of new blood. Although they
had both been educated at the Paris Conservatoire, their close
association with Charles Tournemire—Daniel-Lesur as a private composition pupil, Messiaen as an admiring protégé—
maintained the link with César Franck. Moreover, insufficient
notice has been taken of the marked similarities between
d'Indy and Messiaen, not only in their nature mysticism, but
also in their theological cast of mind and mode of existence.
The latter, as a committed Roman Catholic church organist,
teacher, and pedagogue, also led a dedicated life of unremitting work within institutions. Belief in the dogmas of the
Catholic Church and the urge to system building were at the
root of his own elaborately constructed musical language,
schematically set out in *Technique de mon langage musical*
(1944), which owes much to the example of d'Indy's *Cours de
composition musicale*. And the cyclic principle plays an important role in the formal organization of the large-scale *Visions
de l'Amen*, *Vingt Regards sur l'enfant-Jésus* and the
Turangalîla Symphony.

The years after 1945 saw the triumph of the radical intellectual Left, however, and the discrediting of the Catholic
Church and its moral and cultural values. It is hardly surprising, in these circumstances, that Vallas's biography of

Epilogue

d'Indy (1946–50) reads like a tired defence of a lost cause. Heading the aggressive avant-garde composers infatuated with the second Viennese school, Pierre Boulez launched vitriolic attacks on the representatives of historicism and tradition—even on Messiaen for his 'musique de bordel'—which far exceeded the tone of d'Indy's polemics.

With his anti-Semitic reputation still fully intact, d'Indy received an honoured place in the new demonology. In an essay 'Richard Wagner, the Man and the Works', Boulez makes a sinister implication that the founder of the Schola Cantorum was effectively a proto-Nazi, who 'attempted, in his composition classes to explain "rationally" why a Jew was incapable of writing music of any value'.[1] We have seen how d'Indy's high esteem of Paul Dukas refutes such pernicious nonsense. Other travesties of the truth appear in Jean Barraqué's *Debussy* (1962), where it is asserted that d'Indy 'rapidly succeeded in transforming the Société [Nationale] into a temple of academicism'. And, after the abortive première of Debussy's *Fantaisie pour piano et orchestre* in 1890, the outraged d'Indy allegedly 'showed an extreme coldness towards Debussy from then onwards'.[2]

In the very different political and cultural climate of the 1990s, I have attempted a more balanced, sympathetic portrait of d'Indy. The damaging charge of anti-Semitism can now be seen as a more general and widespread problem in the French society of his time. And as we have seen, his pedagogical work brought a much-needed intellectual foundation and academic respectability to music studies in his native land; he was greatly concerned that Germany should not have the monopoly of high seriousness and endeavour. Above all, he stood as the implacable enemy of cultural trivialization and rampant commercial values in the arts. The battles he fought are no less ours today.

---

[1] P. Boulez, *Orientations*, trans. Martin Cooper (London, 1986), 229.
[2] J. Barraqué, *Debussy* (Paris, 1962), 64, 94.

Catalogue of Main Works*

CHAMBER MUSIC

Suite dans le style ancienne, 1886
Trio for clarinet, cello, and piano, 1887
String Quartet No. 1, 1890
String Quartet No. 2, 1897
Violin Sonata, 1904
Piano Quintet, 1924
Cello Sonata, 1925
Suite for flute, string trio, and harp, 1927
String Sextet, 1927
String Quartet No. 3, 1929
Piano Trio in the form of a suite, 1929
String Quartet No. 4, 1931 (incomplete)

CHORAL MUSIC

Le Chant de la cloche, 1879–83

ORCHESTRAL WORKS

Wallenstein (three symphonic overtures after Schiller), 1873, 1879–81
Jean Hundaye (symphony), 1874–5 (unpublished)
La Forêt enchantée (symphonic legend after Uhland), 1878
Saugefleurie (legend after de Bonnières), 1884
Symphonie Cévenole (*Symphonie sur un chant montagnard français*), 1886
Fantaisie sur des thèmes populaires français, for oboe and orchestra, 1888
Tableaux de voyage, 1891–2
Istar (symphonic variations), 1896
Symphony in B flat, 1902–3
Choral varié, for saxophone and orchestra, 1903
Jour d'été à la montagne, 1905

221

Catalogue of Main Works

Souvenirs, 1906
Symphonie brévis, 1916–18
Poème des rivages, 1919–21
Diptyque Méditerranéen, 1925–6

ORGAN WORKS

Prélude, 1913

PIANO WORKS

Poème des montagnes, 1881
Tableaux de voyage, 1888
Sonata, 1907
Menuet sur le nom d'Haydn, 1909

STAGE WORKS

Attendez-moi sous l'orme (comic opera), 1876–82
Fervaal, 1889–95
L'Étranger, 1898–1901
La Légende de Saint-Christophe, 1908–15
Le Rêve de Cinyras (lyric comedy), 1922–3

* Dates are those of composition.

Bibliography

BOOKS

ARON, RAYMOND. *Main Currents in Sociological Thought*, vol. 1 (London, 1965).

BARRAQUÉ, JEAN. *Debussy* (Paris, 1962).

BARRÈS, MAURICE. *Le Jardin de Bérénice* (Paris, 1891).

—— *Les Déracinés* (Paris, 1897).

BARRÈS, M.; ROSTAND, E.; and GANCHE, E. *Une défense heroïque, Magnard* (Paris, 1915).

BARRICELLI, JEAN and WEINSTEIN, LEO. *Ernest Chausson, the Composer's Life and Works* (Westport, Conn., 1955).

BARTHES, ROLAND. *Mythologies* (Paris, 1957), trans. Annette Lavers (London, 1972).

BÉHAGUE, GERALD. *Music in Latin America, an Introduction* (Englewood Cliffs, NJ, 1979).

Béla Bartók Letters, ed. J. Demeny (London, 1971).

BLOY, LÉON. *Journal* (Paris, 1956–63).

BOULEZ, PIERRE. *Orientations*, trans. Martin Cooper (London, 1986).

BUNÜEL, LUIS. *My Last Breath* (London, 1984).

Cahiers Paul Claudel (Paris, 1961).

CALVOCORESSI, M. D. *Musicians' Gallery* (London, 1933).

CARLEY, LIONEL. *Delius, a Life in Letters* (London, 1983).

—— *Delius, The Paris Years* (London, 1975).

CARRAUD, GASTON. *La Vie, l'oeuvre et la mort d'Albéric Magnard* (Paris, 1921).

CASSELAER, CATHERINE VAN. *Lot's Wife, Lesbian Paris 1890–1914* (Liverpool, 1986).

Catalogue du Bibliothèque de Vincent d'Indy (Paris, 1933).

CHASE, GILBERT. *The Music of Spain* (New York, 1941).

CHIRON, YVES. *Maurice Barrès, le prince de la jeunesse* (Paris, 1986).

CITRON, MARCIA J. *Gender and the Musical Canon* (Cambridge, 1993).

Cobbett's Cyclopedic Survey of Chamber Music (London, 1963).

CORREDOR, J. M. *Conversations with Casals* (London, 1956).

Correspondance de Claude Debussy et Pierre Louÿs 1893–1914 (Paris, 1945).

Bibliography

Correspondance de Paul Dukas, choix de lettres établi par Georges Favre (Paris, 1971).

COSSART, MICHAEL DE. *The Food of Love, the Princesse de Polignac (1865–1943) and her Salon* (London, 1978).

—— *Ida Rubinstein, a Theatrical Life* (Liverpool, 1987).

COURCEL, R. DE. *La Basilique de Sainte-Clotilde* (Paris, 1957).

DANTE ALIGHIERI. *The Divine Comedy*, trans. C. H. Sisson (London, 1980).

DAVIES, LAWRENCE. *César Franck and his Circle* (London, 1970).

DEANE, BASIL. *Albert Roussel* (London, 1961).

Debussy Letters, ed. F. Lesure and R. Nichols (London, 1987).

Debussy on Music, ed. F. Lesure (London, 1977).

DEL MAR, NORMAN. *Richard Strauss* (London, 1962).

DEMUTH, NORMAN. *Vincent d'Indy* (London, 1951).

DENT, E. J. *Ferruccio Busoni* (London, 1974).

DEREPAS, G. *César Franck* (Paris, 1897).

—— *Les Théories de l'inconnaissance et les degrés de la connaissance* (Paris, 1883).

DUFOURCQ, NORBERT. *Autour de Coquard, César Franck et Vincent d'Indy* (Paris, 1952).

DUKAS, PAUL. *Les Écrits de Paul Dukas sur la musique* (Paris, 1948).

DURAND, JACQUES. *Quelques souvenirs d'un éditeur de musique* (Paris, 1924).

EELS, GEORGES. *The Life that he Led, a Biography of Cole Porter* (London, 1967).

ELIOT, T. S. *The Waste Land* (London, 1922).

ENTRÈVES, A. P. D' *Natural Law* (London, 1970).

FAURÉ, GABRIEL. *Correspondance*, ed. J. M. Nectoux (Paris, 1980).

FAY, AMY. *Music Study in Germany* (Chicago, 1881).

FLAUBERT, GUSTAV. *La Tentation de Saint Antoine* (Paris, 1874).

—— *Salammbô* (Paris, 1861).

FRAGUIER, MARGUÉRITE DE. *Vincent d'Indy, souvenirs d'une élève* (Paris, 1934).

FUBINI, ENRICO. *A History of Music Aesthetics* (Basingstoke and London, 1991).

GABÉAUD, ALICE. *Auprès du maître Vincent d'Indy* (Paris, 1933).

Gabriel Fauré, a Life in Letters, ed. J. B. Jones (London, 1989).

GARAFOLA, LYNN. *Diaghilev's Ballets Russes* (New York and Oxford, 1989).

GIDE, ANDRÉ. *Journal 1889–1939* (Paris, 1948).

GILLMOR, ALAN M. *Erik Satie* (London, 1988).

GILSON, PAUL. *Notes de musique et souvenirs* (Brussels, 1942).

Bibliography

GONCOURT. *Pages from the Goncourt Journals*, ed. R. Baldick (Oxford, 1962).

GRANGE, HENRY-LOUIS DE LA. *Gustav Mahler* (Paris, 1973).

GRAY, CECIL. *Musical Chairs* (London, 1985).

GRUNFELD, FREDERIC V. *Rodin, a Biography* (London, 1987).

HARDING, JAMES. *Saint-Saëns and his Circle* (London, 1965).

HASKELL, ARNOLD. *Diaghileff* (London, 1935).

HOLMES, GEORGE. *Dante* (Oxford, 1980).

HONEGGER, ARTHUR. *I am a Composer* (London, 1966).

HORNE, ALISTAIR. *The Fall of Paris, the Siege and the Commune* (London, 1965; rev. 1989).

HUDSON, LIAM, and JACOT, BERNADINE. *The Way Men Think, Intellect, Intimacy and the Erotic Imagination* (New Haven, 1991).

HUIZINGER, JOHAN. *The Waning of the Middle Ages* (Haarlem, 1919), trans. F. Hopman (London, 1924).

HUYSMANS, J. K. *Là-Haut* (Tournai, 1965).

IBSEN, HENRIK. *Brand* (1866).

—— *The Lady from the Sea* (1888).

IMBERT, HUGUES. *Profils des musiciens* (Paris, 1888).

INDY, VINCENT D'. *Histoire du 105ᵉ bataillon* (Paris, 1872).

—— *Cours de Composition musicale* Vols (Paris, 1903–51).

—— *César Franck* (Paris, 1906) tr. R. Newmarch (New York, 1910).

—— *Beethoven* (Paris, 1911).

—— *Emmanuel Chabrier et Paul Dukas* (Paris, 1920).

—— *La Schola Cantorum en 1925* (Paris, 1927).

—— *Richard Wagner et son influence sur l'art musical français* (Paris, 1930).

—— *Introduction à l'étude de Parsifal de Wagner* (Paris, 1937).

KIRK, H. L. *Pablo Casals* (London, 1974).

KOLAKOWSKI, LESZEK. *Bergson* (Oxford, 1985).

LALOY, LOUIS. *La Musique retrouvée, 1902–27* (Paris, 1928).

Landowska on Music, ed. D. Restout (London, 1965).

LAPLANE, GABRIEL. *Albéniz, sa vie, son œuvre* (Paris, 1956).

Letters of Composers, an Anthology 1603–1945 (New York, 1946).

Lettres à Auguste Sérieyx etc. (Paris, 1961).

LEVINSON, ANDRÉ. *La Danse d'aujourd'hui: études, notes, portraits* (Paris, 1929).

LINDEN, ALBERT VAN DER. *Octave Maus et la vie musicale belge 1875–1914* (Brussels, 1950).

LIVERMORE, ANN. *A Short History of Spanish Music* (London, 1972).

LOCKSPEISER, EDWARD. *Debussy, his Life and Mind* (London, 1962).

MAETERLINCK, MAURICE. *La Princesse Maleine* (1889).

Bibliography

MALLARMÉ, STÉPHANE. *Correspondance* (Paris, 1969).

MANN, NICHOLAS. *Petrarch* (Oxford, 1984).

MARIZ, VASCO. *Villa-Lobos, Life and Work* (Washington, DC, 1963).

MAUROIS, ANDRÉ. *The Quest for Proust* (London, 1962).

MAUS, MADELEINE OCTAVE. *Trente années de lutte pour l'art, Les XX, La Libre Esthétique* (Brussels, 1980).

MCKENNA, MARIAN. *Myra Hess, a Portrait* (London, 1976).

MESSIAEN, OLIVIER. *Technique de mon langage musical* (Paris, 1944).

—— *Musique et couleur, nouveaux entretiens avec Claude Samuel* (Paris, 1986).

MILHAUD, DARIUS. *Notes without Music* (London, 1952).

MÜNCH, CHARLES. *I am a Conductor* (New York, 1955).

MYERS, ROLLO. *Emmanuel Chabrier and his Circle* (London, 1969).

NECTOUX, JEAN MICHEL. *Gabriel Fauré, a Musical Life*, trans. R. Nichols (Cambridge, 1991).

NICHOLS, ROGER. *Ravel* (London, 1977).

—— *Debussy Remembered* (London, 1992).

—— and LANGHAM SMITH, RICHARD. *Claude Debussy, Pelléas et Mélisande* (Cambridge, 1989).

NIN, ANAÏS. *The Early Diary of A.N. 1927–31* (London, 1994).

—— *Journal of a Wife, the Early Diary of Anaïs Nin 1923–27* (London, 1984).

—— *The Journals of Anaïs Nin 1931–1934* (London, 1966).

—— *A Woman Speaks* (London, 1978).

NORTHCOTE, SYDNEY. *The Songs of Henri Duparc* (London, 1959).

ORENSTEIN, A. (ed.). *A Ravel Reader, Correspondence, Articles, Interviews* (New York, 1990).

ORLEDGE, ROBERT. *Gabriel Fauré* (London, 1979).

OTTO, RUDOLF. *The Idea of the Holy* (London, 1959).

OUELLETTE, FERNAND. *Edgard Varèse, a Musical Biography* (London, 1973).

PAINTER, GEORGE. *Marcel Proust* (London, 1965).

PATER, WALTER. *The Renaissance* (1873).

PIERRE, C. *Le Conservatoire National* (Paris, 1900).

PROUST, MARCEL. *Correspondance* (Paris, 1991).

Richard Strauss and Romain Rolland, Correspondence, Diary and Essays (London, 1968).

RIMSKY-KORSAKOV, NICOLAS. *My Musical Life* (London, 1974).

ROLLAND, ROMAIN. *Jean-Christophe* (Paris, 1903–12).

—— *Musiciens d'aujourd'hui* (Paris, 1908).

—— *Journal des années de guerre, 1914–1919* (Paris, 1952).

—— *Mémoires et fragments du journal* (Paris, 1956).

Bibliography

—— *Mémoires et souvenirs* (Paris, 1956).

RUBIN, WILLIAM S. *Dada and Surrealist Art* (London, 1969).

RUSKIN, JOHN. *The Seven Lamps of Architecture* (London, 1849).

SAINT-SAËNS, CAMILLE. *Les Idées de M. Vincent d'Indy* (Paris, 1919).

SCHWARTZ, CHARLES. *Cole Porter, a Biography* (London, 1978).

SISSON, C. H. *The Avoidance of Literature* (Manchester, 1978).

SMITH, ROLLAND. *Towards an Authentic Interpretation of the Organ Works of César Franck* (New York, 1983).

STUCKENSCHMIDT, H. H. *Ferruccio Busoni* (London, 1970).

SUBIRA, JOSÉ. *Historia de la música Espãnola et Hispanoamerica* (Barcelona, 1953).

TAPPOLET, ARTHUR. *Arthur Honegger* (Neuchâtel, 1938).

THOMSON, ANDREW. *The Life and Times of Charles-Marie Widor (1844–1937)* (Oxford, 1987).

TOURNEMIRE, CHARLES. *César Franck* (Paris, 1931).

VALÉRY, PAUL. *Charmes* (Paris, 1922).

VALLAS, LÉON. *César Franck* (New York, 1951).

—— *Vincent d'Indy* (Paris, 1946–50).

VARÈSE, LOUISE. *A Looking-glass Diary* (London, 1973).

VIDLER, ALEC R. *The Church in an Age of Revolution* (London, 1961).

VIERNE, LOUIS. *Mes Souvenirs* (Paris, 1939).

VUILLERMOZ, ÉMILE. *Histoire de la musique* (Paris, 1949).

WHARTON, EDITH. *The Letters of Edith Wharton* (London, 1988).

WILKINS, NIGEL. *The Writings of Erik Satie* (London, 1980).

WOOD, HENRY J. *My Life in Music* (London, 1938).

WRIGHT, SIMON. *Villa-Lobos* (Oxford, 1992).

YOUNG, PERCY M. *Edward Elgar* (London, 1955).

YSAŸE, ANTOINE, and RATCLIFFE, BERTRAM. *Ysaÿe, his Life, Work and Influence* (London, 1947).

ZELDIN, THEODORE. *France 1848–1945* (Oxford, 1973–7).

ARTICLES, REVIEWS, ETC.

BALSAN, ALAIN. 'L'Hérédité Drômoise de Vincent d'Indy, notes généalogiques', *Revue Drômoise*, no. 421 (Oct. 1981).

BOLLER, CARLO. 'Quelques souvenirs sur Vincent d'Indy', *Feuilles musicales* (Lausanne), no. 3 (Apr. 1951).

BOUCHER, MAURICE. Review of *Diptyque Méditerranéen*, RM 8 (Jan. 1920).

CHARLTON, DAVID. 'Grand Opera', in *New Oxford History of Music*, vol. 9: *Romanticism 1830–90* (Oxford, 1990).

Bibliography

COEUROY, ANDRÉ. 'Formes actuelles de musique religieuse', RM, 8 (June 1925).

GIOCANTI, STÉPHAN. 'Vincent d'Indy et le régionalisme musical', *La France Latine*, no. 113 (1991).

GIOCANTI, STÉPHAN. 'Vincent d'Indy et Stéphane Mallarmé', *Le Coeur de moulin, Bulletin de l'Association Festival Déodat de Sévérac*, no. 10 (1991).

—— 'Vincent d'Indy et Isaac Albéniz'. *Revue de l'Association Internationale* (forthcoming).

GOICHOT, article in *Revue Dromôise*, no. 421 (Oct. 1981).

GUILLOT, PIERRE. Introduction to de Sévérac's Piano Sonata, Edition musicales du Marais, 3 (Paris, 1990).

HONEGGER, ARTHUR. 'Souvenirs sur la classe de Vincent d'Indy au Conservatoire', RM, 10 (1951).

D'INDY, JEAN. 'Vincent d'Indy en famille', *Revue Internationale de musique*, 10 (1951).

D'INDY, VINCENT. 'Impressions musicales d'enfance et de la jeunesse', *Annales*, 15 May 1930.

—— *L'Harmonie vivante* (undated pamphlet).

LAURENCIE, JEAN DE LA. 'Quelques souvenirs vivarois sur Vincent d'Indy', *Revue du Vivarais* (Mar.–Apr. 1932).

MALHERBE, HENRY. Review of *Istar*, danced by Ida Rubinstein, *Feuilleton du temps*, 30 July 1924.

MILHAUD, DARIUS. 'La Musique en Brésil', RM 1 (1920).

NÈDE, ANDRÉ. 'Pie X et la musique religieuse', in *Tribune de Saint-Gervais*, 1895, repr. in *Le Ménéstrel*, 9 Aug. 1903.

PHOTIADÈS, CONSTANTIN. 'Vincent d'Indy, Souvenirs de Constantin Photiadès', *La Revue de Paris*, 15 Jan. 1932.

PIÉDELIÈVRE, PAULE. 'Louis Vierne à la Schola Cantorum et à l'École César Franck', appendix to Vierne, *Mes Souvenirs* (Paris, 1939).

Programme Général des Assises de musique religieuse et classique, Schola Cantorum, 1900.

PRUNIÈRES, HENRI. Review of *La Légende de Saint-Christophe*, RM 1 (1920), 60–1.

SISSON, C. H. 'Charles Maurras', in *The Avoidance of Literature* (Manchester, 1978).

Index

Index

Index

Index

Index

Index